PRAISE FOR CINEMA NIRVANA

"Dean Sluyter has one of the freshest voices in spiritual writing today. From the common ore of pop culture, he extracts the gleaming diamonds of dharma-wisdom. Take this jolly ride with him, and you'll never see movies—or your own life—in the same way again." **—LAMA SURYA DAS**, author of *Awakening the Buddha Within*

"Entertaining and thoughtful in turn, *Cinema Nirvana* compels you to watch the movies in the way a buddha might see them." **—STEPHEN BATCHELOR**, author of *Living with the Devil*

"If you spliced together DNA from Quentin Tarantino and the Dalai Lama, you'd get Dean Sluyter and he'd write this amazing book." **—MICHAEL GELB**, author of *How to Think Like Leonardo da Vinci*

"From its opening title straight on to its finale, *Cinema Nirvana* is original, amusing, and on the ball. It will help you stay awake at the movies and dream more in real life." **—KATE WHEELER**, author of *Not Where I Started From*

"Sluyter is the movie guru I have longed for. He mines deep spiritual wisdom from classic films with tremendous humor and grace. Virtually every page contains jaw-dropping insights and laugh-out-loud surprises." **—LAMA JOHN MAKRANSKY**, Professor of Buddhism and Comp___ Theology ___

"Dean Sluyter's *Cinema Nirvana* is ___ teaching disguised as cinematic ___ classic movies and these core teac___ constantly felt blown away by the ___ ___ dharmic connections Dean perceive___ ___. *Casablanca* as Mahayana? *Independence Day* as ___ ___ness? But of course! Bravo and emaho!" **—LEWIS RICHMOND**, author of *Work as a Spiritual Practice*

*Why the Chicken Crossed the Road
and Other Hidden Enlightenment Teachings*

*The Zen Commandments:
Ten Suggestions for a Life of Inner Freedom*

Just Being: Natural Meditation (CD)

Author photo: MARGARET KOIS

DEAN SLUYTER (rhymes with "inciter") has taught meditation since 1970 and leads workshops throughout the United States, with topics ranging from "Just Being: The Way of Natural Meditation" to "Shakespeare's Cosmic Vision." An award-winning former film critic, Dean is on the faculty of The Pingry School and New York Open Center. He is chief meditation instructor of Aikido Schools of New Jersey and leads the Dzogchen Center's New Jersey practice group. Information on Dean's books, CDs, teaching schedule, and more is available at deansluyter.com.

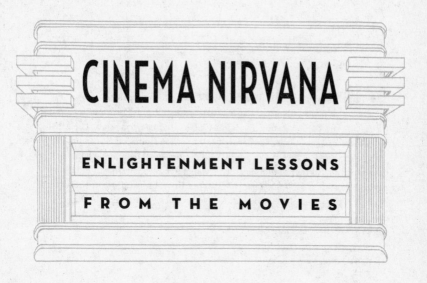

CINEMA NIRVANA

ENLIGHTENMENT LESSONS

FROM THE MOVIES

DEAN SLUYTER

THREE RIVERS PRESS • NEW YORK

Published by
Three Rivers Press,
New York, New York.
Member of the Crown Publishing Group,
a division of Random House, Inc.
www.crownpublishing.com

THREE RIVERS PRESS and the
Tugboat design are registered trademarks
of Random House, Inc.

Design by Karen Minster

ISBN 1-4000-4974-1

Printed in the United States of America

For Maggy

who held my hand at the movies

ACKNOWLEDGMENTS

Many thanks to my beta readers, Stephen Bloom, Koushik Das, John Dean, Linda Dean, Jim Handlin, Amy Lifton, Carol Rahbari, David Rahbari, Kate Riley, Day Rosenberg, Katherine Rosenberg, Joseph Roy, Jim Vincent, Rosie Vincent, and Diane Zeitlin . . . to my alpha listener, Tara Wings Sluyter . . . to Gretchen and Bill Richardson for the inspiration of their wisteria and high biscuits . . . to my stalwart friend and consigliere Jonathan Matson . . . to my publisher and editor, the ever-helpful Shaye Areheart and Julie Will . . . to the Great Communicator, Josh Baran . . . to Our Lady of the Posters, Jamie Jarrard, and everyone at Poster Itati . . . to my precious family . . . and, always, to the one teacher who assumes countless forms: lama of unrepayable kindness, I only remember you.

CONTENTS

Reality is that which,
when you stop believing in it,
doesn't go away.

—PHILIP K. DICK

SNAP OUT OF IT

Go throughout the land and spread the
dharma in the dialect of the people.

—THE BUDDHA
(to his disciples, shortly before his death)

The movies are weird—you actually have
to think about them when you watch them.

—BRITNEY SPEARS
(at the Sundance Film Festival)

TIBETAN TEMPLES SMELL LIKE POPCORN. ACTUALLY,
they smell like the hot buttery goop that's pumped onto popcorn in the lobbies of movie theaters: as I walk from my car on
a clear spring New Jersey evening, past the bank and the vacuum cleaner store, I can smell it a block away. What I smelled in
Tibet were butter lamps, simple cups of yak butter with lighted
wicks, carried by wide-eyed peasants as they walked in silence
from one shrine room to the next, or glowing where the resident monks had set them at the feet of gold-painted buddhas.
Like movie theaters, the temples are windowless and dark. The
butter lamps, burning there for centuries, have coated everything with a fine layer of sooty grease, so that the stone floors,
like the floors of movie theaters, are sticky underfoot.

The earliest of these temples were erected in the eighth century, when Padmasambhava and a few other illustrious teachers carried the *dharma*—the enlightenment teachings of the Buddha—from India. In Tibet they found a preliterate society, incapable of reading the texts they had brought. Fortunately, they had also brought the lavish system of visual symbolism we still see in the remaining temples, where every detail of the paintings and statues, down to the weapons wielded by a wrathful deity or the color of a lama's undershirt, conveys some part of the teaching.

In today's *post*literate society, where people can read books but spend most of their time gazing at various kinds of glowing screens instead, perhaps we can find enlightenment lessons in the movies. Perhaps, if we look close enough, there are dharma teachings in the weapons wielded by Clint Eastwood or the color of Grumpy's eyes. God, they say, is in the details. Maybe, if we take that saying literally, we can find the infinite looming in the way Sonny Corleone dies at the tollbooth or in the shark's-eye-view shot that opens *Jaws*. Of course Disney, Leone, Coppola, and Spielberg are no Padmasambhavas, but, like all great artists, in their most inspired moments they touch places beyond their own understanding. Plato imagined people sitting before a fire in a dark cave, watching flickering shadow shows that hint at the higher reality of the sunlit world and that eventually prompt them to emerge into the light. Perhaps our flickering movie shows can help point us to a higher, more light-filled reality, if only we can decipher the hints.

In a way, I've been trying to decipher them since I was six, when my parents took me to see *Forbidden Planet*. Robby the Robot, Dr. Morbius with his dark secrets and his beautiful daughter, the invisible Id monster stomping giant footprints in the dust of Altair-4, the spooky, quavering electronic music—*Wooo-OOO-ooo!*—all this suggested a mysterious, alluring cosmic dimension. I didn't know where it was or what it had to do with me, but it was out there and I wanted it. I embarked upon a lifelong love affair with movies, eventually spending several years working as a film critic. Meanwhile, my pursuit of the cosmic led me to study with lamas and yogis, attend retreats in the U.S. and Europe, and trek to cave shrines and butter lamp–filled temples in Tibet and Nepal. Maybe it was inevitable that someday these two passions would once again converge.

SO LET'S PLAY. What can *Memento* teach us about the slippery nature of time and "reality"? What can *Casablanca* teach us about *bodhichitta*, selfless commitment to the enlightened happiness of others? What can we learn about the insatiability of the self from *Jaws*, or about God the Father from *The Godfather*, or about sex and liberation from *Jailhouse Rock*? What does *Invasion of the Body Snatchers* say about individuality and conformity on the spiritual path? How can *Fistful of Dollars* help us deal skillfully with a world of craziness and violence? What qualities of enlightenment are personified by James Bond, Snow White, Humphrey Bogart, the Marx Brothers? How does the radiant beauty of our "stars" express our own intrinsic radiance? Most important, how can movies teach us to taste enlightened awareness silently within ourselves and then find that same flavor in our noisy outer lives?

Here's my theory. The Buddha is Cher in *Moonstruck*, slapping us upside the head and saying, "Snap out of it!" *Buddha* means "awakened one," and Buddha/Cher is challenging us to join her in snapping out of our stupor, to wake up and become Buddha/Us. As we do, we discover that the nature of existence itself, just as it is, is so startlingly rich, so infinitely satisfying, that it makes all our old attempts to sleepwalk our way to satisfaction seem laughably clumsy. We've been stumbling after so many things, and missing the One Thing.

> Again, the kingdom of heaven is like a merchant
> in search of fine pearls; on finding one pearl of
> great value, he went and sold all that he had and
> bought it.
> —MATTHEW 13:45–46

This pearl of great value may seem like a mystery, like the glowing contents of Marsellus Wallace's stolen briefcase in *Pulp Fiction:* we never see it, and no one in the film ever names it, but they all stare at it in awe, agree that it's beautiful, and are willing to risk their lives for it. I think most of us catch fugitive glimpses of that pearl, especially in childhood, but later we find ourselves pining away for it, like Citizen Kane pining for the Rosebud of simple, childlike happiness, never suspecting that he's had it in his mansion all along, obscured by the clutter of bigger, better, less satisfying toys.

So this enlightenment, or kingdom of heaven, is already ours. It's like a treasure locked away in a safe, and what religions offer (at their best) is mouth-watering descriptions of the treasure to motivate us, diagrams of the safe, and a box of time-tested safecracking tools. I find that the Buddhist teachings provide especially clear diagrams and especially nifty tools, but when someone hands me a big stick of dynamite with a lighted fuse, I don't spend a lot of time quibbling about who the manufacturer was. So I draw on many traditions. It's all just means to an end. Once we've got our hands on the treasure we lay our tools aside, and we see that the descriptions were hopelessly inadequate anyway.

In *American Beauty*, a teenage filmmaker glimpses it in the form of a discarded plastic bag:

RICKY: It was one of those days when it's a minute away from snowing and there's this electricity in the air, you can almost hear it, right? And this bag was like, dancing with me. Like a little kid begging me to play with it. For fifteen minutes. And that's the day I knew there was this entire life behind things, and . . . this incredibly benevolent force, that wanted me to know there was no reason to be afraid, ever. . . . Sometimes there's so much beauty in the world I feel like I can't take it, like my heart's going to cave in.

In the enlightened state you come to see that that beauty is in the world not just sometimes but always. And by acclimating gradually, you find that you *can* take it. Your heart doesn't cave in but opens out, to meet and embrace everything. And it's all perfectly ordinary and normal.

MOVIES ARE THE EXPRESSION of our collective yearnings, and our yearnings are ultimately spiritual, whether we know it or not, whether we like it or not. But in choosing films to explore, I've deliberately skipped those where the spiritual content is too literal or obvious. That includes most cases where people have told me "Ooh, you have to write about—" Where's the fun in finding what's already spelled out? But if the Force is really with us, so that we can really Wax-On Wax-Off our way to mastery, and thus escape from the Matrix, then such truths must lurk even in films where there's no Yoda or Mr. Miyagi or Morpheus to explain them. And if occasionally I work overtime to find these truths (the Tibetans call this "squeezing the legs out of the snake"), then so be it. I think I still have my first-grade report card, on which Miss Somebody wrote, "Dean has a lot of good ideas, but sometimes he gets carried away." Too late to change now. Like James Brown in "Cold Sweat," all I can say is, "Excuse me while I do the boogaloo."

I've also limited myself to American films (aside from one spaghetti western, which is faux American). I want to stick with familiar, domestic fare as our way into the supposedly unfamiliar, exotic realm of enlightenment. We're Americans, not Tibetans or Japanese or even Europeans. By the nineteenth century, European visitors were shocked to see our alien custom of putting our feet up and leaning back in our chairs. This is the land of peanut butter and jelly, blue jeans and rock 'n' roll. Just as Padmasambhava made the dharma Tibetan by integrating indigenous Tibetan gods and myths into the temple images, maybe we can make it American by integrating it with our blue-jeaned movie gods and their big-screen myths. At the core of the enlightenment experience is the discovery, like Dorothy's discovery in Oz, that there's no place like home. Everything we sought in exotic lands and far-out ideas is right here, far in, so intimate to our own being that we simply overlooked it. The ordinary turns out to be the extraordinary; the boy next door is your friendly neighborhood Spider-Man.

So let's pick a seat (sixth row, right aisle for me, please), put up our feet, and soak up some enlightenment lessons. And don't forget the popcorn. As it happens, our ritual moviegoing snack is an enlightenment lesson in itself, the product of a dramatic transformation. Something small, hard, and unpalatable explodes and turns inside out, becoming tender and tasty as it expands. This is just the kind of transformation we want our own lives to undergo: to explode out of hard constrictedness, to blow open our kernel of truth, to bring to the outside the tender, tasty enlightenment that was already inside. Let's see what we can learn about this process from the movies.

SNOW WHITE AND THE SEVEN DWARFS
(1937)

DARE TO BE DOPEY

So, in planning a new picture, we don't think of grown-ups and we don't think of children, but just of that fine, clean, unspoiled spot down deep in every one of us, that the world has maybe made us forget and maybe our pictures can help recall.

—WALT DISNEY

AS A ROLE MODEL, SNOW WHITE SUCKS. SHE'S AN UTTERLY passive fairy-tale heroine who climbs no beanstalks and slays no dragons. She has no talents but housecleaning and no interests beyond pining away for that Special Someone who will someday come and solve all her problems. Her shrill, girly voice attests to her empty-headed helplessness—she's sisters-under-the-skin with the old politically incorrect Teen Talk Barbie that sighed, "Math is hard!" All she is is young and pretty, and not smart enough to understand that one day, like the Queen, she'll be forty and washed up.

This sort of critique is valid as long as we're viewing the film on a strictly literal level. But on that level, *Jack and the Beanstalk* teaches us to solve our problems by stealing and killing, and Christ's parables are pointless stories about pearls and swine, lost sheep and mustard seeds. If we look at it in the right light and from the right angle, *Snow White and the Seven Dwarfs*, the first feature-length cartoon ever made, turns out to be an extended dharma parable, its teachings as exquisitely detailed as they are unintended.

Back in 1937, when the film was in production, the press called it "Disney's Folly." Even Roy Disney, Walt's brother and partner, wanted to stick to their wildly popular Mickey Mouse shorts, fearful that the project would sink the studio. Walt kept hiring more artists, hundreds of them, and going back to the bank for more money. To realize his vision, new technology was developed (a giant multiplane camera to add layers of perspective), an in-house art school was established, live dancers and dwarfs were filmed and copied, chemists mixed 1,500 custom paint colors, and teams of animators worked around the clock for months, fired up by Walt's relentless perfectionism. As one artist said, "Disney had only one rule: whatever we did had to be better than anybody else could do it, even if you had to animate it nine times."

The result tapped into something universal, and *Snow White* became the first great international blockbuster of the sound era. True, it set in motion the Disney juggernaut-of-cuteness that would eventually crush every delicate, wistful children's classic in sight (poor Pooh!), but that's another story. Visually, the film is still stunning today, in such scenes as the climactic storm, where the fall and splatter of each individual raindrop is hand-rendered with painstaking predigital craftsmanship. But most remarkable is how, out of the intensely concentrated awareness of some 1,000 collaborating artists (writers, animators, colorists, actors, musicians, and more) emerged a self-portrait of awareness itself: our pristine, snow-white inmost being, with its innate yearning to find fulfillment in the arms of the Prince Charming of enlightenment.

BUT ENLIGHTENMENT, in all its expansiveness, is an unfamiliar realm. So the film begins with the all-too-familiar constrictedness of unenlightenment, in the person of Snow White's stepmother, the Queen, closeted in the dark, claustrophobic recesses of her strangely uninhabited castle. Where are the King, the courtiers, the ladies in waiting? She dwells in isolation, just as we dwell (so it seems) alone inside a body, a tiny island of self lost in the wide sea of all that is not our self. Gazing into her mirror, she pronounces her famous incantation—

Magic mirror on the wall,
Who is the fairest one of all?

—just as we try to make ourselves less tiny by being the fairest (or the richest or strongest or smartest or coolest) one of all. But because it merely intensifies the sense of self, such self-aggrandizement is a losing game. Making our island more luxurious just reinforces the sensation that we're stuck on an island.

And all such improvements are temporary anyway; we can't stay the fairest one of all forever. The Queen knows her beauty is doomed, and in straining to preserve it—another self-defeating strategy—she has made herself grotesque. Her high cheekbones and flawless skin, exaggerated by the black cowl pulled tight over her hair and ears, are fixed in a frozen mask that is not beautiful but an ice-cold, Joan Crawfordesque parody of beauty: she's like a walking face-lift with nothing beneath it. When she summons the Spirit for reassurance that she's still the fairest one of all, she addresses him as "Slave in the magic mirror," but *she's* clearly a slave *of* the magic mirror. The words *narcissism* and *narcotic* come from the same root, and the Queen is hooked, a mirror junkie with an expensive habit.

The plot is set in motion when the Spirit puts Mommie Dearest in a rage by revealing that Snow White is now fairest of all. Reflecting the Queen's frozen features, the Spirit is also drawn as a mask—the mournful mask of tragedy, the drama of inevitable loss. The Greek word for mask, *persona*, is the root of our words *person* and *personality*, implying that the "person," the self we work so hard to preserve and promote, is merely a mask and not what we truly are. That's good news. Working to earn more money, get a higher SAT score, or, for that matter, make ourselves more attractive is not the problem; it's the *identification* with these achievements, the illusion that we *are* our faces, brains, or money. Like the Queen, we're happy to be a made-up self as long as it's succeeding on its own made-up terms. But sooner or later others arise to challenge us. Then, because of our identification with the role we've been playing, our very survival seems to require that we eliminate the challenger. We lash out.

> In ignorance, alienated and lonely, we are cut off
> from the world and other creatures by our belief
> that we are all separate entities. . . . Hatred or
> aversion is a direct function of the split mind. . . .
> [D]ue to the fear inherent in "island-consciousness,"
> when any event occurs that is not exuding comfort
> and security . . . the conditions for a possible
> violent confrontation are present.
> —*THE FLIGHT OF THE GARUDA*

Here this spawning of violence occurs when the Queen summons her Huntsman to take Snow White into the woods and cut out her heart.

Fortunately, there's an alternative to isolation, fear, and rage. We can use the daily threats to our precarious security as opportunities for insight, to see that these challenges to the false self bring not doom but redemption. Instead of clutching at the mask with an ever-tightening grip, we can let go.

Turn off your mind, relax and float downstream.
It is not dying, it is not dying.
    —LENNON/MCCARTNEY,
      "Tomorrow Never Knows"

That which overshadows us, we discover by relaxing into it, is not some outer menace but our own true being—represented here by Snow White.

HER NAME, HER VOICE, her face all suggest that Snow White is more than a literal fairy-tale heroine, that she personifies something beyond the realm of human limitation. She is Disney's embodiment of "that fine, clean, unspoiled spot down deep in every one of us," as pure as the driven snow. She was originally drawn with skin so otherworldly white that the female artists in the ink and paint department, it is said, had to go back cell by cell, applying rouge from their own makeup kits to her cheeks. Her voice, so nearly ultrasonic that it's painful, was not a casual choice. Disney, who had sound equipment specially installed in his office so he could listen in on auditions, rejected over a hundred singers before hearing nineteen-year-old Adriana Caselotti and exclaiming, "That's the girl!"

The name Snow White is particularly suggestive. As snow blankets the entire countryside, it implies a beauty that can't be hoarded, a shared asset that's vaster than our island of self. Dharma texts use such terms as *sem karpo* ("white mind" in Tibetan) to describe that which underlies all our masks and is "fairer"—more radiant, more real, more joyously liberative— than any of them. One popular exercise for cleansing the mind of impurities that obstruct this awareness, the Vajrasattva ("white scepter") purification, involves visualizing enlightenment-nectar "the color of fresh snow in brilliant sunlight" pouring down through the top of one's head and flushing out the entire body. In fact, when we first see Snow White she is engaged in cleansing, scrubbing the outer steps of the palace, the Queen's fortress of self-imposed solitude and limitation.

Looking up at that massive obstruction, Snow White sighs with discouragement. She is dressed in rags, neglected by her stepmother, just as our inner being, with no family resemblance to the false self, is shunted aside like a neglected stepchild. Yet her beauty shines despite her rags. Our radiant essence, pure awareness, can never be tainted by the world of mundane experience.

How can that be? Here's an experiment that can help make it clear:

- Examine any two objects—say, a penny and a dollar. Through your senses, you experience the penny as round, brownish, and smooth, the dollar as rectangular, greenish, and crinkly.

- Notice that these sensations of roundness, crinkliness, and so forth are experienced within your awareness. You are aware *of* them.

- Now notice whether your awareness itself is brown or greenish, crinkly or smooth. (Take your time and observe closely.) Plainly it's none of these, since you can be aware of many colors and textures at once. *Awareness itself* is pure—it has no shape, texture, size, or any other sensory characteristic, but is an unchanging luminous clarity within which arises the ever-changing display of sensations.

So, underlying all perception is pure awareness, in the background of every mind-moment. It just needs to be promoted to the foreground. The neglected stepchild must take her rightful place as a princess.

STILL SIGHING, SNOW WHITE carries her scrub bucket a few yards to a well, peers into its depths, and sings about her wish for "the one I love" to "find me today." Our inner nature wants, as it were, to be found. It's not enough merely to *be* that luminous clarity; we must somehow come to *know* it. This knowing is not an idea or a feeling but a direct experience—in fact, *the* experience, *satori, nirvana, rigpa,* the peace that passeth understanding, the kingdom of God within. Here it's represented by the Prince, the one who can draw Snow White out of the background to which she has been relegated. Sages in all traditions say this ultimate experience cannot be adequately described ("The Tao that can be spoken of is not the true Tao"), and, fittingly, the Prince is the one character the Disney artists were never satisfied with. They couldn't find a way to make him visually embody Snow White's ultimate, supremely desirable destiny. Instead he wound up looking the way many descriptions of enlightenment misleadingly make it sound: bland and boring.

Because this enlightenment experience is not anything foreign to us but is the realization of our own basic nature, we're spontaneously attracted to it—the Prince is Charming. Snow White has never laid eyes on the guy, but he's already "the one I love." This preexisting affinity makes her confident that he's the one and that, sooner or later, he'll show up. And the feeling is mutual. Realization is spontaneously attracted to us; in a moment, the Prince will arrive on a horse that is also snow-white, implying that Snow White's own pristine nature carries him toward her. In this context, her Barbie-esque passivity makes sense after all. The essence of meditation—the most stripped-down, straightforward technique of realizing the pure nature of our awareness—is *wu wei,* "not doing," simply letting awareness be. All forms of spiritual doing exist to bring us to this point of not doing, where any exertion would merely overlay complications upon the perfect, snow-white face of what we already are. As a Zen teacher once put it, "Enlightenment, when it happens, is an accident. Spiritual practice just makes us more accident-prone."

This is the utter simplicity that makes even the word "meditation" seem superfluous. Whether with eyes closed or open, whether cross-legged on a cushion after intoning mantras or lounging in the backyard after sipping morning coffee, we just let go, not following our thoughts or repressing them, not manipulating our experience or judging it. As with muddy water, if we don't stir it but just let it settle, the medium in which the mud is suspended spontaneously reveals its innate clarity. We simply sit, simply be, and, in its time, realization comes unbidden, "as a thief in the night," just as Prince Charming now comes riding onto the scene, scales the wall, and steals silently into Snow White's garden.

Oblivious of his presence, Snow White goes on singing, and through her eyes, in a point-of-view shot that's one of the film's most striking images, we see her reflection looking back from the bottom of the well. It's a vivid evocation of the meditative state: awareness simply resting aware of awareness.

> In this there is not a thing to be removed,
> Nor anything that needs to be added.
> It is merely the immaculate,
> Looking naturally at itself.
> —KHENPO JAMYANG DORJE

Oddly, the image recalls the Queen and her mirror, but with a crucial difference. The Queen strikes a rigid, imperial stance, issuing commands at horizontal eye level; Snow White bends in a relaxed, gracefully rounded posture, her head bowed as if in humble prayer, gazing with gentle acceptance into the vertical depths. And while the Queen glares at a hard surface that reflects her own rigidity, Snow White looks into living water, in which circular ripples (a spectacular artistic tour de force) gently radiate outward across her reflection, implying that the self she sees is not static and isolated but fluidly interconnected with everything else. The Queen would be furious if ripples crossed *her* face—they would have her running for the Botox.

A moment later, the Prince appears at Snow White's side—reflected in the bottom of the well. This, her first glimpse of him, reminds us that initially our inner nature can most readily encounter its own realization in the depths of meditation. But it's always available, right here and now, as the Prince indicates by singing back the last word of Snow White's wishing song in an ascending interval that makes it a triumphant declaration: "To-*day*!"

In principle, this is all we should ever have to do: look into ourselves once, see what we truly are, and then live the experience. In practice, though, these glimpses (in Zen they're called *kensho*) are highly unstable, due to their unfamiliarity, as we now see when timid Snow White becomes flustered and runs away. To become permanent, inner illumination must be hauled up, so to speak, from the bottom of the well to the surface. In Judaism, where the Sabbath, or Shabbat, is set aside for such inner experience, a key prayer says

> Help me to extend the joy of Shabbat to the other
> days of the week, until I attain the goal of deep joy
> always.

To live happily ever after (in "deep joy always") with the Prince, Snow White must leave her sheltered garden for the outer world—a journey that will take her to the cottage of the Seven Dwarfs.

THE JOURNEY BEGINS when the Huntsman, who can't bring himself to kill Snow White, sinks to his knees and begs her to run away. This is the first hint that our essence has a kind of immortality, invulnerable to the false self's jealous attempts to obliterate it. Setting forth, Snow White strikes up an easy friendship with the forest animals (nature responds positively to *our* inner nature), and they lead her to the Dwarfs' empty, messy cottage, where, again asserting her purifying power, she starts scrubbing dishes and sweeping away cobwebs, whistling while she works.

Cut to diamond mine, where we meet the Dwarfs, also cheerfully at work, singing about how they love to "dig dig dig dig dig dig dig." In the original fairy tale by the Brothers Grimm (and in the pre-Disney stage and silent film versions), the Dwarfs are anonymous, interchangeable little homunculi who toil away under the earth. One of Disney's most inspired departures was to give each Dwarf a unique name and a vivid personality to go with it. (It's also the beginning of the process that would eventually make his films, with all their friendly teapots and singing candlesticks, so cloying.) Hundreds of names were considered, including Hungry, Jumpy, Puffy, Baldy, Shifty, Helpful, and Awful, before Happy, Sneezy, Grumpy, Bashful, Sleepy, Dopey, and Doc made the cut. This motley crew suggests a different model for functioning in the world than the Queen's rigid fixity. They are a set of varying states, an array of moods and modes, each component essential to the functioning of the whole, none to be identified with as a "self," all to be embraced.

It is through these modes that we interact with our environment and seek to gain fulfillment from it. Like the Dwarfs digging away with their picks and shovels, we try to extract the gleaming gems of gratification from the hard rock of the material world, though we may not understand our own mission. "We dig up diamonds by the score," sing the Dwarfs, "though we don't know what we dig 'em for." When we're, say, selling insurance or playing golf, it's not about insurance or golf. What we really seek in all our doing is the moment when the mind lets go of all doing and seeking, when the customer buys the policy or the ball drops into the hole and we relax, with a momentary "Ah!," into simple, self-sufficient being.

Not surprisingly, neurological studies have shown that our brain-wave patterns at that moment resemble those of meditators deep in practice. The "Ah!" of satisfaction, of course, is not "out there" in the closed deal or the sunk putt, which merely triggers it. It's within us, where (as Jesus assures us) the kingdom of God is, where awareness settles into itself; it's "where we live," separate from the active level where we work. So the Dwarfs dig away, unconscious that Snow White, who embodies this self-sufficient being, is already settling into the home where *they* live. The satisfaction we work so hard to extract from the world of activity is, it turns out, already ours.

> Don't search any further.
> Don't go into the tangled jungle
> looking for the great awakened elephant,
> who is already resting quietly at home
> in front of your own hearth.
> —VEN. LAMA GENDUN RINPOCHE

Actually, not all the Dwarfs work underground. Two remain at the surface to examine and sort what the other five dig up, suggesting two different ways we process our experiences of the world. Bespectacled Doc is the rational intellect. He's all business, with his jeweler's loupe and his carefully labeled bags for different carat weights, reducing gemlike direct experience to abstract categories of quality and quantity. His assistant is mute, beardless, childlike Dopey, the silent holy fool, our naive, blissfully ignorant side (possibly modeled on Charlie Chaplin, whom Disney impersonated in contests in his youth).

But Dopey is the only Dwarf who knows "what we dig 'em for." He doesn't just dig 'em, he *digs* 'em, man. Tapping Doc on the shoulder, he shows him the two big diamonds he has stuck in his eyes, tripping out on the kaleidoscopic display they produce, grinning and flapping his ears. We all have brief, spontaneous moments when we dare to be dopey, when we let go, stop trying to categorize or manipulate our experience, and just enjoy the kaleidoscopic wonder of whatever is before us. But soon abstract thought takes over again. Our inner Doc, set on reducing the world to a Doc-toral dissertation, makes us knock it off and drop that visionary mode—as Doc now raps Dopey on the head, knocking the diamonds to the ground. But that's OK. As the others toil and accumulate, we see Dopey dance about, sweeping up stray diamonds only to throw them away, or locking the vault and then leaving the oversize key hanging conspicuously by the door. When visionary bliss is perceived everywhere, there's no need to hoard it.

The point is not that one component is "good" and the other "bad." All are necessary. We do need to think analytical, purposeful thoughts as well as to dopily space out. We do need an outgoing Happy part to indiscriminately engage and embrace the world; a discriminating Sneezy part to expel anything unhealthful that comes in from the world; a Bashful part to maintain some private space; a Sleepy part as a kind of power-off button, to give the whole system an occasional oblivion break; and even a cynical Grumpy part, a bullshit detector, to keep things real. This synergy is graphically depicted at closing time, when the Dwarfs march home in single file, singing their "Heigh Ho" song. Each has his place, from Doc, who leads the procession with the headlight-white lantern of intellect, to Dopey, who is pushed to the back of the line just as our wordless amazement keeps getting pushed to the back of the mind. But with his taillight-red lantern, he's still an essential part of the vehicle of personality. They're separate states, but they're united: *E pluribus unum.*

WHEN THE DWARFS arrive home, these longtime bachelors are alarmed to find the light on and the place clean. After years without the influence of snow-white pure awareness, we become used to a certain amount of darkness in our consciousness and messiness in our lives. Upon taking up spiritual practice, we may at first be disconcerted to find that old habits—maybe smoking, or hurtful wisecracking, or indulgent self-pity—are being spontaneously swept away. It may be a mess, but it's *our* mess, and when it starts to go we feel as if part of ourselves is going. But something better awaits us. In fact, she's upstairs. Snow White has fallen asleep, stretched across several of the Dwarfs' little beds, as befits the unifying essence that will bring fulfillment to the personality's diverse components.

The intellect reasserting itself as the supposed boss of the personality, Doc tries to lead a reconnaissance mission. But encountering pure awareness requires direct *seeing*, not the intellect's jabbering. Doc's professorial glasses, far too wide for his eyes, are strictly for show, and his blustering commands keep getting tangled up:

> Careful, men! Search every cook and nanny—er, hook and granny—er, crooked—Search everywhere!

Wisely, the Dwarfs recognize that naive, wordless simplicity is the best way to approach our true being, and they send Dopey tiptoeing upstairs for a first look. Jesus says that to enter the kingdom of heaven we must be like little children. Buddhists say Zen mind is beginner's mind. Having taught meditation to hundreds of high school students, I've often found that the ones who take to it most readily are not the valedictorians but the jocks and artists, who are used to experiencing things simply and directly, through their bodies rather than their heads.

But at first even Dopey mistakes the sleeping Snow White, covered by a bedsheet, for a monster, and runs back to mime this information to the others. Such illusory monstrous beings are common in esoteric spiritual teachings. The Tibetan Book of the Dead describes various "wrathful deities," with their dripping fangs and bodies of flame, but emphasizes that they are really nothing but our own inner nature, upon which we project a fierce aspect when we fail to recognize it properly—that may be why we find so many creative ways to avoid it. Intending to kill the monster, the Dwarfs venture upstairs, but just as our first tastes of inner being allay our fears, once Snow White awakes she charms the Dwarfs—all but Grumpy. Our cynical component is determined to resist the light as long as possible, as suggested by Grumpy's eyes, which, being merely tiny black pupils with no irises, can't dilate to let in more light. (The other Dwarfs have brown eyes, except Dopey with his innocent baby blues.)

Snow White has cooked soup for her hosts, pure awareness being the one thing that can feed the outer personality's gnawing inner hunger, but first she sends them outside to wash, a novel experience for them. Most spiritual traditions acknowledge the need for some form of ritual cleansing or baptism before we can ingest the sacred; the Dwarfs use a communal tub, reminiscent of the Sabbath *mikveh*. The last holdout, again, is Grumpy, whom the others finally grab and dunk, giving him the full-immersion, extrathorough soaking he needs. This points up another important—and frequently misunderstood—fact of life on the spiritual path. Before we can enjoy the full feast of inner experience, our personality must be cleansed, but none of its aspects are lost. They are all purified, even (finally) the grumpy, negative ones. Ram Dass says that, despite his decades of psychotherapy, psychedelic experimentation, devotion, and meditation, he has not shed a single neurosis; rather, they have all been gradually transformed from big, scary monsters to harmless, friendly little Schmoo-like creatures . . . not unlike our Dwarfs.

It can be particularly confusing when we encounter people we consider spiritually developed, expecting them to be cosmically bland, colorless characters, and discover that they manifest a full spectrum of colors—opinions, tastes, quirks. What we can't see is that *they* experience those colors as various wavelengths of pure white (snow-white) light, so they can engage in them wholeheartedly without being limited or stained by them. I know a lama who's a longtime devotee of the New England Patriots. When they finally won the Super Bowl in 2002, he was most assuredly not sitting in the lotus pose, drifting in a state of divine detachment, but leaping around the room and whooping like any other crazed, exuberant fan.

IT IS WITH just such exuberance that, after supper, the Dwarfs sing and dance with Snow White in a joyous hoedown, marking the symbolic integration of silent, fulfilling inner awareness and practical, stabilizing outer activity.

> For you shall go out in joy,
> and be led back in peace;
> the mountains and the hills before you
> shall burst into song. . . .
> —ISAIAH 55:12

Being needs doing, doing needs being. This is news worth celebrating: we don't have to choose between being blissful hermits or productive but stressed-out working stiffs. We can, as one of my teachers put it, "live 200 percent of life." Like the football-loving lama, we can participate enthusiastically in the full range of activities and emotions without being bound by any of them.

To see how this freedom works, let's take our earlier experiment a step further:

- Sit quietly and think of some scene from your past that makes you feel happy. Stay with that for a little while.

- Next, think of a scene that makes you feel grumpy, and stay with that.

- In each case, notice that the experience of the scene is a series of remembered sensations experienced within your awareness, like the roundness of the penny or the greenness of the dollar—just more subtle.

- Now, paying very close attention to the happiness and grumpiness that the memories evoke, notice that these emotions are also sensations. That's why we call them "feelings." Happiness has a sort of texture or flavor that is different from that of grumpiness. And notice that these sensations, like all others, are experienced within awareness.

- Notice that *awareness itself*, just as it is neither brown and smooth like a penny nor green and crinkly like a dollar, is also neither this scene nor that scene, neither happy nor grumpy. Rather, it is the pure reflectivity, the luminous clarity, *within which* all these sensations come and go.

So it's never quite right to say "I *am* happy" or "I *am* grumpy." It would be more accurate to say "I feel happiness" or "The sensations of grumpiness have arisen." The great jazzman Lester Young somehow understood this. He never asked "How are you?" but always "How are your feelings?"

As you go through your day and through your life, keep playing with this deceptively simple experiment in one form after another till you really get it. Then you'll get that you're always absolutely free—that, no matter what joy or misery arises, *you* are that which is beyond all joy and misery: pristine snow-white mind.

> The mind's own basic nature is ultimately
> neutral. . . . . When I was young I was quite
> short-tempered. However, the mood never lasted
> for twenty-four hours. If negative emotions are in
> the very nature of our mind, then as long as the
> mind is functioning the anger must remain.
> That, however, is not the case. Similarly, positive
> emotions are also not in the nature of the mind.
> The mind is something neutral, reflecting all sorts
> of different experiences or phenomena.
> —H. H. THE XIV DALAI LAMA,
> *Live in a Better Way*

Many of these moods and modes mutate quickly, arising and vanishing in seconds or minutes. Others may hang around for practically a lifetime, so that we think of them as a permanent, inherent part of the person, a trait rather than a state: "Oh, he's selfish," "She's clever," "They're frivolous," "I'm Jewish," "You're Irish." These are like slow-drifting clouds, which, at a casual glance, appear to be solid, permanent features of the sky. But every cloud changes, moves, and eventually evaporates, while the sky has no beginning or end. Even if it hung around for a thousand years, a cloud would still be essentially different from sky; and sky, no matter how many clouds may float in it, always remains open, empty, untouched, vast.

NOW THAT THE two sides of life embodied by Snow White and the Dwarfs have at last been brought together, the festivities in their cottage, with all their singing and dancing, look almost like a wedding celebration. But then, craving an even deeper, more complete realization—her *real* wedding—Snow White sings "Some Day My Prince Will Come."* Our inmost being cries out to find its match in something as vast as itself. A full-sized princess, after all, can't shack up forever with a gang of Dwarfs (although Dopey, now her most eager dance partner, later keeps trying for the lips whenever she gives each Dwarf a maternal kiss on the top of the head).

So even the 200 percent model, the comfy lifestyle of the bourgeois-bohemian meditator—like me—can be a kind of trap. With the support of our newfound inner expansiveness, our dwarfish outer lives become seductively fulfilling. I get up in the morning in my lovely little Tudor cottage (not unlike the Dwarfs', as a matter of fact), sit in my corner meditation room, go do my teaching, come home, do my writing (on the back patio, if the weather's nice, among the catbirds and chipmunks), whip up some dinner, maybe play my saxophone or go to a movie, and it's all so ridiculously pleasant that I want to stay right here forever, stuck in the divine honey pot. But at the same time, the growing light of realization teases us, makes us crave to face it head-on in some blinding, ultimate form, a form that transcends life and death. And some day that light, that prince, will come.

What precipitates the coming of that day is the acceptance of

---

* To hear a truly poignant version, at this point switch to the French soundtrack on the DVD.

the reality of death—we're really going to leave all this behind. Even as Snow White dances away with the Dwarfs, the Queen is in her *Frankenstein*-inspired laboratory, cooking up the poisoned apple. Just when I feel I've finally paid my dues and learned a few things about life, just when my job has become pretty easy and my relationships fulfilling, just when my neuroses have mellowed to a manageable level, I have to give it all up. So soon? Right now? Maybe. To accept death's reality, we must accept its imminence. It's always just one missed heartbeat away.

This realization, although scary at first, becomes profoundly liberating when we make it a regular practice. Perhaps the simplest way to do this is, in every moment of our lives, to *buy a one-way ticket*. Each time you go down the hallway to the bathroom, abandon the presumption that you'll ever return to the office or the party. Each time you lie down, abandon the presumption (and it is presumptuous) that you'll ever stand up again. Whenever you pray or chant, burrow deeper in with each syllable, abandoning any thought of ever coming back out. Again and again, utterly abandon home, job, family, possessions, whatever you've got. If you happen to see them again, that's lovely. But keep giving them all up *as if* you're about to die, which is, after all, a distinct possibility.

Then you begin to inhabit and savor each moment as *the* moment, rather than a mere stopover. Since the present moment is all we have (besides dubious memories of the past and flimsy projections of the future), this openness to death paradoxically gives you your life. As you hug your friend or sing your song or park your car, you're fully present, fully alive, in the hugging, singing, parking. And when death arrives and letting everything go is no longer optional, you'll have had plenty of practice.

Here death arrives in the form of the poisoned apple, offered by the vengeful Queen, now magically transformed into her own worst nightmare—a hideous Hag. It's an interesting choice of disguises, as if the false self, exhausted by constantly straining toward unattainable immortality and perfection, secretly welcomes its own decay. This is the only time we see her leave the isolation of her castle, and, as she cackles away, the only time she relaxes and enjoys herself. Ironically, accepting the ravages of time and change are the beginning of her liberation, hence her joy. Trailed by a pair of grinning vultures, she makes her way to the Dwarfs' cottage, where she finds Snow White home alone and, speaking menacingly straight into the camera, convinces her that what she offers is a magic wishing apple: "One bite, and all your dreams will come true." Wishing for her Prince to find her, Snow White takes a bite and falls to the floor—off-camera, in a quaintly old-fashioned attempt not to overly upset the kids.

But what we call death, as it turns out, is the death only of the limited, false self. The Dwarfs come home and chase the Hag through a raging storm—a storm of purification, the culmination of the process that started with the water in Snow White's scrub bucket. They corner her on a craggy mountaintop that epitomizes narcissistic isolation. There the Hag attempts to roll a boulder down on the Dwarfs, but, when a bolt of lightning pulverizes her little crag, she falls to her death (in a dramatic plunge echoed in several other films, including *King Kong* and both versions of *Scarface*). In Vajrayana iconography, the lightning bolt symbolizes the surging power of illumination, in which we suddenly see clearly what we are. What we aren't, with all its Queenly arrogance and Haggish twistedness, drops away.

AS SNOW WHITE lies in state before the kneeling Dwarfs, Grumpy sheds the most bitter tears; the part of us that resisted the light the hardest misses it the most when it's gone. But, of course, she is only in a deathlike sleep. The Queen's plan was that the Dwarfs would bury Snow White alive, just as pure awareness is buried alive in the workaday world when the false self rules our lives. The Dwarfs, though, can't bear to bury her, so they keep her in a casket of glass and gold. If inner being is sufficiently integrated with the outer, active personality, it remains in sight, even through the direst crisis.

And now the Queen's promise, that eating the apple will make Snow White's dream come true, is ironically fulfilled. News of the miraculous preservation reaches the Prince, who arrives on the scene to wake Snow White with "love's first kiss." This awakening to the full glory of what we are—pure being, awake to its own nature—is the real resurrection, the real buddhahood. Opening her eyes, Snow White beholds the one who is like herself, the one she saw when she looked deep within at her own reflection in the well. Like her, he is tall and beautiful. Enlightenment is not just one more Dwarfish mood or mode, not just another Queenly fixation, but our own essence fully blossomed. It is therefore our only completely fulfilling destiny. Nothing else will do.

And now, as the Dwarfs rejoice, nothing else is left to do but for the Prince to carry Snow White off to his castle, which, in the dazzling final shot, we behold floating above the clouds, a fantasy structure awash in light, clearly representing not just a nice suburban home for a pair of newlyweds but a radiant spiritual state—the kingdom of heaven. In contrast with the Queen's dank castle shown in the film's opening shot, it's snow-white, the purified castle Snow White was trying to scrub into being when first we saw her.

As we awaken day by day into a more enlightened life, we come to see that everything we regarded as a death—the death of each situation, each concept, each self-image—is not *our* death. What we are, like Snow White, doesn't die but only sleeps. Even when everything else is destroyed (and it will be), our essence cannot be destroyed. Everything that dies has an element of isolation and constriction; if we can just let it go, what remains is liberation. Finally even the body is just one more limitation we once identified with.

So the more thoroughly we immerse ourselves in simple being, and the more clearly we learn to recognize it in our lives of doing, the more we come to suspect that all the talk of an immortal heavenly realm above the clouds is no mere fairy tale. It's a perfectly apt metaphor for the final, crystal-clear realization of our own deathless nature. With all obscurations dissolved at last, we see "that fine, clean, unspoiled spot" not only deep inside ourselves but everywhere we look. And then we live not just happily ever after, but—beyond happy or sad, beyond birth and death—*free* ever after.

THE BIG SLEEP
(1946)

DANCING IN THE DARK

We must examine what is here, now, our neurotic mind.
Once we are completely familiar with the negative aspects
of the state of our being, then we know the "way out"
automatically.

—CHÖGYAM TRUNGPA RINPOCHE,
Cutting Through Spiritual Materialism

If you're going through hell, keep going.

—WINSTON CHURCHILL

THE DREAM HAS MANY VARIATIONS. SOMETIMES, IN A panic, I suddenly realize that back in high school I forgot I was enrolled in a math course and stopped going; my college degrees and my whole subsequent life have all been a fraud. In the most grisly version, there's a body, dismembered and stuffed into a black plastic garbage bag, stashed away in the back of an upper closet shelf—someone I forgot I murdered in the distant past. And always there's the sense of pollution, of deep taintedness, a sense that in some irretrievable past I committed such irredeemable acts that my life is now miserably, irreversibly ruined. I've screwed up, and now I'm screwed.

On bad days, our world resembles those dreams.

JOHNER: Earth? I'm not going to that fucking slum.
—*Alien: Resurrection*

AIDS, terrorism, global warming—there's a sense that *we've* screwed up, and now we're *all* screwed. We're in this big, bad dream together, trapped in the darkness of this big sleep with no Prince Charming to wake us. Some people call it Original Sin and speak hopefully of Redemption; the Buddha called it the First Noble Truth (suffering is our chronic condition) and spoke of the Third Noble Truth (the condition is cured by enlightenment). But to meaningfully embrace a solution, we have to be well versed in the problem. What is it like when we can see no light at the end of the tunnel? And while we're in that tunnel, what are the most graceful methods of dancing in the dark, with the least crashing into others? The cinema of nirvana requires the cinema of samsara; we can't explore enlightenment without knowing endarkenment.

So let us consider dark film: film noir, the stylized crime dramas that emerged in the '40s, with their deep shadows, rainy streets, swirling cigarette smoke, dangerous dames, and wisecracking men in trench coats and fedoras. Because the noir hero is typically a private detective, he's a lot like us. We're also seekers of truth, looking for a solution to the mystery of our lives, a way out of the dark. Like him, we're hunting for the perpetrator of the crime, the cause of suffering. Like the cops in his world, our culture's official truth-seeking establishment is generally too corrupt or incompetent to be much help. In noir, answers are hard to find—or, rather, much too easy. Shady grifters and two-faced women, like our priests and philosophers, give the detective one answer after another, but they all contradict each other. He's like the hero of Borges's "The Library of Babel," who wanders among shelves that extend forever in all directions, filled with books that are just random sequences of letters. Somewhere, one of those books must reveal the truth, the meaning of his otherwise meaningless life. But how would he find it? How would he recognize it?

AMONG NOIR FILMS, *The Big Sleep* is notorious for its impossibly twisted storyline. There are poisoned drinks; hidden cameras; a high-class porn racket; a crooked gambling casino; two or three extortion plots; half a dozen or so killings, including a car plunge off a pier that may or may not be a suicide; a missing Irishman whose disappearance may or may not have anything to do with any of this, and whose friends may or may not want him found; and lots more. If you watch the film three or four times and perhaps read the Raymond Chandler novel it's based on, you may or may not be able to make sense of it. In a famous incident, Howard Hawks, the puzzled director, telegraphed Chandler to ask about that car plunge. Chandler wasn't sure either.

But this baffling convolutedness is precisely the point. Life in the dark doesn't make sense. It's a maze, a labyrinth through which we grope, as does Philip Marlowe, our private-eye hero, played by Humphrey Bogart.

> MARLOWE: It's a funny thing. You're trying to find out what your father hired me to find out, and I'm trying to find out why you want to find out.
> VIVIAN [Lauren Bacall]: You could go on forever, couldn't you?

By the time he more or less solves the mystery, we're still so confused that there's no sense of tidy resolution. The fat lady doesn't sing but coughs spasmodically. Samsara, the confusion that is the lack of nirvana, is like that. Short of waking up, there's no way out of the tangled dream.

> And there are no truths outside the gates of Eden.
> —BOB DYLAN

Hawks reinforces this theme with a visual style that is not overtly dreamlike but always slightly off-kilter. From the creepy way a drugged woman doodles on her knee with her finger, humming childishly, unaware of the corpse lying at her feet, to the odd, unsettling angle at which a car tools up a hill through the rain, everything has a queasy, not-quite-right quality.

We enter this dream-maze as Marlowe enters the mansion of the fabulously wealthy General Sternwood, who is being blackmailed by someone who has the goods on one of his two loose-living daughters. As we follow Marlowe on his quest for answers, the film becomes a guided tour of samsara. Hindu and Buddhist cosmology also provides such a tour, in the Wheel of Life diagram. In Tibet, it's found at the entrance to every temple, always painted on the outer wall because it represents the structure of mundane outer existence, which is to be transcended as one enters the enlightenment-space of the temple's interior. The wheel, crowded with all sorts of busy beings, looks kind of like an extralarge pizza with everything, cut into six slices, each slice depicting a "realm"— a plane or dimension into which we may be reborn, depending on our karma. Karma is *not* some kind of mysterious destiny beyond our control, but exactly the opposite. It literally means "action" or "doing," and implies that our fate is our own doing. ("The fault, dear Brutus, is not in our stars, / But in ourselves. . . .")

The denizens of the six realms—gods, "jealous gods," humans, animals, "hungry ghosts," and hell-beings—are archetypal roles. They might be played as physical forms that we inhabit for a lifetime, or as situations and moods that we inhabit for months or minutes, "reborn" each time things change. The realms are all projections of mental states, so it's not necessary to take them literally (the Dalai Lama doesn't), but they provide a psychologically precise model of nonliberation, of all the ways we keep getting stuck as we go wearily round in circles, till at last we're sufficiently clued in to step off the wheel into nirvana. *The Big Sleep* looks a lot like the six realms.

Marlowe's journey begins at the top of the wheel, in the celestial *deva* realm—General Sternwood's lush tropical greenhouse. The devas, or gods, inhabit a world of power and pleasure. Their youth and beauty unfading, they live a life of ease, pampered with every luxury, feeding from the bounty of a great wish-fulfilling tree that drops fruit in profusion. In our society, the devas are those who have made it, who live lifestyles of the rich and famous. On this planet—as you know if you've traveled in Third World countries—the deva realm is America, land of soft toilet paper, smooth highways, good health care, and overflowing supermarket shelves. Individually, we dwell in the deva realm at the top of the wheel whenever we feel on top of the world. The humidity is low, our team is winning, we're wearing our favorite shirt, we're in love, and we're having a great hair day. "I want things to stay like this forever," we think.

But this too shall pass, alas. What goes up must come down; that's the way the wheel spins. The weather changes, love changes. One day that shirt will be a dust rag and your hair will be gone. The devas, with their life spans of thousands of years, are lulled into thinking they'll be livin' large eternally, but when their good karma runs out they abruptly begin to age and, with great anguish, see their pleasure-realm slipping away—as suddenly, it is said, as a foul smell blows in on a summer breeze.

> I often think how comforting life must have been
> for early man because he believed in a powerful,
> benevolent Creator who looked after all things.
> Imagine his disappointment when he saw his wife
> putting on weight.
> —WOODY ALLEN,
>   "My Speech to the Graduates"

During the tech boom of the '90s, stock analysts wrote seriously of a market that would never decline again. Superstars feel like they'll always be at the top of the charts, but (as VH1's *Behind the Music* reminds us) soon their decade fades and they're playing for tips at a bar and grill in Arizona. Americans think we'll be the world superpower forever, as did the Romans, the Mongols, and every other has-been dynasty. General Sternwood commanded great armies and amassed a fortune, but now his daughters run wild and blackmailers pick his bones. He's wheelchair-bound and broken, reduced to licking his lips as he watches other men drink his brandy. For a film made at the close of World War II, just when General Eisenhower (whose bald dome General Sternwood shares) was leading America to victory, it's a bold insinuation: the high of power and prosperity must eventually give way to a hangover of disillusionment. The general nurses his hangover swaddled with blankets in the overheated greenhouse, trying to warm up his blood, surrounded by orchids that, he tells Marlowe, he finds nauseating:

> Nasty things. Their flesh is too much like the flesh of
> men, and their perfume has the rotten sweetness of
> corruption.

As Marlowe plunges into the Los Angeles underworld in pursuit of the General's enemies, he enters the realm of the *asuras*, translated as "jealous gods," "anti-gods," or "titans." The asuras are wannabe devas. They're hustlers, aggressors, guys on the make. Devas are former asuras who've made it. "Behind every great fortune," said Balzac, "is a great crime," and most aristocratic family trees—Rockefellers, Vanderbilts—have ruthless robber-baron roots. Thus the wish-fulfilling tree whose fruits ripen in the deva realm has its roots in the asura realm, and the two races wage a constant turf war for its possession. Individually, we dwell in the asura realm whenever the passion for success blinds us to all other values. (Macbeth, as he contemplates usurping the throne through assassination, ticks off half a dozen excellent reasons not to do it, but then concludes that "vaulting ambition" trumps them all.)

In *The Big Sleep*, the ambitious asuras are gangsters, typified by Eddie Mars, fittingly named for the god of war. His royal court is his casino, a temple to the get-rich-quick mentality of those who hope to change their lives with other people's money. He's also a blackmailer, preying on Establishment devas like the Sternwoods. Such criminally overreaching American dreamers are our model asuras (Jay Gatsby, Tony Soprano, the Enron execs). For those in the underclass, the asura ethic promises a shortcut out of the exploited animal realm— hip-hop gangstas emulate Mafia gangsters:

> Never prayed to God, I prayed to Gotti. . . .
> You don't know me, but the whole world owe me.
> —JAY-Z,
>   "D'Evils"

THE WORLDS OF DEVAS, asuras, and humans (whom we'll discuss later) are the upper realms, above the equator of our pizza diagram. The first of the three lower realms is that of the animals. Some people fantasize pleasantly about being a cat or dog or bird, especially in devic America where pets eat better than most people in a lot of countries. But wild animals spend most of their waking minutes searching for food and water, their ears cocked for predators; most domestic animals are beasts of burden or livestock raised for slaughter. Animal consciousness is dominated by exploitation and the struggle for survival. It's not easy and it's not cute.

> I believe that life is a mess. . . . It is like yeast, a
> ferment, a thing that moves and may move for a

minute . . . but that in the end will cease to move.
The big eat the little that they may continue to
move, the strong eat the weak that they may retain
their strength. The lucky eat the most and move the
longest, that is all.
        —JACK LONDON,
        The Sea-Wolf

Animals are condemned to this eat-or-be-eaten fate by their
stupidity. If cows were as smart as they are big, they'd gang up
on the ranchers who turn them into hamburgers. In human society, sadly, there is never a shortage of people living animalistic lives: ignorant, fearful, exploited. They're the lumps in the
lumpenproletariat, devoid of self-awareness, preoccupied with
the struggle to make the next mortgage payment, dutifully
yielding up their sons for war and their hard-earned dollars for
shiny trinkets, as seen on TV. The most popular words in the
headlines of the tabloid papers they read are "shock," "shocking," and "shocker," as if they need a constant series of electric
jolts just to remind them they're alive. But, whatever our class,
we all have moments when we choose to be foolish and used, to
let ourselves be led by the nose, possibly to slaughter.

In the noir world the animals are the underlings on both
sides of the law: the ordinary cops who are dull-witted next to
clever sleuths like Marlowe, and the brutish thugs who are foot-
soldiers and fall guys for bosses like Eddie Mars. Marlowe dis-
misses them all with one of the film's best quips: "My, my, my.
Such a lot of guns around town and so few brains!" Like animals focused on survival, most of the film's cops just want to
live long enough to collect their pensions; if they catch a few
crooks along the way, that's all right. For the thugs to survive,
their best bet in the short term is to follow orders, but long
term they're as expendable as veal calves. We're often invited to
laugh at their stupidity, as when Eddie Mars summons his two

inanely strutting stooges to intimidate Marlowe. Pete in his silly hat and bow tie and Sidney with his too-tight suit (named for Peter Lorre and Sydney Greenstreet, Bogart's much-loved supporting players in *Casablanca*) are a sort of lowlife Rosencrantz and Guildenstern. Marlowe eventually bamboozles them into shooting their own boss.

Seriously dangerous, though, is the hit man Canino, the predatory dregs of the animal kingdom. As his name implies, he's a mad dog, a cruel killer with hollowed-out eyes, implausibly played by Bob Steele, one of the great cowboy heroes of the early screen. Mars calls on him when it's time for some particularly brutal violence; fittingly, he shows up only near the end, as we penetrate to the film's heart of darkness. Always in his hat and overcoat—dressed to kill—and shrouded in shadows and fog, he uses an innocent woman for a shield in a shootout, beats Marlowe viciously, and poisons the film's nicest thug.

Also below the equator is the realm of the *pretas*, the so-called "hungry ghosts," with their long, narrow necks, tiny mouths, and stomachs so cavernous they can never be filled. These strange beings are the embodiment of our own insatiability. In most cities, when everything else is closed the bars are still open, filled with people for whom the drink that will finally satisfy them is always the next one. (As we walked past the open door of a local saloon one summer night, my wife said, "Maybe they're just thirsty.") We're reborn in the preta realm whenever we persist in behavior that only exacerbates our hungers. It could be compulsive eating or drinking or shopping, or playing endless computer games, or yearning for the old lover, the one who would have *really* made us happy.

> Lust is the craving for salt of a man that is dying of thirst.
>
> —FREDERICK BUECHNER,
> *Wishful Thinking*

The general's nymphomaniac daughter Carmen, played by the sizzling Martha Vickers, is the film's resident preta. She is, like a dame in another Chandler novel, "a blonde to make a bishop kick a hole through a stained-glass window." Her voracious hunger for drugs and sex are signaled by her habit of sucking her thumb, a gesture that is at once infantile and crudely sensual. Marlowe tells Norris the butler, "You ought to wean her. She's old enough," but there's no Mrs. Sternwood in sight, no mothering figure in the stern woods of the general's patriarchal domain. Do our bottomless thirsts stem from being insufficiently loved and nursed by our mothers? Are they aggravated by patriarchal religions that have banished the infinitely loving, nurturing Mother Goddess of old? Could be.

The lowest of the three lower realms is called hell, but it's not the Christian hell of eternal punishment, externally imposed. Like all the realms—like everything in our existence—it's an impermanent product of our own thought and action. Specifically, hell is the projection of our anger. Whenever we are caught up in blind fury, whenever we fixate upon another person or group as the source of all our problems, the Evil One, we have created a dualistic reality of you versus me, where I must eliminate you. Hell can be an instant of road rage or a Hundred Years' War. It eliminates all fellow-feeling, all appreciation of the other, and leaves only alienation.

> Fathers and teachers, I ponder, "What is hell?"
> I maintain that it is the suffering of being unable
> to love.
> —DOSTOYEVSKY,
> *The Brothers Karamazov*

The hellish explosions of terrorism and war, then, are extensions of hellishly imploding emotions. Because anger can feel cutting or crushing, icy or fiery, the classical descriptions of the hell realm include a suite of subrealms—cutting hells, crushing hells, hot and cold hells—which can be read as metaphors for these inner feelings. And, while all the realms have a quality of fixation, of being stuck, hell is the distilled essence of stuckness. Anytime all you can think is "Get me out of here" but you can't get out of there—stuck on a long elevator ride, say, with your ex—that's hell. That's what makes it *seem* eternal. And while we're stuck there, caught up in rage, we may commit an act (making a truly cruel remark in a family quarrel, tossing a bomb into a marketplace) that will perpetuate suffering and hatred for years to come.

> Hell is a state where, in an attempt to avoid pain,
> you cause yourself as much pain as possible. . . .
> We begin to treat everything as a threat, and
> whatever we treat as a threat becomes a threat.
> —NGAK'CHANG RINPOCHE

The Big Sleep's hell dweller is an angry young man in a leather jacket named Carol Lundgren, the gay lover of Geiger, the shady book dealer who blackmails Carmen with porn photos taken of her while drugged. (In the film, shackled by the puritanical Hollywood Production Code that remained in force till 1968, this is all rather fuzzy. It's clearer in the novel.) Lundgren becomes enraged when Geiger is killed, and, erroneously thinking the killer is a crook named Joe Brody, he goes for revenge. But watching from the point of view of Marlowe, who's at Brody's place to retrieve the photos, we don't exactly see all that. There's a knock, Brody opens the door a crack, and, in one of the film's great subtle, weird, dreamlike images, a single bullet from the unseen shooter rips a hole in the door and Brody falls dead. The image encapsulates what anger does to us. It's as if Lundgren's whole being has been reduced to a faceless, narrowly aimed, explosive propulsion. No longer a person, he has become a stream of hatred so intensely concentrated it can squeeze through that little hole.

AS DIFFERENT AS they are, the one quality shared by these first five realms is that they don't lead directly to enlightenment. In the Monopoly game of samsara you have to pass "Go" to win, and the go, go, go is the active, seeking, dissatisfied, self-aware realm of the humans. Devas are too mired in pleasure and pride—why seek nirvana when you're lolling in samsara's luxury penthouse? The jealousy of asuras, the hunger of pretas, the rage of hell-beings, and the dullness of animals similarly prevent them from conceiving their own higher good. (If my cats could understand for just fifteen minutes that being put in a box and driven to the vet's office for a shot will make them feel better, they could save themselves a lot of struggle.) With vicious circularity, these states of mind grip us so tightly that we don't know we're being gripped.

> That's why he can't see things as they really are. . . .
> How can he see he's got flies in his eyes if he's got
> flies in his eyes?
>   —JOSEPH HELLER,
>   *Catch-22*

So, whether you think of rebirth as a literal reality or a psychological metaphor, finding oneself in the human mode is a rare opportunity, too precious to waste. The Buddha once picked up a bit of dirt on his fingernail and said that if all the dirt in the world represented all the forms we can be born in, the bit he was holding was equivalent to our chances of manifesting as a human.

Marlowe is the film's representative human. He's a person, a mensch, not superhuman like a god or subhuman like an animal, just more or less normal and reasonably virtuous, even if he needs to self-medicate with an occasional drink to stay on course. His habitual wisecracking suggests that he is at least on the path to becoming wise. He has just the qualities that detectives need and that we need to detect the solution to samsara's mystery, the great awakening that ends the big sleep. He's curious and quick to speculate, but slow to draw conclusions.

> MARLOWE: Hmmm.
> VIVIAN: What does "Hmmm" mean?
> MARLOWE: It means "Hmmm."

He's brave (meaning not that he's fearless, but that he does what he fears), he's resourceful, and, above all, he's tenacious:

> VIVIAN: Why did you have to go on?
> MARLOWE: Too many people told me to stop.

He conducts himself with grace under pressure. He's a professional.*

As he stands waiting in General Sternwood's high-ceilinged foyer in the film's opening scene, Marlowe looks with interest at a carved panel depicting a coat of arms topped by a knight's helmet, our first inkling of his strategy for navigating through a world of corruption without being corrupted. But being a knight isn't easy: just then Carmen appears, luscious in her skimpy white shorts, eyeing Marlowe like so much raw meat.

---

* Several character and plot elements of *The Big Sleep* are slyly recycled in the Coen brothers' *The Big Lebowski* (1998). Unlike Marlowe, the Coens' detective is an amateur, a bumbling, shaggy stoner known as The Dude (Jeff Bridges). Yet because he shares Marlowe's essential humanity and integrity, he comes out all right, living to bowl another line. The Dude abides.

(Watch closely and you'll see he's demurely shielding his crotch with his hat.)

> CARMEN: You're not very tall, are you?
> MARLOWE [glancing down into the hat]: Well, I, uh,
> I try to be.

There are two jokes here. One is about Bogart's height of 5'8", unimpressive for a macho leading man. The other is a sexual innuendo about size mattering and about rising, shall we say, to the occasion. But there's also a suggestion of the would-be knight's honorable striving. Despite our limitations, we humans, the animals who have learned to walk on our rear feet, can try to stand tall. Maybe I'm not very heroic or smart or nice, but, well, I, uh, I try to be, and there's honor in that.

> We are all in the gutter, but some of us are looking
> at the stars.
> —OSCAR WILDE,
>   *Lady Windermere's Fan*

When, his jaw set in determination, Marlowe steps into the night and the rain to slog through the trenches for the thousandth time, tying the belt of his trench coat, we know he's suiting up in the right armor and he's got the right stuff.

Much of the film's power comes from Bogart's utter rightness in the role, particularly at just this moment in his life. He doesn't have the height or hair or conventionally handsome features that would let anyone mistake him for a god. Or the voice—his Brooklyn snarl and hint of a lisp, caused by a scarred lip he suffered in the navy, inspired the voice of Bugs Bunny. He doesn't have the emotional range to express the intense passions of the other five realms. But the thoughtful toughness, the tender cynicism, and the confident wit that masks a deeper vulnerability make him intensely human. We sense that he has been there, he has struggled, he is weary of a battle whose outcome is always in doubt, but he soldiers on with dignity. The battle-scarred quality we see onscreen is genuine; as *The Big Sleep* was shooting, Bogart was going through a bitter divorce and drinking heavily. (He once said, "The problem with the world is that everyone is a few drinks behind.") He has faults, but hypocrisy is not one of them. He never, ever pretends to be something he's not.

Thus Bogart embodies the down-to-earth frankness that's necessary for real spiritual progress, unlike the strained posturing and sugary fantasies that often pass for spirituality, from the most fundamentalist churches to the airy-fairyest New Age soirées. You can't move ahead unless you're clear about where you are.

> You are the salt of the earth; but if the salt has lost
> its taste, how can the saltiness be restored?
> —MATTHEW 5:13

Bogart's always salty.

TO BE HUMAN, then, is not to be enlightened, but it's the prerequisite. And you can get there from here. Marlowe, as an ex-cop who was fired for insubordination (that is, thinking for himself), has evolved out of the animal realm, and throughout the film we encounter a cop here or a butler there whose wry smile indicates an intelligence that raises him above the herd, and who helps Marlowe just because it's the right thing to do. The most important evolving character is Carmen's sister Vivian, played by Lauren Bacall, who offscreen was Bogart's tall, slim, deep-voiced lover and wife-to-be. Bogey and Bacall had famously met on the set of *To Have and Have Not.* She was just eighteen, but her seductively knowing delivery ("Just whistle") gave men, including the forty-two-year-old Bogart, the shivers. When she was cast as Vivian, a minor character in the novel, the part was expanded to exploit the celebrated romance.

Although both of the general's daughters are caught up in voracious preta appetites (Carmen for drugs and sex, Vivian for gambling and booze), Marlowe avoids involvement with the sister who is intent on dragging him down, opting for the one who shows an aptitude for climbing up to the human level. Still, their initial encounters are hostile. In the noir world, with its male point of view, woman is the dangerous other, the trap that distracts the detective from the truth he seeks. As a cop in another Chandler novel says, "Dames lie about anything—just for practice."

But even as the two circle warily, wondering whether to trust one another, they trade clever banter that is a kind of courtship display, including some of the raciest double-entendre to make it past the censors up to that time.*

> VIVIAN: Speaking of horses, I like to play them myself. But I like to see them work out a little first, see if they're front runners or come from behind. . . . I'd say you don't like to be rated. You like to get out in front, open up a little lead, take a little breather in the backstretch, and then come home free.
> MARLOWE: You don't like to be rated yourself.
> VIVIAN: I haven't met anyone yet that can do it. Any suggestions?

---

* Most of this banter was added a year after principal shooting wrapped. The war had ended, and the movie's release was delayed to give way to a stockpile of soon-to-be-outdated combat films. Meanwhile, Bacall's debut with Bogey in Hawks's *To Have and Have Not* caused a sensation, and studio head Jack Warner ordered the shooting of new scenes and recutting of old ones to play up the romance. Both the restored 1945 "dark" version and the "romantic" 1946 theatrical release are included in the 2000 DVD.

MARLOWE: Well, I can't tell till I've seen you over a distance of ground. You've got a touch of class, but I don't know how far you can go.
VIVIAN: A lot depends on who's in the saddle.

This is clearly a mating dance, but it's also something more. Just as animals (and people) display their fine plumage and perform their strutting dances to show they're healthy specimens worthy of remaining in the gene pool, Marlowe and Vivian, in their playful battle of wits, are engaged in a mutual display of *knowingness*, of awareness—precisely the quality required to awaken from the big sleep.

Unlike the baby doll Carmen, Vivian is a consenting adult, as signaled by her contralto voice. Not a mere object of carnal knowledge, she's a knower, one of the guys. Both she and Marlowe seek complete freedom (they "don't like to be rated," they like to "come home free"), which is found only in liberation from samsara's cramped compartments. In a tense night scene near the end of the film, their trust becomes total and they become full partners in liberation. The murderous Canino has beaten and bound Marlowe in a remote hideout. Vivian unties him, literally setting him free. A few moments later, he saves her by shooting Canino, as if freeing her from the grip of the lowest, most vicious of animal passions. The would-be knight has rescued at least this one maiden, slain at least one dragon.

These acts are capped by Vivian's finely nuanced declaration, "I guess I'm in love with you," and Marlowe's response, "I guess I'm in love with you too." Here once again, we're saved by the salt. Love in the fullest sense, the sense in which Jesus advises us to love one another, is a beautiful ideal but is difficult or impossible before the enlightened state. In the thick of samsara, the best we can honestly manage is a tentative creep of faith, a provisional assumption—a "guess"—and that's the best we can reasonably expect from others. But that's good enough to treat one another with kindness and to help one another along the path. As an encyclopedia salesman friend of mine used to say, "Let's write it up on that basis."

A CENTRAL FACT of samsara is that it has something to do with sex and death. The rim of the Wheel of Life diagram shows the binding process of cause and effect, depicted in part as scenes of seduction and copulation, and the entire wheel is in the monstrous grip of Lord Yama, the king of death. What keeps the cycle of samsara spinning are our exits, via death, and our entrances, via sex. Usually, sex and death distract us from nirvana by convincingly impersonating it—all three are literally mind-blowing experiences.

The film's key scene is a strange, primal amalgam of sex and death, both embodied by the dangerously seductive Carmen. (Remember the missing Irishman? By the film's end, we learn that she killed him for refusing to sleep with her.) While staking out the darkened hillside home of the blackmailer Geiger, Marlowe sees a flash of white light and hears a female scream followed by shots. He breaks in and finds Geiger dead on the floor and Carmen, heavily drugged, sitting in an ornate chair, dressed in a Chinese brocade lounge outfit. (In the book she's naked, which makes more sense.) On a table in the middle of the room is a flashgun and beside it a large plaster Buddha's head whose hinged back is open to reveal a hidden camera from which the film has been removed. Obviously Carmen has been photographed in a compromising situation, and, almost simultaneously, Geiger has been killed. Sex and death.

The Buddha's head, like Carmen's outfit (and the beaded curtains, the smoking incense pot, and other cheesy Orientalia), is noir shorthand for decadence; in the era of Fu Manchu and Mata Hari, it's meant to evoke the opium den and the Shanghai brothel. But for us it also suggests a crucial dharma teaching. In every chamber of samsara, no matter how dark and confused, the Buddha—the possibility of awakening—is present. In fact, looking closely at the Wheel of Life, we see that in each realm, almost hidden like a "Where's Waldo?" among the hordes of gloating devas and swollen-bellied pretas, is the Buddha, offering help toward liberation in a form accessible to the locals. To inspire the animals, for example, he holds up a book, bringing knowledge to the ignorant. To charm the devas he plays a lute (supporting my theory that, for such creatures of luxury as Americans, dharma is most digestible between slices of entertainment—like movies). Here, in Geiger's den of iniquity, the Buddha is a silent presence, a reminder that, from beginning to end, from sex to death, the entire dream of samsara, even when it becomes the most twisted of nightmares, is always just one waking moment away from evaporating.

How, then, to proceed? One waking moment at a time. The Buddha head on the table, in keeping with tradition, has elongated earlobes, and the camera always shows it in profile, so that we see only the right ear. Oddly enough, Bogart's Marlowe has a habit of tugging at his right earlobe whenever he's ruminating on a clue. As he contemplates each glimmer of light that may ultimately lead out of the labyrinth, it's as if he's pulling his earlobe a little longer, stretching the receptivity of his awareness, making himself gradually more Buddha-like. We can all do that. We have to launch our effort from the human realm, to be as decent and real as we can, and tenacious and resourceful—good detectives. And it helps every time we reach out in trust, like Marlowe and Vivian, recognizing others as seekers of the same truth and happiness that we seek, not mere objects that bring us difficulty or pleasure.

The six realms are just different ways of holding on. The way out of them is to let go. That doesn't mean dramatically renouncing all our ambitions and hungers, or forcibly suppressing our anger and pride. But again and again, by just relaxing for a moment in the middle of the fight or the party or the funeral, and letting in some slack, some neutral spaciousness, we can loosen our grip on the realms and theirs on us. With spaciousness comes awareness. We can find the Buddha in any realm we're in by finding our own awareness, simple and clear, as unblinking and nonjudging as a camera in a plaster head. If we clearly see, even once, that the comforts and torments of the six realms are as empty as dreams, we can never again fully buy into them. Then, one moment at a time, they begin to be under-cut by a spontaneous detachment that feels something like the cool irony of Bogey's voice. No matter how complex or con-vincing our dreams may be, the moment we realize we've been dreaming we start to wake up.

THIS IS IT

Henceforward burn what thou hast worshipped
and worship what thou hast burned.
> —ST. REMY

Blue skies smiling at me
Nothing but blue skies do I see.
> —IRVING BERLIN

YOU'VE PROBABLY HEARD THE ONE ABOUT HOW SEX IS like pizza: when it's good, it's *really* good, but when it's bad . . . well, it's still pretty good. That's how I feel about movies. I can even feel that way about a big, bad, dumb movie like *Independence Day*. It's basically just a bunch of explosions and Hollywood clichés, but I can relax and enjoy it, and if I get relaxed enough I can even start to see some juicy hints about what dharma texts call *shunyata,* emptiness, and why it's the solution to all our problems.

This jumbo alien-invasion pageant was directed by Roland Emmerich, who went on two years later to do a remake of *Godzilla* with the slogan SIZE DOES MATTER. (In 2004, he super-sized the scale of the mayhem with global warming in *The Day After Tomorrow.*) Here, size is apparently *all* that matters. The extraterrestrial warships that hover overhead are fifteen miles across and use 1950s-vintage killer rays to unsportingly incin-

erate whole cities, with cars, fire trucks, people, and flaming de-
bris blown straight toward the camera at alarming velocities.
The biggest spectacle, and the film's central image (first pre-
viewed in the '96 Super Bowl commercial derby), is the shot of
the White House being blasted to smithereens.

The earthlings' response is also big. The invaders foolishly
launch their attack a couple of days before the Fourth of July,
inspiring Americans of all stripes to unite, fight, and prevail.
But this rainbow coalition quickly degenerates into a fiesta of
stereotypes. Air Force pilot Will Smith is the smooth-movin',
trash-talkin', alien-whuppin' black man; computer wonk Jeff
Goldblum is the clever, neurotic Jew (Judd Hirsch, as his Yid-
dishe poppa, can barely get through a sentence without an *oy
vey* or a *schlemiel*—he does everything but dangle matzoh balls
from his ears); Randy Quaid is the addled, substance-abusing
Vietnam vet; and Harvey Fierstein is the silly, fussy fairy, who
cowers under his desk making frantic phone calls to his mother
and his shrink. Foreigners don't fare much better. When the
fight goes international, it's like a bad day at "It's a Small
World," with panicked Arabs in turbans running for the hills,
jabbering Africans hoisting their spears skyward, and stiff-
upper-lipped RAF pilots declaring, "It's about bloody time!"

True, the film has a weirdly prophetic quality. Five years
before the September 11 attacks it shows iconic American
buildings being destroyed from the sky, with the response led
by a trim, swaggering president (Bill Pullman), a former fighter
pilot who gets back into his flight suit to rally the troops. In
fact, the film's anticipation of Bush attitude is downright creepy.
We're encouraged to cheer at the president's moment of moral
clarity—when he growls "Nuke 'em!"—as well as the fate of the
sign-waving demonstrators who gather on an L.A. rooftop to
welcome the aliens and are the first to be zapped. Bye-bye,
pesky peaceniks!

Most of the liveliest bits have been lifted from *War of the*

Worlds, Star Wars, Alien, The Right Stuff, Dr. Strangelove, even *Frankenstein* (the ominously moving finger of the not-dead-after-all alien on the operating table). The script reads like an encyclopedia of the trite, with not one but two ticking count-downs and the obligatory cute kid and cute doggie that tag along to keep our heartstrings tugged. At one crucial moment, Goldblum, trying to save the planet by uploading a virus to the aliens' mainframe, actually says—with a straight face—"All we can do now is pray."

And yet . . .

AND YET THERE'S SOMETHING that keeps us looking at the screen. There's an almost irreducibly gratifying and even wisdom-conferring element of movie-watching, and I've deliberately included this clunker to try to isolate that element. (In fact, with movies as with people, sometimes too much unrelenting intelligence is like a hard shell; you need some space of dumbness to let the wisdom in.) There's something good about sitting in that dark, open space in a crowd of silent stranger-companions, all facing the same way, gazing on the same dancing shapes and glowing colors that evoke the unfolding of existence. As we witness those big, noisy doings, it's as if we join with our *sangha,* the spiritual community of our fellow audience members, to generate a collective silence as big as the noise, and to feel that silence deepened and enlivened by all the commotion it beholds.

And nothing enlivens it quite like watching stuff blow up. Our attraction to that supposedly crude spectacle arises, like tragedy, from the nagging intuition that anything constructed is artificial and therefore cruisin' for a deconstruction. The second-to-last thing the Buddha said on his deathbed was that all com-pounds disintegrate. The skyscraper stays vertical, the king stays in power, for a limited time only. Entropy wins: all things must crumble. The higher a thing stands and the longer it impersonates solid, permanent reality, the stronger the corrective compulsion to pull it apart. It's exciting and strangely refreshing to see some great edifice we thought would last forever vaporized in a moment. Blam! Cool!

> The harder they come, the harder they'll fall.
> One and all.
> —JIMMY CLIFF

Like the climax of a tragedy, an explosion is an epiphany, a revelation of deeper truth. When the object bursts into flame, we're seeing the release of stellar energy, the stored starlight of the Big Bang, of which all things including ourselves are created. What remains is the primordial existence that is prior to creation, the boundless empty space that underlies structure. Thus in the Hindu tradition, Shiva, the lord of enlightenment, is also the lord of destruction, the Demolition Man whose ecstatic dance blows apart the rigid structures of stale situations and concepts so that a fresher, vaster clarity remains.

> Barn's burnt down—
> now
> I can see the moon.
> —MASAHIDE

In *Independence Day*, that vast clarity is the sky. There are lots of panoramic shots of crowds staring dumbfounded at the huge, menacing spacecraft that hover over their cities, looking oddly like the soles of giant sneakers that have stepped in dog poop. What's far bigger and more astounding is the sky itself, which has room for countless such craft. But in the film as in life, we don't see crowds gazing in wonder at the open sky—until the end, of course, when the invaders have been destroyed and everyone suddenly appreciates that empty blue expanse.

When the Taliban dynamited the two giant Buddha statues at Bamiyan, of course it was a terrible crime. And yet I can't help thinking that the Buddha himself, a bit puzzled that people had made graven images of him in the first place, would have no trouble enjoying the emptiness that was left in their place.

When people hear that Buddhists revere emptiness, or shunyata, they often presume that it means some kind of depressing void or terrifying black hole. But empty means empty of, free from, all concepts and characteristics, including "depressing," "void," "terrifying," "black," and "hole."

"Oh, so it must be like—"

Nope.

"Well then, it must be like—"

Nope. (Repeat as needed.)

Far from being some impenetrable mystery, this emptiness is that very same ever-virginal snow-white awareness that we've seen to be our very core. Far from being some exotic Eastern concoction, it also lies at the heart of the Judeo-Christian-Islamic tradition. The magnificent temple at Jerusalem, the spiritual center of ancient Judaism, outwardly resembled the hundreds of temples of Zeus and Mithras and Aphrodite that dotted the Mediterranean world. But while each pagan temple contained at its hub a graven image of its god, the Jewish inner sanctum was empty. Worshippers encountered an absence that, lacking any specific, limiting form, affirmed an omnipresent, limitless formlessness. Perhaps we could call it omni-absence. The gentiles must have considered this omission hilarious—"Hey, Abey, who stole your statue?"—but it's an expression of the same brilliant spiritual insight that has God, when Moses asks his name, answer with empty self-referral, "I am that I am." The two I am's are like two facing mirrors with nothing between them, reflecting one another into infinity: pure am-ness, infinite being, which cannot be named or grasped or depicted, but in which all beings are.

BUT HOW CAN WE *KNOW* this infinite, formless dimension of existence, not only symbolically, by beholding a blue sky or an empty altar, but directly? It's all in the movie. To clear the sky of obscurations, Goldblum with his trusty laptop and Smith with his hotshot piloting skills commandeer a recovered alien pod, fly into the bowels of the mother ship that has been coordinating the attacks, and knock it out. In the film's stereotypical vocabulary, this is Jewish brains and Negro brawn, Einstein and LeBron James, working in coordination. In the same way, we can taste the clarity of empty openness by throwing ourselves wholeheartedly into any activity that fully engages mind and body together—and then letting both go. The letting go part is crucial; here it's the bit where Goldblum sets the virus to upload and then says there's nothing to do but pray. We can take it a step further and say there's nothing to do.

Hopefully, you already have some such letting-go process in your life. My friend Roberta does. She sells mortgages for a living, but her passion is singing barbershop harmonies in her local Sweet Adelines chapter. She and her sister singers work hard at polishing their arrangements, but when she's onstage belting out a tune she loses both work and self (and all those variable interest rates) in the simple act of pouring forth sound; and she loses her individual sound in the bigger sound of the chorus. At that point she's letting go into a big, open, skylike space, making a joyful noise unto the Lord even if the lyrics are about being Alabamy bound. No wonder Sweet Adelines jokingly call their organization "The Cult." It provides essentially the same liberative expansiveness, the same sense of unrestricted, omnidirectional flow, as religion confers—on religion's better days.

The nonviolent martial art of aikido (pronounced "*eye*-key-doh") is *my* cult, or at least one of them. (I've also got Shakespeare, body surfing, the blues, and a few others.) There, part of the letting-go training is *tsuburi*, practice cuts made with a *boken,* a wooden sword that is gripped with both hands, samurai style. In the most basic cut, I raise the boken overhead, then swing it out and down, as if slicing someone from the crown to the navel. Then I do it again and again, dozens or hundreds of cuts per session. From the outside, all this chopping air must look pointless. But each cut has many nuances to engage the body and mind: back straight, head up, elbows in, sink into the knees, pull the hilt toward my center while flinging the tip into space. And when I'm in my groove and the cuts becomes frictionless, full of space, glorious—like a clear, empty sky—I go beyond body and mind and fling *myself* into space.

Independence Day's symbol for this flung self is the Randy Quaid character, the drunken, bumbling, war-damaged cropduster with a habit of dusting the wrong crops, a disappointment to his kids, apparently abandoned by his wife. Even if we're outwardly happy and successful, there's an intimate, private sense of our self that each of us, I suspect, feels is the real one: confused, alone, a screw-up. But Quaid is redeemed when he helps save the planet in a triumphant suicide mission, reflecting the flip side of our secret sense of self—the hunch that we are somehow destined for great things. As a matter of fact we are, but the greatest things come when, like Quaid here, the self is dissolved and transcended.

> Compared to begging one hundred times,
>   "Save me, protect me!"
> It is much more effective to say once, "Devour me!"
>   —MACHIG LAPDRON

So, when practicing tsuburi, you're supposed to visualize someone in front of you that you're slicing in half. I slice me—not out of some twisted self-loathing, but with the idea of slicing open my shell of constriction.

You can engage mind and body and lose the self in fishing, dancing, painting houses, riding horses, grinding lithography stones, or doing just about anything else. (If you're smart, like my chef friend Gretchen, you arrange to get paid for it.) But it does take a certain focus, a vivid presence in the letting go. There's a documentary film showing the great Isaac Stern teaching a master class to young violinists in China. One of them plays a passage with perfect technical virtuosity, but it's missing something essential that leaves it lifeless. Stern plays the same passage back to him, and suddenly it makes you weep. "Every note is your life," he explains. That's why, when I practice tsuburi, I don't count, "One, two, three," but "One, one, one." Only by being fully present, bringing your whole self to bear on every note of the music or every cut of the sword, can you let go of self and connect with skylike freedom.

Then you're in your groove, time goes away, and even though your body's still there you no longer feel stuck in it. Certainly sex can confer that sense. The thousands of gracefully copulating pairs of male and female buddhas in Tibetan temple art imply that the transcendence encountered in sex is of the same nature as enlightened awareness. We can eventually encounter it everywhere; we can't mate all the time, but we can let go and be present all the time.

Still, there's one special transcendent activity that is the distilled essence of all others. In English, it goes by the unfortunate name of "meditation"—unfortunate because for many people the word suggests either something strenuous (straining to concentrate or block out thoughts) or something mushy (listening to New Age tapes of rolling surf or rain forests, thinking rose-tinted thoughts about God or love). Meditation in its purest form steers clear of both these traps, hard and soft, by being something supremely simple: full engagement of mind and body in doing nothing.

Doing nothing. To immerse ourselves in the liberating

dimension of omni-absence, our technique itself must have the nature of absence. To grasp the ungraspable we must practice nongrasping. How can you hold the sky in your hand? Leave your hand open. How can you find the sky in yourself? Leave yourself open. So the technique is to just be and allow things to come and go. Sit, breathe, and rest in the skylike panorama of whatever happens to arise. Like Jerry Rice of the 49ers, be a wide receiver. Don't space out, but remain vividly alert to each moment's experience, yet completely at rest in that alertness. Don't resist any thought or sensation, but let it dissolve in its own time as naturally as it arose. Don't try to hold onto anything, don't try to change anything. All experience, as you may notice, is in the present, and it's always too late to change the present.

This structureless approach doesn't mean that the traditional structures of meditative practice—sitting postures, breathing techniques, mantras, rituals, visualizations, and so forth—have no place. They're very useful (and I use a lot of them) for initially engaging the body and mind in functioning harmoniously, like pedaling your bike with both feet.* But after a bit of pedaling it's time to let both mind and body coast. This may sound tricky, but even if you've never formally "meditated," you already have extensive practice doing something a lot like it:

Watching movies.

Maybe *that's* what makes watching even bad movies pretty good—it's a surprisingly close approximation of the meditative state. People who claim they could never sit still for fifteen minutes routinely do it in the cinema temple for two hours at a

---

* If it hasn't happened already, someday someone will try to convince you that the brand of bike he's selling—his prayer or mantra or ritual—is the only one that works. No matter how impressive his credentials or how cosmically benevolent the glow in his eyes, on that point he's full of shit.

time. (They sit even longer in front of the television, but something about TV tends to numb the mind, producing dullness rather than alertness.) In meditation we just nonjudgmentally watch the movie called *The Present Moment*, which is the only show in town. The dousing of the house lights at the start of a movie even resembles the closing of the eyes at the beginning of a session, although with this panoramic doing-nothing approach you'll eventually realize there's no need even to close your eyes. There's no need to block out anything.

Why? As it happens, this lame movie provides the answer, and in its lamest line. A few moments after Goldblum's bit about praying comes an even cheesier cliché, possibly the cheesy movie cliché champion of all time: "Gentlemen, this is it!" I grew up hearing it in one World War II film after another, always uttered by the commanding officer just before the crucial battle, the do-or-die charge, to make sure that even the most clueless viewer sits up, gives the scene his full attention, and gets its *ultimacy*—its quality of being The Big Thing we've been waiting for. Here, delivered by the wonderful character actor Robert Loggia as a gravelly-voiced general, the line kicks off the final clash, with hundreds of nuke-toting earthling pilots in dogfights with their alien counterparts.

As it happens, "This is it!" is also the pithiest of enlightenment teachings. If infinity (or God, or emptiness, or whichever inadequate name you prefer) is truly infinite, then there cannot be anywhere that it is not; there cannot be any*thing* that it is not. So every allegedly finite thing we behold, including those we consider distracting or problematic, must be none other than the infinite. Within the open sky of realized awareness, everything we once regarded as obscuring clouds (or alien spacecraft) turns out to be part of the sky itself.

So don't block out anything. Open to everything. Just rest purposelessly in whatever's there, not making anything of it, not interpreting it as pleasant or unpleasant, interesting or boring. (Again, relaxing and enjoying bad movies can be good training in nonjudgment.) Everyone tells you to stop and smell the roses, but stop and smell the bus exhaust too. Whatever you hear, smell, taste, touch, see—gentlemen, this is it. Unenlightenment is just nonattention. By giving *every* moment the same full attention we once saved for The Big Thing, we can wake up and perceive ultimacy (the biggest thing, the only thing) everywhere. As the Zen monk Ryokan wrote two centuries ago:

Do you want to know what's in my heart?
From the beginning of time: just this! just this!

Don't save it for "meditation" time, as if that were different from any other time. The rolling pressure of the parking lot under the sole of first one foot and then the other, the soapy-ashy smell of the first raindrops on the warm asphalt, the swoosh of the upholstery under your butt as you slide into the seat, the grind of the ignition as you turn the key, the complex distortion of images through the accelerating rain on the windshield, then their sudden simplification as the wipers clear it away, then distortion, then clearing, distortion, clearing, to the thumping sound of each beat of the blades—this is it, this is it, this is it.

In fact, this natural, unstructured, moment-to-moment opening to the world of ordinary experience, and not some strained effort at otherworldly detachment, is the most traditional of meditative teachings, going back to the Buddha himself:

When he [the meditator] is walking, he knows he is walking; when he is sitting, he knows he is sitting; when he is standing, he knows he is standing; when he is lying down, he knows he is lying down.
     —ANAPANASATI SUTRA

Whether walking or lying down or driving or scrambling an egg or "meditating," just keep coming back to that natural state, resting evenly in each moment's never-to-be-repeated pixel-array of sensory input. This is at once the most basic and most advanced technique of meditation, the one to practice day after day and moment after moment, effortlessly but persistently. Thus we gradually wear down the *myth of specialness*—the illusion that any moment or thing or experience is more "it" than any other. With no specialness anywhere, ultimacy remains everywhere. Then nothing blocks our sky.

WHICH RAISES THE QUESTION, What blocked it in the first place? What are those "obscurations to realization," in Buddhist terms? In *Independence Day*, of course, they're the alien invaders and their lethal spacecraft. But the clue to their deeper identity comes from two of the film's many illogicalities, which are raised by Smith and Goldblum's duo flight in the alien pod. Why would the seats and controls of a spacepod built for nine-foot-tall, multitentacled extraterrestrials be such an ergonomically perfect fit for a pair of humans? And why would the aliens' computer system be so conveniently compatible with ours that it could be discombobulated by a virus that Jeff Goldblum could write on his laptop? (Guess they run Windows—lucky break for us!) Again, this is the dumbness that lets the wisdom in. The alien pod fits because we have built it. The alien computer system crashes because we have programmed it. *We are the aliens.*

That is, we have created the aliens in our own image. The truth is not out there, it's in here. Both the dream of cuddly, messianic E.T.'s and the nightmare of killer aliens are our own projections. Even if we do get visitors someday, that's beside the point. Existence itself is skylike openness—it is that it is— emptiness beyond all our hopes and fears, as we come to discover through consistent practice of this-is-it. The idea that anything that confronts us *isn't* it is simply our own creation; that big dog-poopy sneaker that blocks the sky is our own. That's the best possible news, because it means all we have to do is lift our foot and the sky is clear.

The Buddha described this situation in the Four Noble Truths, the radical teaching that he gave in his first discourse and then doggedly reiterated for the next forty-five years. We can paraphrase them very simply:

1. **THE OLD (BAD) NEWS:** We encounter one kind of unhappiness after another in our lives.

2. **THE NEW NEWS:** But it doesn't come from the outer circumstances we usually blame it on. We create it ourselves by grasping.

3. **THE INCREDIBLY GOOD NEWS:** Therefore we can end it by letting go.

4. **THE FINE PRINT:** In the long run, that requires taking a mature view of things, behaving responsibly, and meditating.

One hot summer day a few years ago I was on the board-walk in Rehoboth Beach, Delaware (eating a bag of delicious Thrasher's fries, heavy on the malt vinegar), and saw a couple pushing their daughter, who was about five, in one of those expensive strollers that look like bonsai'd SUVs. Clearly, she was well fed and nicely clothed, had loving parents, and presumably lived in a comfortable house with plenty of toys. But she was crying bitterly because she wanted a Hello Kitty sticker book and she wanted it now. Completely enveloped in her misery, she could barely hear her parents' frantic explanation that the store was closed.

The Second Noble Truth says we're all that little girl. We've generated our own unhappiness by fixating on something we're sure must be added to or subtracted from our experience of the present moment before we can experience the this-is-it of boundless satisfaction. The Third Noble Truth says that because we are the problem, we are the solution. In any moment we can choose to snap out of it. Just stop looking for external answers to the question of human happiness. As Jesus taught:

> Neither shall they say, Lo here! or, lo there!
> for, behold, the kingdom of God is within you.
> —LUKE 17:21

In a few years Hello Kitty will be forgotten. The girl will want a prom dress or a car and will probably get them, which is fine. But how many fixations must we suffer through before we get the idea? It's as if we need, oh, let's say a virus to upload to the whole system of fixation and bring it to a crash. And since we've written all the code for the system, we can write the virus.

It may seem impossible that a failing grade from your chemistry teacher or an indictment from the district attorney is not really the cause of your unhappiness, just as it seems impossible to the little girl that the lack of the sticker book is not the cause of hers. But much as we grow out of our childhood fixations and their attendant traumas into a broad sense that things are basically OK—what we call maturity—there's also a higher maturity, an extension of this natural growth to the nth degree, into the realized or enlightened or heavenly state, the experience that things are *boundlessly* OK. Of course, you don't abandon common sense; you hire a good lawyer to handle the indictment or you study harder for the next chem test, but you don't depend on any particular outcome to perceive that the open sky of unobstructed being is always there, whether you pass or fail, whether you're home or in jail.

This is not just a matter of philosophy, attitude, or belief. It's open to direct experience. Certainly, complete liberation takes time and conscientious practice (per the fine print of the Fourth Noble Truth), but you can have a life-changing glimpse of it in one moment. All metaphysics, like all politics, is local. If it can't be experienced and applied in this room right now, it's a load. The dharma invites people to investigate for themselves, to "come and see," as the Buddha said. In Jesus' teaching about the kingdom of God, please note the word "behold." Behold that kingdom, see it for yourself. Check it out, don't take his word for it. As Ronald Reagan said, "Trust but verify." A car parked around the corner from my house has a bumper sticker that says REAL MEN LOVE JESUS. I think real men (and women) *emulate* Jesus (and Buddha); they're determined to closely encounter that kingdom of God for themselves, as he plainly urges us to do, and they're willing to take responsibility for their own happiness, to put in the time and practice.

Then, in time, every moment of your life becomes the moment of clearing, every experience the experience that this is it. The alien invaders—the confusion and suffering that are alien to our own true nature—are destroyed. And then, when we no longer depend on this object or that situation for our freedom and happiness, every day is Independence Day.

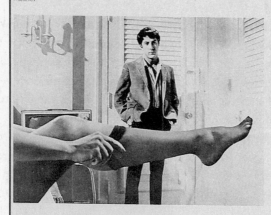

WHADDAYA GOT?

[E]verybody's youth is a dream, a form of chemical madness.

—F. SCOTT FITZGERALD,
"The Diamond as Big as the Ritz"

ADOLESCENCE, SOMEBODY ONCE SAID, IS A FORM OF temporary insanity from which most Americans never recover. Its symptoms include mood swings, impulsiveness, restless dissatisfaction, free-floating aggression, hostility to authority—all the traits that make adolescents the despair of their parents, and America the despair of diplomats.

But the delight of moviegoers. We may be reckless cowboys but we look good on that horse, and our antics make us both more scary and more fun to watch than, say, your average Belgian. We are, as the signature tune of *Easy Rider* puts it, born to be wild.

There must be a reason. In the case of adolescents, sure, they're crazed by flooding hormones, but I think there's something more. Between childhood and adulthood they float briefly in a space of formlessness, where the shape and borders of their future lives have not yet solidified. (Floating in his parents' swimming pool and asked by his father, "What are you doing?," the young hero of *The Graduate* replies, "Well, I would say that I'm just drifting. Here in the pool. . . . It's very comfortable just to drift here.") At that moment, if they're alert, adolescents glimpse freedom and attempt to seize it. This in-between situation is closely parallel to that described in the Bardo Thödol, the so-called Tibetan Book of the Dead. The *bardo*, or transitional state between death and rebirth, is a prime opportunity to let go into the clear light of nirvana, one's own true nature.

But most people miss this chance and so find themselves so-lidifying into another body, in which they must slog through yet another round of samsara. As adolescents sense the fleeting nature of their freedom, they see the painful contrast between it and the sharply delimited adult life they're about to be born into, with all its routines and responsibilities. It makes perfect sense that they flail away at that life and the adults who are its ambassadors. Rebels without a cause, they may not know what they want, but they see what the grown-ups are offering and they know that that ain't it.

> **GIRL IN BAR:** What are you rebelling against, Johnny?
> **JOHNNY** [young Marlon Brando in motorcycle leathers]: Whaddaya got?
> —*The Wild One*

In the case of America, the perpetual unruly teenager in the family of nations, we've been blessed and afflicted with many such freedom-glimpses, starting with the vast expanse of an un-carved land.

> [F]or a transitory enchanted moment, man must
> have held his breath in the presence of this
> continent, compelled into an aesthetic
> contemplation he neither understood nor desired,
> face to face for the last time in history with

something commensurate to his capacity for
wonder.

—F. SCOTT FITZGERALD,
The Great Gatsby

When we ran out of continent we left our farms in Ohio or Ken-
tucky for the gold rush, and ever since have felt that limitless
wealth is our birthright, that if we haven't made it we just
haven't figured out how—yet. This is the country that keeps
hurling gizmos and humans into limitless space, even if they
blow up from time to time, the country where Ford sells its lumbering SUVs under the slogan NO LIMITS and people buy them.

Of course, this vision of life without limits is silly and im-
practical, the source of endless frustration. But it's also what the
enlightenment traditions tell us is the ultimate reality. "There is
an endless, world, O my Brother!" wrote the poet Kabir. "No
form, no body, no length, no breadth is seen there: how can I
tell you that which it is?" Maybe teenagers and Americans are
like the inmates of mental asylums who produce fabulous visionary art, their supposed insanity not so much a descent into
unreality as an overflow of reality, of the indescribable "that
which is," too intense for them to handle.

The Graduate captures that intense, transitory, enchanted
adolescent moment incisively, right from the opening close-up,
where we see the head of young Ben Braddock (Dustin Hoffman) against a stark white background. In that strange whiteness he could be floating in the purity of Kabir's endless world,
dreaming of omnidirectional possibilities, but from his expression he looks more like a patient etherized upon the table, help-
lessly submitting to the removal of some vital part. As the
camera pulls back we see that the whiteness is a pillow and he
is aboard a commercial jet, surrounded by the drained, dispir-
ited faces of silent adults—postop cases who have already un-
dergone the freedomectomy.

That theme is underscored when the plane lands at LAX and, as the opening credits roll, Ben, fresh from his Ivy League college in jacket and tie, is carried forward by the automatic walkway toward unseen waiting parents, his face an impassive Buster Keaton deadpan, almost dehumanized, as if he's a machine part on a conveyor belt ("Please hold the handrail and stand to the right," says the mechanized voice) being conveyed into the prefabricated future that awaits him if he doesn't do something to break out of it—a future of sterile inauthenticity that a family friend, offering poolside career advice in a happy conspiratorial whisper, will soon summarize in a single, terrifying word: "Plastics." Plastics, of course, are manufactured by pouring fluid into a mold and making it congeal—the samsaric solidification that Ben and all adolescents abhor.

As Ben rolls toward the future it is to the strains of "The Sound of Silence." The moody Simon and Garfunkel score that is such an integral part of the film immediately establishes the inchoate yearning of adolescence, the sense that one briefly has a chance to pluck some strange and wonderful fruit, but that the chance is easily and tragically missed. These early Paul Simon songs, with their fervent, somewhat sophomoric lyrics, work perfectly here, suggesting both the gangly, pimply awkwardness of adolescence and the poignancy of its yearning, which is not diminished but made more poignant by its awkwardness.

Ben vaguely articulates this vague yearning in the next scene, which opens on another severed-head close-up, this time as he broods in his old room upstairs in his parents' suburban home, his face half in darkness, against the background of a large fish tank. When his father appears, summoning him downstairs to his graduation party, Ben asks for more time alone.

MR. BRADDOCK: What is it, Ben?
BEN: I'm just . . .

MR. BRADDOCK: Worried?
BEN: Well . . .
MR. BRADDOCK: About what?
BEN: I guess about my future.
MR. BRADDOCK: What about it?
BEN: I don't know. I want it to be—
MR. BRADDOCK: To be what?
BEN: Different.

The question that is never asked is, Different from what?, but as Ben descends the stairs into a Holden Caulfield nightmare of vapid middle-class twittering, a sea of clinking cocktail glasses and tinkling voices, all sing-songing his praises as his mother reads from his college yearbook about his achievements as scholar and track star and editor, we know that the answer is, Different from *this*. Different from all of you, from empty success, from what has been laid out for me. I don't know what I want, but I know what I don't want, which is your shallow and unsatisfying life. Whaddaya got?

I've spent time at some of the toniest prep schools in New Jersey. Most of the kids there are, like Ben, multitalented, with impressive résumés. They sense the vast array of opportunities that are open to them, and many have dreams of pursuing lives of creativity or service. When they turn seventeen they get their drivers' licenses and, usually, a very expensive birthday gift: a gleaming new vehicle of their choice, and in recent years they've mostly chosen SUVs. But this "free" gift carries a price tag—that NO LIMITS business is strictly a matter of bait and switch. Now they've been inducted into the club, now they're living a style of life to which they will quickly grow accustomed, and to maintain it they will probably have to relinquish any dreams that don't pull in six figures. They've exchanged the possibility of being real explorers of some real outback for an Explorer or an Outback. Gelded by the gelt, they give up the chance of their lives being "different."

IT IS THIS yearning for something different that makes Ben vulnerable to Mrs. Robinson's famous seduction. His affair with the fortyish family friend, played by Anne Bancroft in a wickedly funny, deservedly Oscar-winning performance, is a way of reaching for that something different: sex as rebellion. Every generation of adolescents (it has also been said) thinks they invented sex. They think they're getting away with something subversive, somehow beating the system, when in fact sex is their initiation *into* the system. All those *Playboy* magazines hidden under all the mattresses of our youth were just nature's way of priming us to propagate the species into the next generation.

So, what looks like a way of breaking out of samsara turns out to be the way of breaking into it. Sex is the doorway into involvement—at the very least, emotional involvement with another human (no matter what yesterday's free-love doctrine or today's casual-hook-up culture says) and, in due course, babies, families, jobs to support them, and the wheel goes round and round. Mrs. Robinson herself, we learn, was once an art student; her alcoholic suburban life, in which all such aspirations are now bitterly forgotten, came out of the one wild moment in the backseat of a Ford when her daughter was conceived. Disguised as a way of attaining something "different" from our parents' lives, sex is precisely our way of attaining their lives.

At the end of a montage that wordlessly depicts the unfolding of this joyless affair as Simon and Garfunkel sing more songs of unfulfilled yearning, Ben dives into the pool of comfortable drifting and lands on a gray inflatable raft, clutching at it as if at deliverance, but in the next moment it becomes the naked body of Mrs. Robinson, the embodiment of youthful hope that has been transformed into midlife despair. She's not only "the most attractive of all my parents' friends," as Ben lamely puts it, but also the smartest and most sensitive; she's cursed with knowing just how pointless and unfulfilling her life is. (In a subtle touch, she's always called Mrs. Robinson— she's so emotionally impoverished that she doesn't have a first name.) Her body is not the raft that will convey him to the far shore of liberation, but part of that relentless conveyor belt that leads to a future of plastics.

In fact, his involvement with her recalls the Bardo Thödol's (rather strange-sounding) warning that we can be reborn into another round of samsara as a result of being attracted to the point of union of a mating couple, which turns out to be our new parents in the act of conceiving us. Ben's seduction by this "most attractive" stand-in parent suggests some such attraction, with the result that he is "reborn" from his free-floating in-between state into the samsara of adult suburban life. In one of the film's funniest scenes, Ben's first hotel-room tryst with Mrs. Robinson, he awkwardly puts his hand on her breast, just as she turns away to rub irritably at a spot she's noticed on her blouse—suddenly and disconcertingly transformed from lover to housewife/mom. Ben responds by walking to the wall and banging the top of his head against it, like a baby pushing to emerge from the confinement of the womb it has entered.

But this is a comedy, and good news is on the way. The very things that pull us into samsaric involvement also offer fresh opportunities for nirvanic transcendence, sex included. An essential element of the appeal of sex is the way it lifts us into a realm where time and space and the state of our 401(k) are left far below. The problem is that, like everything else, it's fleeting. If sex is the only expansive experience shared by two people, it becomes like a ten-minute roller-coaster ride preceded and followed by hours of waiting in line, only these waits usually involve all kinds of complicated psychodrama and buying of drinks or drapes. This arrangement can work in the long term only if that expansive, transcendental element can somehow come to suffuse the twenty-three to twenty-four hours of the day when we're not copulating.

This can happen through what we call romantic love. The fact that we speak of being "in love" implies that we're *in* something, immersed in a different medium, dwelling in a different state or on a different plane. "Fly Me to the Moon," "April in Paris"—a thousand love songs with a thousand metaphors have tried to describe it. Sages of various traditions speak of *ananda* (sublime bliss), nirvana (the blown-away state), or the kingdom of heaven, and advise us to find it within ourselves; failing that, we seek it from others, and that seeking, like many things, has a special sharpness in adolescence. I was in desperate love with a couple of girls in high school, and they've visited me a few times over the years in dreams, set in a dewy, enchanted space at the dawn of time, where virginal purity and unashamed sensuality are one—some pristine Rousseau jungle where they gently take my hand and kiss my brow, gazing at me with sad, serious eyes, and healing all my damage with the touch of their cool skin. I now live on another coast and am unlikely to meet them again in the waking world—luckily. Let them remain ever-youthful angels of my imagination.

Romantic love, then, is the primordial bliss of one's own inner essence experienced in the outer form of another. Here that other is Elaine, Mrs. Robinson's daughter, with whom Ben falls in love after reluctantly taking her on a family-arranged date. Hiding behind sunglasses, treating her with deliberate callousness, he brings her to a seedy club where a big-breasted stripper, deftly rotating her tasseled pasties in opposite directions, crouches closer and closer to brushing them against the top of Elaine's head, till Ben, in a moment of clarity, shouts "No!" He suddenly realizes that the angel of romantic tenderness has entered his life and he has almost succeeded, as so many of us do succeed, in crushing that delicacy with the gross lust that the stripper personifies. It's like feeling the delicate tickle of the breeze blowing on the hairs of your arm and deliberately scratching the tickle away. To take delicate angels, messengers of our own subtle, overlooked inner being, and make them victims of aggressive, violative sexuality is to blind ourselves to that being, just as the men of Sodom are struck blind when they try to gang-rape the visiting angels of the Lord.

The angel here is played by Katharine Ross, her radiant face evoking an aesthetic transcendence that is the visual echo of what Ben is really looking for—a "different" life in which his own authentic essence is unburied and unsmothered. After the crisis in the strip club, he begins to unbury himself by removing his sunglasses, and they go to a noisy drive-in restaurant where, for the first time in the film, he looks relaxed, and his declaration that "You're the first thing for so long that I've liked" shows that he has taken a big, healthy step out of his Holden Caulfield isolation. (Holden's sister tells him, "You don't like anything that's happening. . . . Name one thing.") The ease of their banter hints at the utter relaxation of abiding in one's own essence, of being home at last, all seeking and posing left far behind. This is how ordinary people feel when they're in love, and how enlightened people, who are in love with existence, feel all the time.

"AND THEY GOT MARRIED and lived happily ever after." From the most ancient fairy tale to last week's chick flick, that happy ending has its enduring appeal certainly because it reenacts our biologically mandated courtship ritual, but also because it represents our settling into the enlightened state (the only real state of perpetual happiness). But between our first glimpses of that state and our final attainment of it, there is usually a long, harried pursuit, with plenty of thrills and spills courtesy of the forces of samsara. This occurs in the film when the scorned and furious Mrs. Robinson reveals her involvement with Ben to

Elaine, Elaine flees north to Berkeley, and Ben, in the little red Alfa Romeo convertible that is his graduation present, goes after her.*

After a string of attempted reconciliations and further misunderstandings that are familiar to all spiritual seekers who find themselves alternately encouraged and spurned by the elusive essence, Ben learns that Elaine has again fled, this time south to Santa Barbara to marry one Carl Smith. If Ben is the film descendant of Holden Caulfield, Carl "the make-out king" is the descendant of Holden's despised classmate Ward Stradlater, expert and insincere straddler of girls who deserve better, the violator of Holden's angels. (The writers keep Ben and Elaine's relationship conveniently chaste by having him fall in love with her and her flee Los Angeles after just one date.)

The producers of *The Graduate* originally pictured Ben as a tall, blond, vapid Southern California type, what they called a "surfboard." Everything changed when they instead cast the short, dark, ethnic Hoffman. His lack of conventional Aryan prettiness became an emblem of his authenticity, and the bland surfboard quality was all transferred to Carl Smith. (By 1967, most surfboards were made of molded plastics.) The first time Ben meets him, in the awkward three's-a-crowd scene at the zoo, Carl is puffing ridiculously on a pipe, adding collegiate-intellectual pretension to his romantic phoniness. He is, in short, Ben's Mr. Hyde, the externalization of all his own most gross, inauthentic, plasticky possibilities, and thus the one from whose crushing grip Elaine must be rescued. To the tune of Simon and Garfunkel's "Mrs. Robinson," Ben tools down Highway 101 in the Alfa, desperately trying to reach the church in time to stop the wedding, finally running out of gas and (at last putting all that track training to good use) sprinting the last

---

* The car, auto buffs, is a 1966 Duetto Spider 1600. The U.S. importer was a relative of Hoffman's.

stretch on foot. He arrives a moment too late, and as the groom kisses the bride Ben raps on the glass balcony door he's locked behind, yelling, "Elaine! Elaine!"

As the families curse Ben violently, Elaine hesitates a moment, then, face turned upward, slowly begins walking toward him, like a waking sleepwalker, and finally answers his primal call with her own: "Ben!" It's a wonderful moment of old-fashioned movie magic, straight out of the screwball comedies of the '30s, but it's also more than that: it's the romantic angel of our own essence, refusing to be crushed, recognizing us and affirming us as her own.

Fighting off the angry relatives and escaping from the church, Ben and Elaine hop aboard a yellow city bus and ride off, first laughing triumphantly (his only hearty laugh in the film), then subsiding into a wordless, straight-ahead gaze, as "The Sound of Silence" comes up once more. They certainly appear to be riding into some version of happily-ever-after. But almost everyone who writes about this film is at pains not to be taken in by the ending, to say that Ben and Elaine are now as lost and confused as their parents and headed for the same lives of quiet desperation. Mike Nichols, the director, said as much in later interviews. But, no matter what he says, *that's not what's on the screen.* In spite of his perfectly reasonable cynicism, Nichols here has allowed himself a moment of romantic transcendence, of redemptive love in all its radiant, unreasonable glory—the kind of brief moment that can make bearable so much tedium and turmoil before and after. As if in answer to Ben's anguished solitary straight-ahead gaze in the opening close-up, this side-by-side gaze at the end is one of contented reverie, of contemplation of a life that is, at least for now, transformed—different.

Plastics may await, but for this moment all mundane considerations magically vanish from Ben and Elaine's awareness and from ours: the impossibly complicated family repercussions of their intention to be together, Ben's need to earn a living in some presumably conventional, plastic way, even that nice little Alfa left abandoned on the shoulder of the road. Nichols may well be right about Ben's future, but even if we don't escape the wheel of samsara this time around, if we can have a few such moments that let the light in, there's that much more available the next time, whether that means in the next chapter of this life, in the next life, or perhaps in the next generation. "And the vision that was planted in my brain / Still remains," sing Simon and Garfunkel. Each time around we can at least leave some artifacts of freedom. The '60s may have crashed and burned, but they left the songs of Dylan and the Beatles, the myth of Woodstock, the speeches of Dr. King, and films like this. More than that, they left about a million small and large ways in which people are more relaxed and real and determined to Do Their Thing, so that, no matter how hard some preachers and politicians may try, they can never quite make it the '50s again.

Crazy, impetuous youth (adolescents and Americans) want everything right now, via a short, straight line, but in time we see that we're on a wide spiral of incremental change, in which things keep being different but the same, same but different. Ben has not abolished or even seriously challenged his stifling bourgeois world, and thus some critics have assailed *The Graduate* as essentially conservative, unworthy of its '60s cult status. True, he's still in that world, but there's a little less of it in him. There's a hint of that as he and Elaine sit at the back of the bus, where the rowdy, trouble-making kids always sit, unlike the model student the college yearbook describes. As he was at the beginning of the film, here at the end Ben is on a vehicle full of alien adults. It's yellow like a school bus, yet full of oldsters, as if signaling how quickly we go from the beginning of a cycle, a life, to the end. Ben's bus (our bus) is headed down the road to inevitable decay and death, but he's got his angel with him to make it OK.

The film ends as it begins, in silence, again made eloquent by

Paul Simon's song. The lyrics of "The Sound of Silence" are ambivalent: silence grows like a cancer, but it's also where the words of the prophets are whispered. Ben's silence at the beginning is one of loneliness and confusion: he says nothing because he doesn't know what to say and has no one to say it to. The silence he and Elaine share at the end is sublime, the silence that lovers and meditators know, in which everything's clear, everything's fine, and nothing has to be said. The vision that was planted in my brain still remains.

EASY RIDER
(1969)

WE BLEW IT

Are birds free from the chains of the skyway?
  —BOB DYLAN,
  "Ballad in Plain D"

EASY RIDER OFFERS A DIFFERENT TAKE ON THE ADOLESCENT-
American crazy quest for transcendental freedom. This shaggy,
largely improvised travelogue of two dope dealers on a motor-
cycle odyssey across the Southwest—one of them with an
American flag sewn onto the back of his leather jacket—
explores a fleeting moment of opportunity not just in the life of
the individual, but in the life of the nation.

Disclaimer: I'm an old hippie—a veteran, as my brother Ross
puts it, of the Acid Wars—and I'm particular about films that
try to portray what I lived. I dropped out of college in 1967, and
for the next couple of years I hitchhiked back and forth across
the country, built geodesic domes in the communes of the
Northwest, hung out in the crash pads of the Haight-Ashbury,
rode freight trains with hobos, shared jail cells with winos,
slept in parks with girls whose names I didn't know, protested
the war, dodged the draft, danced all night at Monterey, and
came very close to meeting my own *Easy Rider* ending at the
hands of some hippie-hatin' cowboys in a small town in Arizona. In those days, copies of *The Urantia Book, The Psychedelic
Experience,* and *The Aquarian Gospel of Jesus the Christ* were
passed around with feverish underground excitement. People I
knew talked seriously about ending the war by cutting their

hair, getting a job in the White House kitchen, and slipping LSD into LBJ's coffee; or about waiting for The Big One, the earthquake that would shake California loose to become a groovy autonomous island. Like many people in those heady times, I started to feel that some kind of apocalypse—some spectacularly radical spiritual resolution of the world's over-wrought situation—was on its way. *Those* '60s, I can testify, were a different planet, and there's probably no way to fully convey its alien atmosphere and topography to those who weren't there. But I'm very interested in films that try.

Easy Rider and, to a lesser degree, *Hair*, God help us, seem to be the films left in the '60s time capsule, the ones that people watch now to see how it supposedly was then. But *Hair* is based on a musical that was always sort of a theme-park version of the hippie revolution. While sellout crowds in Las Vegas tapped their toes to a road company's rendition of "Aquarius" and "Let the Sunshine In," the Vegas cops were unceremoniously rousting any real hippies they spotted on the street. The '60s shown in *Hair* aren't the ones I remember; maybe the surviving apostles and centurions felt the same way about the curious forms that Jesus' story took a few decades later in the retellings of people who weren't there.

That leaves *Easy Rider*. No doubt it's an historically impor-tant film, marking the moment when the studios recognized that *Mary Poppins* and *Funny Girl* were inadequate responses to a culture that was blowing up all around them. The inspira-tion of Peter Fonda (producer, writer, star) and Dennis Hopper (director, writer, star) to combine their background in B motor-cycle pictures like *The Wild Angels* with California psychedelia and French art-film sensibility was a brilliant and unrepeat-able gesture. The exclusive use of contemporary rock music for the soundtrack was groundbreaking, as was cinematographer László Kovács's handheld, shot-from-the-hip vision of an open-air America as seen from a Harley. As a document of the '60s, though, much of it is embarrassing. The question is, how much of it, like your dorky high-school yearbook photo, is embarrassing because it's accurate?

Was I anything like Dennis Hopper's hopped-up character Billy? Well, no, but worse, I had much in common with Peter Fonda's pretentiously cool, insufferably solemn Wyatt, aka Captain America. Almost everything he says is wrong, and all of it is pompous. In the excruciating sequence at the desert commune, when Billy points out that the hippies, who are sowing their seeds in dust, are not likely to make it through the winter, Wyatt piously intones, "They'll make it. Dig 'em—they'll make it." Clearly they *won't* make it, as, on most of the '60s communes, they *didn't* make it. When Wyatt introduces the boozehound lawyer George (Jack Nicholson) to pot, he hands him a joint and commands, "Do this instead," in an accurate reflection of the hippie dogma that marijuana and psychedelics were the mind-expanding cure for alcoholism. Wrong again. Perhaps most offensive is his patronizing speech to a rancher that he meets early in the film:

WYATT: It's not every man that can live off the land. You do your own thing in your own time. You should be proud.

Well jeez, kid, thanks for your approval. What's missing from all of this is any drop of irony. Did we really take ourselves this seriously? I hope not.

Inadvertently, the most appealing people in the film are the ones in the supporting roles—the "straight" people. Many of them are bigots and rednecks, presented as foils to the counterculture heroes, but at least they're real. In some cases they're *literally* real. Perhaps the most daring aspect of the film is how, at a time when tensions between hip and straight were genuine and sometimes turned murderous, director Hopper plunked his cast down in southern hamlets and invited the locals to express their feelings in improvised situations. One of the film's strongest moments is the tense scene in a small-town café, where the local high-school girls ogle the exotic out-of-towners and their sexy bikes, while the authentically menacing menfolk growl abuse, a couple of them quipping, "Look like a bunch of refugees from a gorilla love-in." "A gorilla couldn't love that."

The film was also groundbreaking in its portrayal of drug use. Coming out of the generation that was raised on health-ed films that showed how one puff of the devil's weed would send you straight down the road to prostitution, insanity, and early death, it's remarkable that Hopper and Fonda managed to sell Hollywood and audiences a film where the heroes are not only dopers but dealers. The soundtrack's apologetic use of the Steppenwolf song "The Pusher" ("God damn the pusher man") is unconvincing; it bears no relation to how Wyatt and Billy are presented or how we feel about them. Yet in its own backward way, *Easy Rider* winds up making a more credible anti-drug argument than did the old reefer-madness films.

The '60s doctrine that drugs would make us all ecstatic, visionary poets and sensitive social activists collapses, as it did in real life, of its own ponderous weight. Wyatt's New Orleans acid trip is hellish, and Billy is a stupid man whom pot just makes stupider. It also inflames his hyperactivity and paranoia; the moment he arrives at the peaceful commune, he picks up a short stick, aims it in all directions, and shouts "Bang! Bang! Bang!" The film's only evidence that pot might enhance creativity is a couple of stoned ad-libs in the night scene shot in the Crater Park ruins. Reclining beside a smoky fire, Wyatt, Billy, and a hitchhiker they've picked up (Luke Askew) are passing around a joint (clearly a real one) and are far gone, having one of those conversations that seem deep only when you're very stoned. With his usual solemnity, Wyatt/Fonda asks, "You ever want to be somebody else?" Piercing through all that serious bullshit, the hitchhiker replies, "I'd like to try Porky Pig." We can't help feeling that Fonda, and this overly serious film, need more of that.

"WE BLEW IT." Spoken by Wyatt the night before he and Billy are killed by a particularly cretinous redneck firing a shotgun from an old pickup truck, this is the film's most famous line, but everyone argues about what it means. This is as it should be. Wisely, Fonda and Hopper cut the long speech that was supposed to explain it. As it stands, this is the film's koan, the question that defies tidy answers but, if asked insistently enough, can be a spur to realization.

What they have blown is pretty clear: the chance to be free, for life to be, as Ben Braddock puts it in *The Graduate*, "different." The opportunity to achieve some higher level of individual liberation is rare enough—the Buddha compared the odds to those that a blind turtle, which surfaces once every hundred years, will accidentally pop its head through a hole in a single piece of wood adrift upon the ocean. For a brief moment circa 1967 we had, or at least had a vivid impression of having, a shot at generational or cultural or even global liberation—hey, it was the dawning of the Age of Aquarius. Sure, that sounds silly now, but it *was* an unprecedented moment in history, when suddenly thousands of people in dozens of countries were simultaneously searching for ideal states of inner consciousness and outer social organization, with the perhaps crazy yet touching faith not only that such states were within reach but that in just a few years the world would adopt them. When the apocalypse didn't arrive but Monday morning did, it's natural that many of the faithful felt we had blown it.

Let us count the ways.

Hopper and Fonda are both on record as saying that the phrase is about "going for the money." It's true that many people who swam naked at Woodstock are now corporate suits.

Early in the film, Wyatt inserts dozens of rolled-up hundred-dollar bills from a Mexican drug deal into a long plastic tube, which he then stuffs into the red-white-and-blue gas tank of his Harley. It's an image, Fonda has said, of "fucking the flag with money," and certainly it's not news that money has repeatedly corrupted the American dream. But at the same time, money *is* the American dream. The real question is, What do you do for it and how do you use it? Some people have made and used great fortunes with extraordinary creativity and generosity. Billy and Wyatt's problem is not so much that they go for the money as that they obtain it destructively (wholesaling cocaine, a drug that wasn't considered benign even in the '60s) and that their plans for it are so unimaginative. With all they've done and seen, their big ambition, the best they can come up with, is to retire to Florida. Talk about turning into your parents!

In fact, part of how we blew it was by not understanding and respecting money. Eastern cultures traditionally recognize that having full-time seekers is important for the spiritual well-being of the whole community, and everyone drops something into the monk's begging bowl. Lacking that tradition, the hippies just became parasites. An "easy rider" is a man who lives off a prostitute's earnings, who's along for a free ride. That was us. We didn't realize we were easy riders, that our freedom depended on the postwar prosperity generated by the straights working the nine-to-fives we derided. I spun starry-eyed neo-Thoreauvian theories about everyone sleeping contentedly under bushes, conveniently forgetting that not every place had warm weather like California's. I scorned the government while sponging off my sometime girlfriend, who got welfare checks because she was pregnant by her former boyfriend.

Another way we blew it was our methodology—trying to usher in the age of peace and love with chemicals. Psychedelics certainly gave a lot of people a lot of powerfully motivating glimpses of a higher reality. The first time I took acid was in the fall of 1965, when it was so new it was still legal in California, and what I took was pure LSD, straight from Sandoz Pharmaceuticals, before the advent of street acid cut with who knows what. I had been raised with virtually no spiritual training and had read no dharma books. All I knew was that my high-school friend Candi said that the stuff was amazing and important, and one Sunday afternoon on her rooftop terrace in Van Nuys I swallowed this capsule. Forty-five minutes later the sky melted and I *knew*—I ecstatically experienced—that there was a God, or an infinite, that that's all there was, that it and I were not two but one, and that this was what everyone was looking for all the time, whether they knew it or not: the answer to all questions and solution to all problems, the only important thing in life. I knew that all human pain and conflict resulted from the tragic lack of this experience, and that love in its purest and widest form was the simple recognition in others of this same infinity that was myself. I had entered the inner sanctum, the Garden of Eden, and desired nothing but to continue to sit and be in that bliss.

And for eight hours I did just that, with an occasional word of guidance from my friend (thank you, Candi, wherever you are) or an eventful stroll to the local Cupid's Hot Dog stand for One With Everything. But then, as the bliss began to fade, I found myself facing the infinitely intolerable situation of being kicked out of the Garden. I think that was the first time I experienced suicidal depression.

> But the children of the kingdom shall be cast out
> into outer darkness: there shall be weeping and
> gnashing of teeth.
> —MATTHEW 8:12

From that day I knew that my life would be about seeking a way or ways to move into the Garden and stay there, and to help open the gate for others. The mission was, in the graffiti slogan of the time, END THE COMEDOWN. A daunting task, but I was bolstered by the knowledge that thousands of others had experienced the same thing and were on the same quest.

Or were they? Gradually I noticed that people were coming to the Age of Aquarius with a lot of their old baggage in tow, and I started to question my assumption that everyone was seeing the same things on chemicals as I had. In San Francisco's Haight-Ashbury district, the mecca of the psychedelic revolution, I met sincere seekers who had come from all over the world to fill their little cups with some kind of enlightenment. But I also met local poseurs who came on weekends in longhair wigs to try to pick up some of those free-love chicks they'd heard about, and runaway kids from Texas or Minnesota who were just mad at Mom and Dad for making them mow the lawn. One night in Golden Gate Park, I watched three or four college athletes in letterman jackets pass around a joint. As they got high, they started arguing about whether this one was hogging the dope or that one was an asshole anyway, and soon their smoke session broke down into shoving and punching. Again, it sounds naive now, but I was shocked. My plan for drugs to convert everyone to peaceful visionaries was not working out.

We also blew it through a time-honored form of confusion. Many of us, having had a couple of powerful transcendent experiences, assumed that we were now "there" and went around presuming to straighten everyone else out. (Several characters in the Bible exhibit the same syndrome.) When others failed to see things our way, we retreated into self-righteousness and a polarized us-versus-them perspective, the virtuous enlightened ones versus the benighted ones. And that, mixed with the deepening confusion brought on by more drugs, began to breed violence. I can tell you the week that the Age of Aquarius and, for that matter, the golden age of hitchhiking ended. Too perfectly, it was at the exact end of the '60s. Before that, I and hundreds of other backpack-wearing wayfarers had traveled all over the country by thumb, meeting every kind of person from farmers to truckers to lonely salesmen, sharing our stories, then getting out, wishing them a happy life, and waiting for the next ride. But in the last week of December 1969, the black-and-white mug shot of the just-apprehended psycho killer Charles Manson, long-haired and crazy-eyed, appeared on the cover of *Life* magazine, and it was all over.

In a way, Wyatt's realization about blowing it almost makes his being blown away by the grotesque redneck in the pickup truck OK, or at least fitting—the self-knowledge that redeems the tragedy. We missed the brass ring last time around; let's try again. Remember, he's Captain America. His epiphany, so bleak on its face, may also suggest the hopeful idea that America is the place where, even if we keep blowing it, we have the intense dynamism of self-destruction and re-creation, first Shiva then Brahma, that empowers us to keep being immolated and then rising again in another form that will try for freedom yet again.

"He not busy being born is busy dying," the Dylan song played at the opening of the last scene says, then goes on, "It's alright, Ma, I'm only sighing." From some bigger perspective it's all right, it's all part of the process.

> BILLY: I don't know, man.
> WYATT: I do. Everything's fine, Billy.

The breathtaking last shot of the film gives us some taste of that perspective. From Wyatt's mangled, flaming bike, the camera swoops back and up, up, in the film's only helicopter shot, a widening vista of lush American countryside, with fields and forest and a rolling river, the ruins of the bike now invisible yet still sending its thin, hopeful stream of smoke signals up into the sky.

BEFORE THE OPENING credits of *Easy Rider*, there's a scene where Wyatt and Billy sell their haul of Mexican coke to a big distributor who shows up in a Rolls-Royce—played, weirdly enough, by Phil Spector. (He got the part because he had his own Rolls.) The deal goes down near a landing strip at LAX, in silence except for the whistle and roar of landing jets. Ben Braddock might well be on one of them, flying into the opening scene of *The Graduate*. In a way he's the real easy rider, accepting the ticket for the bourgeois ride, while Billy and Wyatt, crouching under society's radar as they crouch here under the jets, are doing things the hard way by trying to take it easy. "To live outside the law you must be honest," sings Dylan; they lack the exceptional integrity and intelligence it would take to make their out-of-bounds existence viable.

Following this scene, the motorcycle trek begins with Wyatt tossing his wristwatch into the dust on the side of the road. It's a gesture of dropping out of the straight world's schedules and workweeks, perhaps of transcending time itself, of embracing the freedom of an open-ended, on-the-road lifestyle that looks like a shortcut out of the plastic future Ben dreads. But half a generation before the hippies, the beatniks learned that it's not so simple:

> who flung their wristwatches off of rooftops
> and alarm clocks fell on their heads every day for
>   the next twenty years
>   —ALLEN GINSBERG,
>   "Howl"

In the long run, we've learned, compulsively radical lifestyles usually bring conflict and suffering. But the "straight," normal, middle-class life, with its workaday routine, can range from the merely tedious to the truly soul-crushing, as in the case of

Lester, the Kevin Spacey character in *American Beauty*, who
writes the following job description:

> My job consists of basically masking my contempt
> for the assholes in charge, and, at least once a day, re-
> tiring to the men's room so I can jerk off while I fanta-
> size about a life that doesn't so closely resemble Hell.

There is a way to resolve the dilemma. If you wanted to sum it
up in a slogan you could put on a T-shirt, it might be REBEL, GO
CRAZY, OR PRACTICE DHARMA.

We used to drive through the carwash stoned—wow! amazing! But meditation in the various forms we've been discussing
has shown me that it wasn't just the drugs talking. The carwash
really *is* that amazing. So is the blueberry on the end of my
spoon, so is the quiet hum of the refrigerator. You just have to
pay some attention. Take your focus off the radio news (fighting
in the Middle East? jitters about the economy? call that news?)
and *dig* that trip through the carwash—grok it, as we used to
say. When you're wide open to the essential electricity of being,
doing just about anything is just about as good as doing just
about anything else. Dharma practice, which is fundamentally
the practice of looking past our dead concepts ("Oh, this is just
a process that washes my car") to the experience of the living
moment, gives you the wow without making you stupid and
confused, so that you can *function* in the state of wow. Which
means that, unlike Billy and Captain America and my entire
hippie cohort, you're not forced to choose between joyless nine-
to-five and ecstatic but doomed outlaw. You can have your job
and grok it too.

In *Tales of Power*, the fourth of Carlos Castaneda's books
about his (possibly embellished) adventures with don Juan
Matús, a Yaqui Indian *brujo* (sorcerer), Castaneda confronts
don Juan about psychoactive substances. In the first three

books, don Juan has used such traditional "power plants" as
peyote and jimsonweed to guide Castaneda through extensive
explorations of an astonishing "separate reality." Now Castaneda tells him that he has begun to question whether the
plants are necessary for accessing that reality.

> "Why did you make me take those power plants so
> many times?" I asked.
>   He laughed and mumbled very softly, " 'Cause
> you're dumb. . . . And there was no other way to
> jolt you."

I suspect that we had to take psychedelics in the '60s because as
a culture we were dumb—we needed something to collectively
jolt us out of the lunkheaded dumbitude of the *Leave It to
Beaver* '50s. Now that's been accomplished, and, like Castaneda
after this confrontation, our culture (I like to think) doesn't
need them anymore. I suspect that these substances work by
adding, we could say, a new *flavor* to awareness, which brings
your attention to the fact that you have awareness in the first
place. It's actually the attention, not the flavor, that allows us to
see the luminosity that surrounds us and is us. If we can just
keep paying attention, the exotic flavors become superfluous.
(Once a student was questioning me about meditation when
suddenly his eyes lit up. "Oh," he said, "you mean you just sit
there and trip!" Fair enough.)

Possibly the most profound experience of my three-year psychedelic period occurred while I was still in high school. One
night my best friend Eddy Cheng and I dropped some acid at
his house in Van Nuys, with the plan of doing an all-night walk-
about: wandering around the Valley, discussing everything we
saw, seeing if we could penetrate to some kind of deeper insight. We had gotten only two or three blocks when I found myself on a quiet corner, face-to-face with a fire hydrant, and

stopped right there. It was the most overwhelmingly wonderful thing I had ever seen. Not that it was radiating Day-Glo rainbow colors or sprouting angel wings or speaking to me with the voice of God. Quite the contrary. It was an absolutely ordinary fire hydrant, exactly as I had always seen it—only now, for the first time, I was *seeing* it, and seeing that there could never be any higher beauty or any deeper truth than the fire hydrant in its perfectly ordinary form.

"This is *it*, Eddy," I said, or words to that effect. (Gentlemen, this is it.) "I'm stopping right here. You can go on without me. I'm just gonna look at this fire hydrant for the rest of the night."

Fortunately, Eddy was wiser about these things than I was. "Come on," he said. "There'll be a lot of other things that are *also* it." We walked on and had a memorable evening of adventures, ending in the foothills of Sherman Oaks, where we watched the sun rise over the undulating Van Gogh cypresses.

Now, forty years later, am I living in the Garden of Eden? Not to the point where I could move my furniture in. But, like anyone who practices dharma with some diligence, I often find the gate left open and can take an occasional little stroll down the garden path and around the first bend or two. And the more I see of it, the more surely I know that its nature is not purple haze or Lucy in the sky with diamonds, but something much simpler and closer to hand than we imagined. Whatever's there—the glow of the nightlight at the end of the hallway, the crick in my neck, the faint vibration of the water in the flower vase as the truck rumbles past the house—is indeed it, just as Eddy promised. The descendants of that fire hydrant are all around me; the more I polish the clarity of my attention, the more I realize I'm still on that all-night walk.

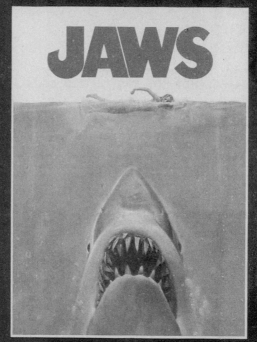

ALL YOU CAN EAT

The more you eat, the more you want.
—CRACKER JACK SLOGAN

A TYPICAL DINNER FOR THE GILDED AGE RAILROAD MIL-
lionaire Diamond Jim Brady began with two or three dozen oys-
ters, followed by six crabs and a few bowls of turtle soup. Then
came the entrees: half a dozen lobsters, two ducks, turtle meat,
a sirloin steak, and vegetables, with a platter of pastries for
dessert, all washed down with a gallon or two of orange juice
and topped off with two pounds of candy. At Brady's favorite
New York restaurant, spectators would crowd around his table
to place bets on whether he would make it through the meal
without dropping dead.

There's a scene early in *Jaws* where Hooper, the shark expert,
and Brody, the chief of police, cut open a dead shark's belly to
see if it's the one that's been eating people. Out spill undigested
whole fish, a tin can, even a license plate. As Hooper explains,
"The digestive system of this animal is very, very slow." Perhaps
we "consumers" (interesting thing to call oneself), like sharks,
are better at consuming than digesting. *Jaws*, Steven Spielberg's
first great work, is usually seen as a movie about terror, but I
think it's about insatiable hunger—*our* hunger.

Producer Richard Zanuck has said that he didn't want to
spend money on big stars because "the star was the shark." The
star of a film is usually the character with whom the audience

identifies. That is, the shark is us; the shark is the self. Hooper, Brody, and Captain Quint are supporting characters who exemplify three different ways to confront the hungry self—what we could call the fundamentalist, the Hinayana, and the Mahayana approaches—with three very different results.

THE SHARK-AS-SELF is established in the film's first moments, when a traveling underwater shot runs beneath the opening credits, the camera cruising a few feet above the ocean floor, nosing through the seaweed as if looking for prey, making us see from the grazing shark's point of view. We've been empathizing with monsters in horror films ever since Boris Karloff's brilliant, sensitive performance in *Frankenstein* made us feel that *we* were being pursued by all those torch-and-pitchfork-wielding peasants in lederhosen. And the first-person POV shot has been a staple of the genre at least since *Halloween,* when six-year-old Michael Myers's first heavy-breathing slasher murder was shown through the eyeholes of his clown mask. Why does this identification with the monster feel so psychologically right unless the monster is somehow our own self?

Buddhist teaching agrees that the self is the monster that stalks and stomps through this world, causing immeasurable suffering. But the theory of *anatta,* "no-self," gives a revolutionary explanation why. The self has no solid reality. It doesn't, in any substantial sense, exist. Obviously we function, acting and interacting, but if we look closely for a solid, definite, irreducible core to all that functioning, an actor behind the action, we can't find any. The self is *shunya,* empty. That's why, we could say, it's so hungry: it keeps trying to fill itself up. Dimly intuiting our lack of essential solidity, we keep trying to concretize ourselves, to get something to stick to our ribs. The problem is, all the objects we consume are also empty. It's like the old cliché about Chinese food, back when it was still a novel alternative to a hearty, all-American steak-and-potatoes dinner: "Funny thing about that Chinese food. You eat and eat, and half an hour later you're hungry again."

But the emptiness of self turns out to be a good thing. Since the self is the supposed recipient of all our anguish, the addressee, if it doesn't exist there's no one to take delivery. It's a little like seeing another driver angrily cussing you out and giving you the finger, then realizing that no, it's all aimed at the guy in the next lane. Certainly wars and divorces still happen, lightning and headache still strike, but in the realized state we see that there's no self, no one to be stricken. And seeing through the "I" pulls the rug out from under our worst behavior: without a self, it's hard to act selfishly. No "me," no "my."

Anatta also means we're not closed off. We're not isolated units in a fragmented universe, but of a wholeness. We all probably had tastes of this wholeness in early childhood, when we spent the afternoon alone inventing little games or sitting under a tree humming tunes and watching the bugs crawl about, so unselfconsciously absorbed in the aimless, timeless simplicity of experience that there was no sense of a separate experiencer, no subject-object split. When athletes are in their zone, when artists are in their flow, when jazz musicians are cooking, they also get a taste—that's what makes those moments so exhilaratingly liberative. But the same thing can happen while you're trading bonds or hanging out laundry. This liberation is something like seeing the movie we call life on the wide screen, from the audience, rather than being trapped in the narrow, fragmented point of view of one character . . . like the hungry-self shark's-eye-view shot that opens this film.

In the fragmented state of unenlightenment (or, as I optimistically like to call it, pre-enlightenment), we're always searching for that wholeness. Ironically, it surrounds us like an ocean.

People will not be saying, "Look, it's over here" or
"Look, it's over there." Rather, the Kingdom of the
Father is already spread out on the earth, and
people aren't aware of it.
          —THE GOSPEL OF THOMAS

Failing to notice it, we keep trying to reconstitute our wholeness the hard way, like tunnel-visioned sharks that are too busy
to see the ocean as they relentlessly consume one fish after another. And since our consumer goods, like us, lack any solid,
separate existence, they never satisfy us for long. Still, we get
fooled again and again. There's always the new new thing—the
new shoes or handbag, the new boyfriend or girlfriend—that
must be what we lack because it's so enticingly *other*. Wanting
so much to dance the dance of seduction one more time, we
conveniently forget how, in all our previous encounters, once
we consumed the other it became part of our domain, annexed
into the emptiness: it lost that new-car smell and started to
smell like us.

     Anatta is not an article of faith but a hypothesis to be tested.
Keep looking for a self. Keep asking, Who or what hears the bus
engine, sees the headlights, smells the carbon monoxide, feels
the annoyance? We say that "I" see the blur of the electric fan's
blades and feel the breeze against my skin, but where is that
seer-and-feeler? For that matter, where are the fan, the bus, and
the other alleged objects that allegedly give rise to all these sensations? If you observe carefully you'll notice that all you ever
actually experience is sensation (as well as thoughts and feelings, which are subtle sensations). We experience sensations in
dreams too, but later conclude that there were no solid objects
behind them. What's different about the waking state? The cor-
roborating testimony of other people? What experience do we
have of *them* but sensation?

Be a good scientist. Keep searching—diligently, rigorously— for any actual experience (not mere inference) of a self for yourself or for anyone or anything else. If you keep not finding one, as centuries of dharma scientists have not found one, the reality of anatta will dawn for you. Then what you're left with is a continuum, an ocean of sensory awareness, and you will see that your old habit of separating out some of the sensations as self and some as other was just a concept.

THEN YOU'RE READY, among other things, to watch *Jaws*, where that opening point-of-view shot so eloquently portrays the empty self: there's movement through the water, minnows and seaweed pass to the left and right, but, since the camera *is* the shark/self, there's no one there for all this moving and passing to happen to. Later, the shark is identified as a "great white"—a big blank, we could say. And in fact this most famous fish in movie history, like the self it represents, never existed. It's a composite of a couple of large mechanical sharks that were shot off Martha's Vineyard (including a hollow one that had only a left side and another that had only a right side— literally empty), and several live but smaller sharks filmed attacking a midget in a shark cage off Australia.

The first victim is Chrissie, the long-haired blond girl who runs off from the beach party to skinny-dip at sunset, a naked Eve calling to her passed-out-drunk Adam to join her. Shown in long shot, she swims tranquilly in the twilit water, which glows with a jewel-like radiance and fills the screen with its vast expanse, a tiny figure easily at one with the ocean of wholeness. Then, as she treads water and the unseen shark approaches, we see her from below. Again, it's the shark's-eye-view, from which she is a beautiful, strangely foreshortened silhouette, devoid of a head (the supposed seat of the self), like a rare black orchid in the gathering dusk, perhaps the delicate flower of our unselfconscious childhood, the Eden of our lives.

Then the shark of self tears that innocence to pieces. We still don't see the shark, but we hear it, or hear its essence, in John Williams's famous two-note theme, that urgent, accelerating pulse of double basses. Spielberg laughed when Williams first played it on the piano, thinking he was joking—this was far too simple. But, perhaps as powerfully as the simple four notes that open Beethoven's Fifth Symphony evoke the forces of nineteenth-century revolution pounding at the door of the old order, this ba-*bum* ba-*bum* evokes the chugging of the primal two-stroke engine of dualism: the lub-*dub* of the heart, the out-*in* of sex, the shit-*eat* of metabolism, day-*night*, live-*die*, win-*lose*, yes-*no*, stop-*go*, and, of course, me-*you*, self-*other*, all in the musically imagined sound of the shark's jaws' soundless up-*down*.

This first attack inconveniently occurs just days before the Fourth of July weekend, all-important to Amity Island's tourist trade. Amity, as the film's grinning, blow-dried, loud-sports-jacketed fool of a mayor loves to point out, means "friendship." To live in amity—to dwell in a civilization, as embodied in this tidy white-picket-fence community—we must somehow deal with the voracious shark of self that imperils it. If our hungers are allowed to run rampant, it will all be rape and pillage, and eventually everyone will be gobbled up. But the mayor's solution, as the big tourist day approaches, is denial—our usual polite solution when company's coming. He won't let Chief Brody declare the cause of Chrissie's death to be a shark attack any more than we, as we decorously sip wine at the charity banquet or stand motionless in the packed elevator, let ourselves declare our hunger for the money of the well-tailored gent on our right or the body of the slinky vixen on our left. Whenever two or three humans are gathered together, the shark is in their midst, and we usually work pretty hard at pretending it isn't. The silliest of the mayor's silly sports jackets is festooned with teeny-tiny anchors, symbols of this at-all-costs-don't-rock-the-boat attitude—and its futility.

Denial just doesn't work. The next two attacks bring the shark ever closer as it emerges from the inky waters of night, the closet of our repression. Rather than in twilit solitude, the second killing takes place amid a crowd of afternoon bathers, the shark no longer completely invisible but now a dark shape that momentarily rises out of the water to engulf little Alex Kintner and his yellow raft, the blood spreading in broad daylight. Then, in the intensely public setting of the Fourth of July, as tourists throng the beaches and a brass band plays cheerful American tunes, a man in a dinghy is killed—we see his severed leg sink to the bottom, and we get our first clear, unhurried view of the shark as it mauls him. Never mind that problems getting the mechanical shark to work forced Spielberg into this game of peekaboo. He winds up expertly teasing and terrifying us by revealing his monster bit by bit, meanwhile showing how the insubstantial self, as it continues on its destructive path, seems progressively more real and concrete.

Something clearly must be done. The mayor's denial strategy is replaced by a more aggressive one, in the form of a chaotic mob of amateur bounty hunters, eager for the reward offered by Alex's mother. Some of these bozos having come from as far away as (gulp!) New Jersey, they race out of the harbor in their overloaded boats, haphazardly flinging bloody chum and lighted dynamite into the water. But those who seek the self in the wrong way (in a pack, with clumsy tools) or for the wrong reasons (for money and fame, like preening artistes or entrepreneurial gurus) are doomed to failure. The bozos do come back with a shark and cheerfully line up to have their picture taken with it ("Just like in high school," exhorts the local news photographer), but it's the wrong shark. The Way that can be spoken of is not the true Way, says the Tao Te Ching, and the self that can be hunted down for money and displayed as a trophy is not the true self. Not only in spirituality but in art or sport or anything else, you may end up with something that looks like the real thing but it won't be the real thing. Your whole enterprise will be as frivolous and false as the "Killer Shark" video game that kids play on the Amity boardwalk.

A serious hunt calls for serious hunters, on a lone boat in deep water. These, of course, are Quint, Hooper, and Brody. They leave ashore the crowd of "ordinary people," as Buddhist texts call nonpractitioners of dharma, who live in amity with their perfectly respectable concerns of raising their families and tending their knickknack stores. Such people are too caught up in petty domesticity to confront the deep stuff; this is comically demonstrated earlier when Chief Brody, while trying to respond to the first shark attack, has to brush off a merchant's frantic complaints that local nine-year-olds are karate-chopping his fence, no doubt one with white pickets.

THESE THREE MEN in a tub are not ordinary. Their decision to take on the problem of self makes them adventurers and real spiritual practitioners. Spielberg signals this deeper commitment, with its greater peril, by carefully shooting all the scenes aboard the *Orca* so that land is never seen, even though it's completely illogical for the boat to go that far out to hunt a shark that's been menacing the beaches. It's a testament to the power of Spielberg's visual storytelling that viewers, caught up in the film's narrative sweep, rarely question this inconsistency.

As we've already seen, the ocean is a symbol of oneness, the wholeness of unfragmented being. This wholeness is both the ground and the goal of the spiritual path, both the primordial nature of our existence and the content of our ultimate enlightenment. It's an apt (and universal) symbol: the ocean manifests as inexhaustibly changing wave activity at its surface, yet is silently changeless at its depth. And the whole world shares it. I remember as a kid looking at a classroom globe and trying to figure out why different areas of the ocean were labeled Atlantic, Pacific, and so forth, when there was clearly only one big ocean. People of earlier times lacked the global perspective to see that everybody's little backyard ocean goes on and on without limit, nonseparate from everybody else's; until enlightenment we don't see that the same is true of our own being. So limitless, oceanic nonduality doesn't need to be created. It's the reality of our situation all along, temporarily obscured by the empty, imagined duality of subject and object.

> This is our birthright, our true nature. It is not
> something missing, to be sought for and obtained,
> but is the very heart of our original existential
> being. It is actually inseparable from our
> uncontrived everyday awareness. . . .
> —NYOSHUL KHENPO RINPOCHE,
> *Natural Great Perfection*

Quint, the boat's nail-spitting captain, played brilliantly by the leathery Robert Shaw, goes after the shark with harpoons and rifles and then tries to drag it ashore with his boat's sheer horsepower. This is the fundamentalist approach to the self and its hungers, the two-fisted attempt to pound it into submission. Whether through Bible-thumping or Koran-thumping condemnation of sin, a fundamentalist can turn the gentlest, most loving of teachings into a club for beating himself and everyone else. This is the way of aggression, rooted in dualism. It's spirituality as a perpetual struggle against an adversary conceived as other than the one who struggles. Quint reminds me of one of my favorite Zen stories, about the monk who finds himself growing increasingly angry at a spider that dangles in front of his face every time he meditates. Finally he asks the *roshi*, the Zen master, for permission to borrow a knife and kill the spider. "Fine," says the roshi, "but first take this piece of chalk and mark an *X* on its belly." Later, when the monk returns and reports that he has done so, the roshi tells him to pull back his robe. There, on his belly, is a large *X*. The roshi chuckles. "Good thing I didn't give you the knife."

It's called projection, and it's like the old fill-in-the-blank Mad Libs game: "If only it weren't for __(noun)__, I could __(verb)__, and then everything would be __(adjective)__." We always think the problem or the enemy is something outside us. But because it's our own self, the more passionately we pursue it, the more quickly we hasten our own destruction. Such pursuit is especially dangerous when joined with an iron will, as dramatized in the long-ago arm-wrestling contest Quint describes "in an Okie bar in San Francisco" with a "big Chinese fella," where he incurred permanent damage to his arm rather than give up. In his unbending determination to go mano a mano with the shark, an enemy that, like the monk's spider, Quint doesn't realize is himself, he's headed for disaster as clearly as a televangelist who thunders against fornication right up to the moment he's caught in the motel parking lot with the whores.

Like fundamentalists of any stripe (all religions have 'em; some religions have 'em in charge), Quint is engrossed in self-loathing and a sense of sin. Appropriately, the original sin that shaped his warlike approach was committed in wartime. As he relates in the solemn below-decks monologue that lies at the film's center of gravity, he was on the crew of the *Indianapolis,* the ship that delivered the atom bomb that was dropped on Hiroshima, then went down in shark-infested waters.

> We didn't know that our bomb mission had been so secret no distress signal had been sent. . . . Sharks come cruisin', so we formed ourselves into tight groups. . . . Sometimes that shark he looks right into you, right into your eyes. You know a thing about a shark, he's got lifeless eyes, black eyes, like a doll's eye. When he comes at you he doesn't seem to be living, until he bites you and those black eyes roll

over white, and then—ah, then you hear that terrible high-pitched screaming, the ocean turns red in spite of all the pounding and the hollering, they all come in, they rip you to pieces. . . . I'll never put on a lifejacket again. . . . Anyway—we delivered the bomb.

A moment later, with a rueful smile, Quint sings a melancholy sea chantey:

Farewell and adieu to you fair Spanish ladies,
Farewell and adieu, you ladies of Spain.

The song anticipates doom and even welcomes it. As if Quint's horrendous war experience were not punishment enough, like all fundamentalists from Ahab to bin Laden he must drive both himself and his supposedly external enemy toward an apocalypse of total destruction, preferably engulfing as many bystanders as possible. The willpower and aggression that war calls forth are exactly the qualities that mobilize the empty self into its greatest dynamism, giving it power, making it look real and really separate: the more yellow flotation barrels Quint shoots into the shark, the more power it displays. ("Can't stay down with three barrels on him, not with three barrels he can't.")

As Quint and the shark approach their apocalyptic convergence point, in a perverse manifestation of their oneness they come to resemble one another more closely—the shark attacks the boat, turning from hunted to hunter, and Quint grows as monstrous as the monster. Early in the film, Hooper finds one of the shark's teeth embedded in the hull of a boat it has attacked; and Quint, just before telling his *Indianapolis* story, wordlessly removes his own false tooth and leaves it out for the rest of the film, as if revealing that he too is a shark, and that both he and that other shark have bitten down too hard.

Sometimes we all bite down too hard, whether on our religion, our job, our creative work, our children, our relationship, or even our meditation. Then the harder we try, the harder it gets, until most of us, having the germ of sanity called laziness, give up. A few people, the true fanatics, keep pushing to the end, just as Quint, trying to tow the shark into shallow waters, pushes the boat faster and faster ("Full throttle!"), wearing a twisted grin and singing "Farewell and adieu," sensing with satisfaction the approach of the destruction he seeks, till black smoke billows from the burned-out engine. Eventually his all-consuming war ends as it must, with him consumed. As the enemy drags him below the surface, his head and torso still sticking out of its mouth, he looks exactly like the lifeless doll to which he earlier compared the shark.

THE YOUNG SHARK EXPERT Hooper (Richard Dreyfuss) is type B to Quint's type A, embodying a shrewder, gentler approach. Although he can match Quint scar for scar, by his own admission he loves sharks. As the three men pursue their prey in a high-speed chase he exclaims, "Fast fish!," in the same admiring tone in which Rocky Balboa, in the corner after his first round with Apollo Creed, says, "He's good!" Trying to get a photo of it, he calls, "Come here, darling." Hooper has specialized equipment, designed more intelligently than Quint's crude weapons, including electronic tracking devices and a cage and diving gear for getting in the water with the shark, getting down with it in its own element. This is what is called *upaya*, skillful means, the smarter alternative to Quint's dualistic antagonism. By understanding and respecting the shark, Hooper hopes to finesse it through the right hoops, while Quint ("five") just curls his five fingers into a fist of rage.

They also stand on opposite sides of 1975's cultural divide. Quint is of the World War II generation—the first two choices for the role were Lee Marvin and Sterling Hayden, both Marines and war veterans who starred in movies like *Hell in the Pacific* and *Fighter Attack*—while Hooper, with his rimless, hexagonal glasses and his bushy hair and beard, is mid-'70s mellow, of the generation and the class that sat out Vietnam smoking dope in college and still prefers to make love, not war. After Quint tells his bloody *Indianapolis* story and sings his death-wishing "Farewell and adieu," Hooper answers with a cheerful drinking song that suggests the more optimistic, life-affirming brand of spirituality that his generation embraced:

> Show me the way to go home.
> I'm tired and I wanna go to bed.
> I had a little drink about an hour ago,
> And it got right to my head.

Our true home, our source and our goal, the wholeness of enlightened life, promises a cheerful end to our travails, as long as there's someone to show us the way. Human suffering is not the dark imperative of our twisted natures but just a confused little detour, a one-hour stop at the tavern. We'll sleep it off by morning.

Hooper works *with* the shark's nature rather than against it. Since its nature is to eat everything it sees, his plan is to go down in the cage and shoot a cylinder of poison into its gaping mouth. This is the path of gentle, systemic transformation rather than heavy moralizing: if the self wants to consume, don't clobber it but give it something new to consume that will eventually kill its unbridled appetite. Some forms of Buddhism, especially the early (Theravada) forms, specialize in such poison-pill methods, emphasizing contemplations designed to develop "revulsion for the world," seeing all its pleasures as fleeting, illusory, and inextricably bound up with pain. In the Theravada, meditation practice is mostly limited to monks and nuns, who devote their lives to dharma as single-pointedly as Hooper is devoted to sharks. The self and its desires are considered so dangerous that the monks must live constrained by the 227 rules of the Vinaya to protect them, just as Hooper must be constrained and protected by the shark cage.

Yet no matter how many rules we follow, the hungry self can find a way around them or force its way through them. The shark first bumps the cage from behind, knocking the poisoned spear from Hooper's hand to the ocean floor, then rams its way through the bars. It was five centuries after the Buddha's death that some practitioners, seeing the inadequacies of the monastic rules-and-revulsion approach, reshaped the dharma as the Mahayana, or "greater vehicle." They gave the Theravada a new, mildly pejorative name: Hinayana, "smaller vehicle," as befits a shark cage built for one. The impulse that sparked this reformation is portrayed here when Chief Brody, alone on deck, suddenly gets an unexpected, almost nose-to-nose look at the shark, staggers below deck, and speaks the film's juiciest line: "You're gonna need a bigger boat."

But since the shark of self, being completely empty in nature, is limitlessly hungry, how big is big enough? In designing their greater vehicle, their bigger boat, the Mahayanists realized that it must be as big as the ocean itself. Then there can't be any more threats from the outside because there *is* no outside. The Mahayana approach is to handle the shark the way Lyndon Johnson handled one of his political enemies, by giving him a high post in his administration, telling his puzzled aides, "I'd rather have him in the tent pissing out than outside the tent pissing in." Rather than develop bigger and better cages to sequester the practitioner from the world, make the whole world the field of practice. Don't try to poison desire—that's just disguised fundamentalism. The real problem is not desire but the false duality of desirer and desired.

Perhaps even more than they are two historical movements within Buddhism, Mahayana and Hinayana represent two *attitudes* that can probably be found in any religion, organization, or activity. Depending on how open or constricted you are, you can be a Mahayana or Hinayana Presbyterian, or Republican, or guitarist. (Shakespeare was a Mahayana playwright, who broke the prevailing rules of formal composition and wrote for the people, earning the condemnation of the Hinayana "university wits." Their work, which followed the rules scrupulously, is now forgotten.) The contrast between the two attitudes is dramatized in the oft-told tale of the two Zen monks Tanzan and Ekido, who, walking along on a rainy day, happen upon a beautiful young woman in silk finery, trying to cross a muddy road. Without hesitation, Tanzan hoists her onto his back and carries her across. Later that night, Ekido finally says, "You've broken an important monastic rule. We're not supposed to go near women, especially beautiful ones." Replies Tanzan, "Oh, are you still carrying her? I put her down after we crossed the road."

So, as Mahayanists, we don't have to drop out of human society but can embrace each person as our bro'. That's the attitude embodied by Brody. We can be serious practitioners without being rule-bound monks—unlike the specialist Hooper, Brody's a land-hugging layman. And, just as the chief of police is responsible for the peace and security of all the residents of Amity, the Mahayana looks beyond mere individual enlightenment and aims for the enlightenment of all beings.

Devout layman that he is, Brody avoids the showdown with the shark/self as long as possible. Aboard the *Orca* he defers to Quint and Hooper; for three-quarters of the film he hides behind those great oversized '70s aviator glasses he wears like a shield or mask. But as the shark violently yanks the third yellow barrel overboard, it knocks Brody's glasses off, stripping him to the required state of naked vulnerability. And now, with Quint swallowed and Hooper missing underwater, Brody must act. The shark has turned the tables, wrecking the boat, which is sinking rapidly, stern first.

But that's fine—perfect, in fact. The Buddha said the dharma is like a raft that we ride to the far shore of enlightenment. Then we discard the raft rather than carry it around on our backs. Our methods of enlightenment, all our doctrines and practices, are merely means, which become extraneous when the end is reached. This applies not only to our ultimate illumination, but to every present-moment encounter with the non-dual. Our concept of oneness and our desire to transform our lives get us to the meditation cushion; but once we're there, we must let go of all concepts and desires. They're just thoughts, and, as Lama Surya Das says, "Enlightenment is not what you think." Our raft is obsolete, our boat breaks up so we may sink unencumbered into the ocean of nonduality. *Emaho!* (That's Tibetan for "Yahoo!")

Pursued into the flooding cabin and struggling to hold the shark at bay, Brody spots one of Hooper's oxygen tanks and heaves it into its mouth. Here we see a crucial difference between Mahayana and Hinayana. Brody's strategy, like Hooper's, is to exploit the self's reliable trait of nonstop consumption, but instead of poison he feeds it compressed oxygen—just O_2, a bunch of air, as insubstantial as the self itself. He feeds nothing to nothing. This is the purest form of meditation: no effort, no goal, no content, no nothin'. (Yet it's not enough to just hang around. We do need the structure of formal meditation practice. To be powerful, the air must be concentrated, compressed within the structure of the tank.) As the shark swims off, Brody grabs a rifle, climbs up the tilting mast, and waits for it to come back around. With seconds left till the mast will be submerged, the shark bears down on him and Brody fires away, trying to hit the tank. But one element is still missing. So Brody utters the film's other great line—"Smile, you son of a bitch!"—and hits it.

This is more than mere metaphor. I've heard lamas, in teaching meditation, summarize a lot of technical instructions by saying simply, "Sit back and smile." Research has shown that facial expressions not only express emotions but can help stimulate them, and smiling can help catalyze the kind of relaxed acceptance that is the key to meditative practice. As the Swiss dharma teacher Charles Genoud says, "The best way to be tense in meditation is to have a goal." Just smile, relax, give up all goals, and rest in whatever arises.

AND THEN, QUIETLY, something detonates, just as the oxygen tank now detonates, blowing the shark of self into the ocean of being, which is *also* nothing. Nothing blows nothing into nothing, and we do it by doing nothing. The self blows up in a single explosive moment (signified by the exclamation *"Kwatz!"* in Zen, or *"Phat!"* in Dzogchen). The frenzy of *rushing* through time to consume the next object and the next, which is the essence of sharklike existence, is suddenly stopped short and blown away. ("Blown away" is a literal translation of *nirvana.*) In that timeless moment both subject and object, whose complex structure of separateness can only be maintained through time, spontaneously deconstruct. Boat and shark vanish simultaneously into ocean.

Then the self that never was joins with the wholeness of being that it always really was, as the exploded shark sinks beneath the surface, dissolving into red blood that disperses into colorless water, accompanied by a piano tinkling celestial descending arpeggios. *Jaws* has many moments that are clever or thrilling, but this is the one moment that is sublime, a clear evocation of transcendence, an inverted miracle in which the red wine of intoxicated desiring is converted to the clear water of being.

In the denouement, when Hooper resurfaces and he and Brody paddle toward shore on a board lashed between two of those yellow barrels, their banter suggests this new, enlightened situation.

> BRODY: Hey, what day is this?
> HOOPER: It's Wednesday—uh, it's Tuesday, I think.
> BRODY: I think the tide's with us.
> HOOPER: Keep kicking.
> BRODY: I used to hate the water.

Having accomplished their encounter with vast, oceanic being in the dimension of timelessness, they are reorienting themselves to time, returning to the day-to-day world of domestic Amity, but now with a larger friendship, aligned with the timeless power of that ocean: the tide (the Force) is with them. That's Brody's Mahayana emphasis. Hooper, ever the striving Theravadan, emphasizes the need to keep kicking. Christians call these two approaches being saved by grace and being saved by works. Here the two are seen as complementary. Our inner Theravadan and our inner Mahayanist can cooperate (there's a place for both), having purged our inner fundamentalist (good riddance).

The film's final moments, under the closing credits, show an extreme long shot of the ocean and, at the right side of the screen, the beach, where two almost invisible figures, so tiny we can't tell which is which, come ashore. It's a visual echo of Chrissie's tranquil, pre-attack swim, as if a restoration of her innocence. Wisely, Spielberg skips the cheap shot, the *Star Wars*–style triumphal welcome to the conquering heroes from the grateful townspeople, a tawdry prize that would merely start feeding the self all over again. Instead, he leaves them here: happily, interchangeably selfless, dwarfed by the great ocean of being, the only real prize.

SO THE ESSENTIAL METHOD for realizing this infinite, oceanic freedom is the infinitely simple practice of goalless resting in present awareness. This is the direct escape route from narrow, driven, tunnel-visioned shark awareness. It's most effectively cultivated through regular sessions of silent sitting ("meditation," to use the word that always threatens to make it sound strenuous and goal-oriented), along with numerous moments of informal letting go and letting be in the midst of the day's activities.

One way of letting go into those moments, one that's particularly relevant here, is simply this:

Put down your fork.

You can do this quite literally. Sit down to a meal, and every time you take a bite, put down your fork and rest your attention in the fullness of the experience of the mouthful you're chewing. Don't hover the way ordinary people do, poised to stab the next forkful. In fact, break it down further. As each forkful travels upward from the plate, take your time and rest in the experience of that long series of moments, rather than be lost in anticipation of its reaching your mouth. If you happen to have a weight problem, you'll probably find that this style of eating *in* fulfillment rather than eating *for* fulfillment helps.

Then do everything else like this. Whatever you're doing, locate your mental fork. Note that poised, ravening anticipation of the *next* thing that keeps you from fully experiencing *this* thing, whatever it is. Note what that anticipation feels like, and then put it down, let it go.

As you open more and more to the fullness of each moment's experience, the *content* of experience begins to matter less. The moment of raising the fork or lowering the fork is just as "good" as the moments of chewing and swallowing. *Every* moment is, as Jack Nicholson says in another film, as good as it gets; what Jack's character doesn't understand is that that's plenty good, infinitely good, infinitely full. The moments of lacing up your running shoes are as full as the moments of running; the moments of driving to the theater are as full as the moments of watching the movie; the moments of flirtation and cuddling are as full as the moments of orgasm, and so are the moments of separation. Like everything in dharma, this is not a doctrine to be believed or an attitude to be faked. Just pay attention and decide whether it's true—come and see.

> Any moment decide, "This is enough"—
> and become enlightened.
> —OSHO

Then whatever you're doing becomes meditation. Meditation is not about seeking an extraordinary experience. That's been our whole life of *non*meditation, whether we're walking into Ben & Jerry's and choosing Chocolate Chip Cookie Dough or thumbing through the sex manual and choosing position #37(a). Meditation is the absolutely ordinary experience of the present moment. The only thing extraordinary about it is that, for once, we're resting in its ordinariness rather than registering vague (or intense) dissatisfaction and rushing into the next moment in hopes that it will be better.

I made up that fork business—Indians in the time of the Buddha didn't have forks. But here's some traditional advice:

Be generous.

Meditative practice is much more powerful when supported by an honest effort to practice the Six Paramitas, the transcendental virtues: generosity, morality, patience, diligence, meditation, and wisdom. We'll discuss these later, but here note that the first listed is always generosity, *dana* (pronounced "donna").

True generosity, whether what we give is tangible or intangible, helps loosen up our sense of stuckness within the confines of self. Sharks are not known for saying "After you."

> Take food from your own mouth and give it as alms.
> —MILAREPA

When we give food or money or goods or time or emotional support, it feels expansive and liberating because it helps free us from the role of obsessed subject seeking gratification from often uncooperative objects. Every act of generosity affords a glimpse of that nonduality where there is no subject/object separation. Through doing, generosity helps accomplish what meditation accomplishes through being. If you don't want to be caught up in life-as-feeding-frenzy, if you don't want to be the self-fish, don't be selfish.

> Upon opening ourselves to these vast infinities,
> we . . . see how narrow, constricted, and
> shortsighted our usual self-centered concerns are,
> in the light of the infinite, shimmering void.
> —NYOSHUL KHENPO RINPOCHE,
> *Natural Great Perfection*

THE TRUMAN SHOW
(1998)

THE REAL WORLD

Live no longer to the expectation of these deceived and deceiving people with whom we converse. Say to them, "O father, O mother, O wife, O brother, O friend, I have lived with you after appearances hitherto. Henceforward I am the truth's."

—EMERSON,
"Self-Reliance"

LEELA: Fry, this isn't TV, this is real life. Can't you tell the difference?
FRY: Sure, I just like TV better.

—*FUTURAMA*

GIMME A BEER, BUT FIRST LET ME TELL YOU THIS GREAT joke: Guy walks into a bar and says to the bartender, "Gimme a beer, but first let me tell you this great joke: Guy walks into a bar and says to the bartender, 'Gimme a beer, but first let me tell you this great joke: Guy walks into a bar . . .'" And so on.

Question #1: Is this a great joke?

Question #2: Are any beers served, and if so how many?

Jokes within jokes, mirrors within mirrors, patterns within patterns. Repetition and also repetition. And running through it all, a search for something real, something to quench our thirst.

Truman Burbank's life is full of patterns and repetition. He gets up every morning in his lovely home, greets his lovely wife, drinks a hot cup of Mococoa, and dresses for work. On the way to his lovely car he gives the lovely family next door a cheery greeting—"Good morning! And in case I don't see you, good afternoon, good evening, and good night!"—fends off the pesky neighborhood Dalmatian, and drives off to work, through the lovely, pastel, sun-drenched (a little *too* sun-drenched) island town of Seahaven, Florida, which has obviously sprung fully formed from the forehead of some architect in love with patterns and repetition.

What Truman doesn't know is that Seahaven is set under an artificial sky within the world's largest studio (next to the HOLLYWOOD sign), that he has been conditioned since childhood to fear setting foot outside it, that he is the star of a nonstop TV show that began with his birth, that all the other residents are shills, and that when his blond, dimpled wife (a little *too* blond, a little *too* dimpled) smilingly extols the virtues of Mococoa she's holding the box up to one of the 5,000 hidden cameras that beam his every move to a rapt worldwide audience. "All-natural cocoa beans from the upper slopes of Mount Nicaragua, no artificial sweeteners!" For the film's first half hour or so, before the artifice is clearly laid out, it's subtly hinted at by the odd angles and porthole framing of tiny cameras set in curbsides, shirt buttons, car radios, and oversize rings.

On one level Peter Weir's *The Truman Show* is a witty, ingeniously worked out parody of our inverted media culture, the logical extension of the world where so-called reality shows crowd the airwaves and, increasingly, broadcasts of everything from the Olympics to standup concerts have mikes and cameras in the wings to make the performer's private moments public—and thus just as contrived as the public moments. At the end of the film, when Truman (Jim Carrey) finally sees through the scam, he confronts the disembodied voice-in-the-sky of

Christof (Ed Harris), the show's godlike creator, who directs it from his command center concealed in Truman's moon:

> TRUMAN: Was nothing real?
> CHRISTOF: You were real. That's what made you so good to watch.

One of the things that make our reality shows so *bad* to watch is that the people in them are *not* real. When Andy Warhol foresaw the world in which everyone would be famous for fifteen minutes, he didn't mention that by the time the thousandth person gets his turn he has watched the first 999 perform. Each new media protagonist has progressively less real life beyond what he has absorbed from previous camera-conscious media protagonists. Unlike Truman, they're not true men. TV offers the spiritually useful opportunity to work through lots of vicarious incarnations quickly by trying out the values and personalities of different heroes and then moving on. But when we and the heroes all become bland clones of one another, what's left to try?

In 1968 the other key slogan of the media age besides Warhol's was born in the streets of Chicago, when antiwar demonstrators froze a phalanx of club-swinging policemen by calling their attention to the new, lightweight news cameras that were getting it all on film. "The whole world is watching! The whole world is watching!" chanted the demonstrators, in a line repeated in this film. But in our reality-show culture the whole world is watching the whole world watching the whole world . . . Gimme a beer!

THE TRUMAN SHOW offers a snazzy take on this tail-swallowing media snake, but it also goes deeper, sharing profound insights into the journey of spiritual discovery.

The journey often begins with the noting of a discrepancy,

an encounter with something inconsistent with our received description of reality. When astronomers first observed the precession of the orbit of Mercury, it was impossible in their Newtonian universe; it eventually required Einstein's universe of general relativity. For Huck Finn the journey begins when he overhears Jim, who as a black slave is not considered fully human, mourning for his absent children: "I do believe he cared just as much for his people as white folks does for their'n. It don't seem natural, but I reckon it's so." For Truman, it begins when a small spotlight falls out of his artificial sky; picking it up, he sees that it's marked SIRIUS (9 CANIS MAJOR). It usually takes some kind of star falling out of our sky to get us going: maybe an intense experience of transcendence or love descends upon us unsought, maybe someone close to us dies or suffers a terrible injury or disease that doesn't jibe with the way we thought a loving God would run things. The usual sequence, which this film so nicely illustrates, follows what we could call the Fats Domino theory of spiritual awakening. First something happens to shake us up. Then we let its implications rattle around inside us for a while (and perhaps we rattle on to others about it). Finally we roll out of our old world into some more expansive vista.

> Launch out into the deep, and let down your nets
> for a draught.
> —LUKE 5:4

As the film goes on, Carrey uses his superb physical acting skills to portray the gradual dawning of insight. An electrifying moment of epiphany comes when, in his first dramatic break from old habit patterns, the suspicious Truman enters the revolving door of his office building but then, instead of falling into the routine of his normal workday, comes out again. His 180-degree turn reflects a 180-degree turn of consciousness, a true Copernican revolution. As he wanders about the town commons, sizing up the fishiness of all the bustle that surrounds him, we see him walking and see him *seeing* with the stunned deliberateness of a man from whose eyes the scales have suddenly fallen away. Phrases like "transformation of awareness" and "liberation from illusion" can sound pretty abstract; here Carrey concretely conveys how it looks and feels.

By glorifying Truman for questioning his reality, the film encourages us to question ours. The enormous Seahaven set, with its choreographed crowds and made-to-order weather, practically leaps out of the pages of Descartes, who, in his quest to ascertain what's unquestionably real, applied a "methodological doubt," speculating that everything he saw could be an elaborate hoax perpetrated by an "evil genius"—like Christof. (Christof's best line: "Cue the sun!") We assume a lot. When we drive past rows of office buildings, we assume that they are full of workers working away, and not, as they are here, empty props. If we have had a best pal since childhood, we assume that he is a sincere friend, and not an actor being fed lines through a hidden earpiece. (In honor of Brando, the actor's actor, the pal is named Marlon; in honor of Streep, the actress's actress, Truman's wife is named Meryl. Her acting duties presumably extend into the bedroom—she's a pro all the way.)

Descartes's doubt is astute not only philosophically but emotionally. It taps into a sort of restless low rumble that most alert people feel at some time in their lives, a queasy mistrust of everything they have bought into as real—real not only in the absolute sense but in the sense of being worthwhile and important. We may laugh off such doubts with jokes about midlife crises, but something's going on there that deserves attention:

And you may find yourself in a beautiful house,
    with a beautiful wife

And you may ask yourself—
Well . . . How did I get here?
—TALKING HEADS,
"Once in a Lifetime"

How did I get here? Out of all of life's boundless possibilities, how did I wind up signing on for this one, forsaking all
others? These are valid questions.

If your house and wife and other comforts are sufficiently
beautiful, it's easy to be lulled into accepting them as all there
is. Anytime you start to feel a stab of doubt, there'll be some
Marlon to come over with a six-pack of brewskis to take the
edge off, always friends with their joshing guy talk or gushing
girl talk to convince you your quest is foolish. The longing for
something more—something unrealized, maybe the crazy unfulfilled dreams of youth—can take many forms, all of them
easy to mock. The lost romance never consummated, the faraway places never visited: here they're rolled into one in the
person of Sylvia, Truman's almond-eyed college crush who is
suddenly removed from the cast when she threatens to reveal
the charade, yanked out of his grasp by her "father" and supposedly relocated to Fiji. (She wears a button reading HOW'S IT
GOING TO END?, implying an element of open-ended free will.)
Truman spends his adult years nurturing a secret life where he
fantasizes about traveling to Fiji; he rips pieces of models' faces
from fashion magazines, trying to reconstruct Sylvia in a paste-
up like that of a criminal suspect and hiding it in the back of a
picture frame, behind a photo of his wife.

Cultivating the fantasy lover as the secret face behind the
spouse's—that's an incisive, subtle take on the restless spirit in
the bourgeois world, and the film is full of them. Truman talks in
cutesy-pie clichés like "the whole kit and caboodle" (shades of
The Simpsons' Ned Flanders), but with a gradually sharpening

edge that eventually hashes them into angry absurdity: "The early bird gathers no moss! The rolling stone catches the worm!" Seahavenites are fond of smarmy spiritual platitudes and off-the-rack emotions; sighing over their wedding photos, Meryl coos, "That was the happiest day of our lives," Truman almost imperceptibly squirms, and that's that. (Like the women in *Huckleberry Finn*, Meryl has the job of "sivilizing" all the spirit out of the hero.) As an insurance salesman in the tradition of Jim Anderson, the prototypical '50s comfort dad of *Father Knows Best*, Truman fortifies folks against the same risks and insecurities he has been trained to dread. The straight-arrow hairdos, the cornball golfwear-inspired clothes—available to viewers through the Truman Catalog, operators are standing by—the bright, flat colors, and the unanimously happy faces give Truman's world a creepy-normal *Invasion of the Body Snatchers* feel, like an old *Dick and Jane* reader with a pervert uncle lurking somewhere in a closet.

What holds Truman as well as his audience in this world is a delicate balance of reassuring sameness and mildly stimulating change: repetition and variation. Life works this way and TV especially works this way. We tune in to see Ross and Rachel and the gang predictably hang out at Central Perk and have predictably sexy, funny problems, but with their problems unpredictably scrambled from week to week by such randomizing factors as new lovers or jobs. Truman's friends Ron and Don could be a symbol of this principle of same-but-different, asymmetry-symmetry; they're identical twins except that one is, bizarrely, a head taller than the other. The same principle can be heard in the tinkling Mozart rondo that plays on the car radio as Truman drives to work—Mozart as sedating aural wallpaper, where the doubling and redoubling of phrases is like the mitosis of cheerfully reproducing cells, same-but-different little units assembling themselves into happy organisms as seamlessly integrated as Truman's world of same-but-different houses, people, days, and years. Good afternoon, good evening, and good night.

When the light starts to dawn for Truman, he starts to see his way through the patterns that structure his world, noticing, for instance, that the traffic flowing past his house is an endless loop: "I predict that in just a moment we will see a lady on a red bike, followed by a man with flowers and a VW Beetle with a dented fender." This leads him to defy the patterns. He walks into nonprescribed buildings and catches cast members scurrying to pretend to work at jobs; he drives in wild, nonprescribed nonpatterns, shouting, "Somebody help me, I'm being spontaneous!"; he indulges in wide-eyed talk about chucking everything and heading for Fiji. Underscoring this mood of discovery is Philip Glass's pulsing music (some of it from *Powaqqatsi*), which here serves as the darkly noble anti-Mozart, using the same elements of fractalizing repetition and variation not to happily assemble patterns but to broodingly contemplate and deconstruct them.

BUT *WHO* HOLDS TRUMAN within those patterns? The short answer is Christof, the autocratic God at whom we and eventually Truman shake our fists, the Oedipal daddy that we congratulate ourselves for vicariously rebelling against. We'll always root for someone who defies "society," but that's too easy, too sophomoric. (When Meryl scolds, "You're talking like a teenager," she has a point.) As individuals we resent society's imposing patterns on us. But who is society other than us individuals in the aggregate, and each one of us sure as hell wants to impose patterns on the others. We have a legitimate interest in making sure they don't get too spontaneous while they're driving—let's have no creative interpretation of traffic signals, please. When I'm in an airplane or a crowded elevator, I want everybody's behavior to be nice and predictable. The increasingly defiant, desperate Truman eventually does things like walking in front of buses and holding his wife at knifepoint. We'll lock you up for that sort of behavior, and rightly so. When you break society's rules you're betting against the house, and the house always wins.* There's a reason why Holden Caulfield is the favorite hero of psycho killers.

So which do we do? Conform and be robots, or defy and be psychos? That's a trick question. Challenging the Oedipal daddy is just the flip side of venerating him. Either way we're giving him credence, affirming his place at the head of the table. The way of authentic freedom is to see that there *is* no head of the table. There's no man in the moon, no Christof in the sky—or if there is, we've created and empowered him at least as much as he's created us. In his black mandarin jacket and chocolate-brown beret, Ed Harris cunningly plays Christof as a pretentious, self-stroking artiste—a fake. What if our creator is as fake as Truman's, a little nothin' behind a curtain posing as The Great and Powerful Oz, perpetuated only by our fear and unreflective belief? Then, for Truman as for his namesake, the buck stops here.

That's a central tenet of Buddhist teaching. In his dialogues with representatives of other faiths, the Dalai Lama is very liberal about acknowledging their commonality, but this is where he draws the line: "No creator God." It's not just an abstract doctrinal point; it changes everything. If there's no ultimate authority figure imposing the patterns of your existence upon you, you must somehow be generating them yourself. Then to seek liberation is to take responsibility for these patterns, as a first step toward liberating yourself from them. When Christof tells an interviewer, "If [Truman] was absolutely determined to leave, there's no way we could prevent him," he's right. Truman cheer-

---

* Except, of course, when it doesn't, and then you change history.

fully perpetuates recurring cycles of mornings, afternoons, evenings, and nights, and, like any other self-satisfied creator, declares them good. We're spiders caught in our own ingenious webs.

This taking responsibility is a kind of spiritual maturity, a growing out of our Holden Caulfield phase. We realize that blaming everything on God or society or existence as if we're not as much a part of it as anyone else is like complaining about a traffic jam as if we're not as much a part of it as every other driver. I once attended an ecology rally in front of Zellerbach Hall at UC Berkeley. One of the speakers pointed out that the building was named for a founder of the Crown-Zellerbach paper goods company. As he put it, "They chop down trees and turn them into shit paper." I was impressed till I thought, Wait a minute—what does *this* guy wipe himself with?

This film's crucial enlightenment teaching is that, as much as we're Truman, we're Christof—lining up camera angles, bringing up the music, exclaiming, "There's the hero shot!" We orchestrate the elements of experience and fantasy into our own hero shots, to enshrine and romanticize the self even as we define and limit it. There's a clue to this near the beginning, when we see Truman in front of his bathroom mirror, acting out a melodramatic daydream of being a dying mountaineer, urging his companions to save themselves by eating his flesh. As a kid I used to spend fantasy time in front of a full-length mirror in my parents' bedroom; my specialty was being gut shot, clutching desperately at the wound, and dying very slowly and photogenically. As we get older, our scripts may become less glamorous, more grounded in our jobs and relationships, with occasional input from the newspapers, but they're still The Drama About Me. She makes *me* so angry. Will the recession affect *my* paycheck? Will the terrorists get *my* family?

TRUMAN: Who are you?
CHRISTOF: I am the creator—of a television show
that gives hope and joy and inspiration to millions.
TRUMAN: Then who am I?
CHRISTOF: You're the star.

For playing both of these roles so expertly without letting either one realize it's the secret identity of the other, we all deserve Emmys.

Hindus have a rich metaphor for this situation. Unlike Buddhists, they have a creator God, Lord Brahma, but no one worships him. In fact, he's considered a bit of a screw-up. After he makes the world, he's seduced by his own creation, committing incest with his daughter. This eventually leads to one of his five heads being cut off, suggesting that when we get lost in our own projections our awareness is diminished—we lose our head. As we're Christof, we're Brahma, but Brahma is just the first person of the Hindu trinity. We're also Lord Vishnu, the maintainer God, the loving, bountiful God who promotes ease and status quo happiness within the created world, the kind of God most Christians really have in mind when they address their prayers to the creator. (Crew members in the *Truman Show* control room wear T-shirts that say LOVE HIM, PROTECT HIM.) And, most important of all to those of us who seek liberation, we're also Lord Shiva, the destroyer, the lord of enlightenment, who deconstructs what Brahma has constructed, dissolving the universe of boundaries once again into boundlessness. Hindus call this boundlessness *brahman* and understand that Brahma, Vishnu, and Shiva are all simply different faces of brahman—as is everything else, as are all of us.

Descartes takes a different angle. I think, therefore I am: his methodological doubt leads him to conclude that, since he experiences his own thinking even as he's thinking doubts, the one thing he cannot doubt is the reality of the thinker, his own existence. ("Was nothing real?" "You were real.") Everything else and everyone else could be his dream. Nowadays brain surgeons can stimulate various parts of a patient's cortex with electrodes and make him experience music, colors, or his fifth birthday. Per Descartes I know *that* I am, but I don't know *what* I am. Maybe I'm a brain floating in a nutrient bath, with electrodes inducing all the experiences I take to be real, from the form of my body to all my so-called memories. Maybe I'm Marilyn Monroe or a Martian or a ball of wax or something I can't conceive of, dreaming up this whole peculiar universe.

If so, then right now I'm dreaming that I'm sitting in my backyard, enjoying the July breeze and the sound of the fountain as I type away on my iBook, wondering if the words I type are real and if there are any real people out there to read them (or if there's any "out there" at all). If I'm *not* dreaming it—if you're real too—then just about now you should be wondering whether *you're* the only real one and the experience of reading these words about dreaming is just the latest ironic plot twist in *your* dream universe. Since all experience takes place within the sphere of personal awareness, just as all of Truman's experience takes place within the painted dome of the Seahaven sky, we can never know any reality outside that sphere.

BUDDHISM, ESPECIALLY IN its later, Mahayana, forms, assumes that everyone else is just as real as I am. And just as unreal. As we have seen in earlier chapters, the self is an entity as suspect as the creator. A few sentences back, when I referred to "the sphere of *personal* awareness," I slipped a joker into the deck. Any sense that awareness has personal qualities, "us" qualities, is just another dreamlike sensation experienced within awareness itself; and awareness itself, as we have seen, is qualityless, like the crystalline emptiness of a mirror that reflects all colors. So, while we can't escape into another person's head, we can discover that we were never really stuck inside our own. We've been looking at things inside out: awareness is not located in our head or anywhere else. If I pay close attention, I can notice that my sensations of having a head, like my sensations of hearing the leaves rustle and feeling the chair against my back and butt, take place *within awareness*, and awareness is not within anything.

Within this unowned, nonpersonal awareness-space, without a separate creator or creatures, what remain are mutual projections of creation, maintenance, and dissolution—a beginningless, endless mesh of interactivity that belongs to everyone and no one. All apparent sentient beings are simultaneously projecting and projected, directing and acting, in a relationship that Thich Nhat Hanh calls "interbeing":

> Interbeing means that you cannot be a separate
> entity. You can only interbe with other people and
> elements. You could also call it true self, the
> awareness that you are made wholly of non-self
> elements.

Or as Bob Dylan put it:

> I'll let you be in my dreams
> If I can be in yours.

This recognition that we're all equally real and unreal, dreamers and dreamed, creators and created, important (stars) and expendable (supporting cast) is what saves us. We're all in the same boat (Mahayana, big vehicle) and can only arrive on the far shore of liberation together. In the film's climactic escape sequence, Truman is literally in a boat, at the tiller of a little sloop, finally confronting his morbid fear of the sea, our fear of the primordial being-soup in which our meticulously constructed lives and identities dissolve. Sailing away from Seahaven just as we must set forth from our comfortable haven of illusions, he's headed toward freedom. Defying the great waves and lightning bolts sent by the Old Testament wrath of Christof to destroy the disobedient servant who has eaten the fruit of knowledge (Christof is pissed off), Truman summons just the kind of chutzpah such a quest requires, shouting, "Is that the best you can do?" At one point he even appears to drown, symbolically undergoing the necessary death of self.

In keeping with the Mahayana spirit, what drives him on his journey is love, signified by the paste-up picture of Sylvia he pulls out his pocket as if consulting a map. Even if our love is a paste-up job, a collage of romantic fantasies, impressions, and desires ripped out of the media, it's good enough to give us the direction, to get us started navigating on the journey of realization.

> It is an ever-fixéd mark
> That looks on tempests and is never shaken;
> It is the star to every wandering bark . . .
>   —SHAKESPEARE,
>   Sonnet 116

Love is the map because it reaches beyond self. Descartes's dead-end logic concludes that the mind can never know the reality of another. But love is a kind of blind crashing through the limits of the mind, to the heart-place where we *feel* the reality of the other.

Of course we don't know what we're getting ourselves into when we set forth. We think love is going to be some cozy gratification of self, but it turns out to be the drowning of self, a voyage from the narrowest attachment to the widest compassion. Buddhists define love very expansively (and provocatively) as the desire for the happiness of others. In that sense, love makes the impossible leap to the conviction that others are real—again, "real" meaning not only existent but worthwhile and important. This is what made it possible for the firefighters to run up the stairs of the World Trade Center, and what makes such selfless acts strike a deep chord in the rest of us. In them we recognize the smashing of the boundaries of our own small-ness. Our wandering bark can follow the star of love "even to the edge of doom," sailing all the way to the edge of our self-constructed reality—the edge that Truman now reaches when, in the film's most astonishing moment, his boat reaches the horizon and bumps up against the sky.

Beyond that edge, the mutual reality of the other awaits us, as Sylvia awaits Truman in her Los Angeles apartment, watching him (as does the rest of the world) on TV, rooting for him to make it. Movingly, silently, he pounds his fist, hand, elbow, shoulder against the sky, as we all at some time pound in desper-ation against the inside of the life or the skull in which (we think) we're trapped. Interestingly, it's when he gives up pound-ing and relaxes a bit that his God speaks to him from the sky and spills the beans, divulging the knowledge Truman seeks. As Christof tries to tempt him to stay, Sylvia briefly glances skyward and whispers, "Please, God!," in what is either the film's one false note or its shrewdest irony—she's begging *her* patriarchal sky-deity to save Truman from *his*. Is this a cop-out, a fuzzy surrender to *our* all-powerful Christof? Or perhaps it's a sly warning that we "real" people in "real" life are caught in the illusion of a yet bigger show—that, as we leave the theater feeling good about seeing Truman deconstruct his projections, our own deconstruction job is just beginning. Worlds within worlds, jokes within jokes.

> "Reality" is the one word that should always appear
> in quotation marks.
> —VLADIMIR NABOKOV

In any case, Truman resists temptation, finds the exit—the studio door through the sky—bows to the camera, and leaves.

Sylvia pulls her coat on and hurries out her door to meet him, a reminder that she was never in Fiji at all, that he and the Sylvia he sought were in the same L.A. all along. We don't have to go anywhere. We don't have to change anything. The lost girl-friend and the exotic island are just external representations of the freedom and happiness that are already right here (wher-ever we are), cut off from us only by the superimposed dome of our own constrictive patterns of self. The solution is to disas-semble the patterns not on the superficial level of behavior, but on the level of consciousness, which is where we built them in the first place. Pierce through them, see them as empty even while leaving them in place.

Rendered weightless by their emptiness, some destructive or superfluous patterns will certainly drop away, but that's almost beside the point. We can achieve total liberation within the con-text of a totally conventional life. Thus, as Truman takes his final bow, he says one more time, "And in case I don't see you, good afternoon, good evening, and good night." It's like a final, friendly endorsement of the routine; as his smile of triumph in-dicates, having seen its emptiness, seen that it's a kind of joke, he can be graciously tolerant of it. Without that sense of toler-ance we never get beyond pounding our fist against the sky. We have to find that door, *penetrate* the sky. It's something far sub-tler and less romantic than quitting our jobs and sailing to Fiji, which is why most people overlook it.

> Knowing the world in full directly,
> the whole world just as it is,
> from the whole world he is freed.
> —SUTTA PITAKA

And because we're not separate beings but interbeing, our individual liberation is involved with the liberation of all. All for one and one for all, as the Latin inscription on the arch over the Seahaven town commons reads. When Truman walks through the sky, his loyal viewers throughout the world (some wearing I'M A TRU-BELIEVER T-shirts) celebrate joyously, but then transmission ceases. He's liberated from the show and they're liberated from watching it—although there's a droll stinger at the film's very end, when two parking attendants who have been following the show obsessively in their little booth now say, "What else is on?" "Yeah, let's see what else is on." "Where's the *TV Guide*?" Even presented with a shot at freedom, most beings will sign right up for another round of samsara, another vicarious incarnation to get lost in.

LOVE IS THE MAP. All religions advise us to free ourselves by loving one another, or words to that effect, but how? Just saying the words or having the intention or giving some awkward "sign of peace" in church on Sunday morning clearly doesn't do it. Vajrayana Buddhism offers many practical techniques for actually developing love, for breaking through our illusory sense of isolation, piercing that sky. I've been fortunate to study a particularly effective one, called *exchanging self and other*, with my teacher and friend Charles Genoud.

- Sit with eyes closed, first settling down with a few minutes of meditation.

- Then bring some person to mind, as if he or she were sitting before you. At first use a "neutral person" such as a casual acquaintance from your neighborhood or work.

- Note the sense of you, the meditator, the one sitting on the chair or cushion, as *self*—our usual, normal sense of ourselves as the center of all experience, the one to whom everything is happening, the one who is happy or unhappy. Also note the sense of the person in front of you—let's call him Bob—as *other*, someone "out there" and therefore less important, just another peripheral person. Notice what the sense of selfness and the sense of otherness *feel* like, their subtle textures.

- Then switch them. Shift the sense of being self, the center of everything, to Bob; shift the sense of being other to the meditator. This doesn't mean that you now see through Bob's eyes or visualize Bob sitting on your cushion or imagine yourself inside his body, but simply that Bob is now the important one, the center of all experience, while the one on the cushion is just another person.

- For a few minutes let your awareness marinate in that Bob-ness, letting Bob be your whole world just as the old you has been your whole world for so many years. As you do so, let the old you languish in the shadows, practically forgotten.

- Try this with various people, one at a time. When you feel you've made the shift successfully, try giving things to Bob (or whoever you're on now). Don't get hung up on specifics, but in your imagination pour a glowing shower of money, luxuries, and wonderful achievements on Bob, leaving nothing for the half-forgotten old you. Since Bob is now the self and the old you is just another person, you should find that heaping all these boons on him generates great happiness.

Later you can move on from neutral people to those who provoke more intense feelings, whether positive or negative. You can also expand the technique to include the development of compassion, which is defined as the desire for others to be free from suffering. Here you imagine (again, without being too specific) heaps of miseries piled upon Bob. If you have successfully made the exchange of self for other, you should be feeling the misery acutely. Then divert all the miseries away from him, putting them on the old you that's languishing in the shadows, and you should feel a sensation of great relief.

Once you start feeling at home with this practice, you can expand it further by sometimes using groups of people—say, your family, your colleagues, all abused children, all victims of war, and eventually all sentient beings. You can also take the practice off the cushion and into daily life. Pick people out of the crowd while you're shopping, pick fellow motorists or pedestrians while you're commuting, and for a few moments let them be the center of the universe instead of you. Or simply reflect, as you drive down the street, that all those houses you pass are full of people, each with a family she loves and worries about as much as you do yours, each with an entire life that's just as important to her as yours is to you, each of whom is the star of the show as much as you are and for whom you are merely one of thousands of extras.

These are powerful practices. They blow big holes in the old sense of separateness, of being stuck inside our little skulls or under our private skies. They help free us from the labor of lining up all those hero shots, and from the exhausting full-time job of trying to rearrange the world so that, against all odds, the happiness always lands on the one person out of six billion we call "me." Practiced regularly, they engender love as something natural and spontaneous rather than a strained virtue, and omnidirectional rather than exclusive. As the old obsession with my-me-mine falls away, and you find yourself consciously interbeing with others, being you stops feeling so tightly constrictive, so excruciatingly localized.

At the root of all suffering, I know only one cause:
the cherishing of self. At the root of all happiness,
I know only one cause: the cherishing of others.
    —SHANTIDEVA

Whenever I think of this film, I think of Jim Carrey's beautiful smile as he takes that final bow and exits through the sky. When you finally give up being the star, it's such a relief.

MEMENTO
(2000)

NOW, WHERE WAS I?

Nothing is known, everything is imagined.
—FEDERICO FELLINI

"It's a poor sort of memory that only works backwards,"
the Queen remarked.
—LEWIS CARROLL,
Alice's Adventures in Wonderland

THIS WAS THE ONLY TIME THIS EVER HAPPENED TO ME.
When Maggy and I went to see *Memento*, after the film ended
and the lights came up we found ourselves still sitting with half
a dozen other viewers, all in varying stages of bafflement.
Within moments we were engaged in a spontaneous sympo-
sium, trying to sort out what the hell we had just seen. The one
thing that was clear to everyone was that, although the film was
confusing, it wasn't because it was sloppy. Its intricate structure
was highly precise—actually more precise, because it had to be,
than many far simpler films. Its protagonist, in case you haven't
seen it (and if you haven't, you should stop reading right now
and watch it), has no short-term memory, so he knows who he
is and what's going on right now but not what happened ten
minutes ago. What's disorienting is that the film puts you in his
shoes by telling the story backward. "Live in the present" is a

popular spiritual cliché. *Memento* gives you no choice. It conveys, more powerfully than any other film I can think of, the reality that the present moment is where we're *always* living because it's all there is, and it presents a cunning picture of how we construct the myths of past and future and then lose ourselves in them.

The hero, Leonard Shelby (Guy Pearce in spiky blond hair), is obsessed with finding the intruder who raped and murdered his wife. In the ensuing scuffle, Leonard suffered a head injury that resulted in anterograde amnesia—the inability to form new memories. A former insurance investigator from San Francisco, he has now checked into a seedy Los Angeles motel to conduct his own amateur investigation, despite such serious handicaps as not being able to remember the beginning of a conversation by the time he gets to the end, and not knowing whether he's meeting someone for the first time or the twentieth. He always carries a Polaroid camera and a pocketful of snapshots with scrawled captions to remind himself where he's staying, which car is his, who people are, and which ones to trust. His system, though, is far from foolproof. In one scene he tells a barmaid (Carrie-Anne Moss) about his condition; she proceeds to test him by spitting into a beer, getting him and a few other patrons to do likewise, and then serving it to him minutes later. And a guy named Teddy (the terrific Joe Pantoliano, who played Ralphie Cifaretto on *The Sopranos*)—a gum-snapping, wisecracking character in a crew cut and mustache, who may or may not be a cop or a thug or both—keeps mysteriously popping up, either to guide Leonard on his mission or to manipulate him for his own purposes. It's hard to tell.

The unreliability of memory is an easy case to make. I have a perfectly vivid recollection of sitting beside the swimming pool with my father at our house in Woodland Hills, California, early one Friday or Saturday evening circa 1962. My older brother

Ross, then about fifteen, comes to say good night. He's going out with friends, and he's all duded up in the style of the time: Brylcreemed hair, pointy Italian shoes, peggers, and a sporty aqua-and-cobalt Sir Guy shirt. Seeing how flawlessly put together Ross looks, my father is seized by a sudden impulse, jumps up, grabs him by the elbows, and throws him into the pool. As clearly as I see this morning's breakfast, I can see my fully clothed brother, sputtering with rage as he treads water in the early evening light.

But here's the problem. A few decades later, in a long-distance phone conversation with my mother, I brought this story up. "That never happened," she insisted. "Your father never threw Ross in the pool with his clothes on. He would never do something like that." She checked with my dad and he agreed. A little worried, I called Ross. He said he couldn't specifically remember it happening but couldn't rule it out either. So there you have it. Three witnesses: one says yes, one says no, one says maybe, and we'll never have any further input. (My father has since died.) Was it my fantasy? Did I dream it? Or did the other principals block out what was, after all, a pretty ugly incident? All I can do with that memory, unless I adopt the dangerous policy that everyone else is always wrong, is to stash it in my ever-expanding Question Mark Zone.

Memento opens with an unnerving backward close-up sequence in which Leonard's hand shakes a Polaroid that fades, rather than develops, and then retracts into his camera; blood runs back into a body he has just shot; and a bullet jumps out of the body and back into his gun. After that each scene runs forward, but the scenes appear in reverse order, first showing us Leonard shooting his man, and then, in chunks of about five minutes or so, what happened before that, and before that, and before that, always with a line of overlapping dialogue to help us string the pieces together. But—and this is where it gets really complicated—alternating with these scenes, which show the main action in color, is another set of shorter black-and-white scenes, in which Leonard sits in his motel room, explaining his situation to us in voice-over or to an unnamed caller on the phone, apparently a police officer. These scenes are arranged in normal order. The very last scene of the film starts in black-and-white and then turns to color, as the two streams of chronology join up, the end of the beginning flowing into the beginning of the end.

But none of this is complicated for the sake of being complicated. It's all ingeniously devised to put us in Leonard's shoes, struggling to navigate our way through a world of labyrinthine bewilderment toward some final truth that will make sense of it all. A graphic model of his labyrinth is the sprawling mess of a map/diagram he has constructed and constantly revises with a marking pen. It's a tangle of snaking lines, arrows, and question marks, each one indicating a possible relationship between places, people (represented by Scotch-taped Polaroids), or events. Apparently the first thing he does when he checks into a motel room, with a purloined police report of his wife's case under his arm, is to tape this monster over his bed as a kind of under-construction mission statement. Always in fear of sabotage and his own forgetfulness, whenever he establishes something crucial he has it tattooed on his skin. His body is now a twisted skein of inked clues to the killer's identity (FACT 1: MALE, FACT 2: WHITE, . . . FACT 6: LICENSE PLATE NUMBER SG137IU) and guidelines (HIDE YOUR WEAKNESS, NEVER ANSWER THE PHONE, REMEMBER SAMMY JANKIS—Sammy Jankis being a man with a similar condition who wound up killing his diabetic wife by giving her too many insulin shots). One spot over his heart is left clear, reserved for his final, triumphant declaration of vengeance.

Here we see how Leonard resembles us. His elaborate chart, constructed so painstakingly and with such slim chance of success, is like our own attempts to figure everything out, our hopeful philosophical and religious systems, our sprawling, endlessly amended art and science. Distilled from all that theory, his tattoos are like our hard-won credos, the few truths we're so sure of that they've become a part of us, have gotten under our skin. We all have our own (perhaps subtle) tattooing methods: we write the epiphany in our journal, we enthusiastically explain it to others (who may or may not share our enthusiasm), we put it on a bumper sticker or our yearbook page or make it the epigraph to our book or the epitaph on our headstone. If we're assertive types, we might even compile a set of such vital truths, have them calligraphed on a scroll or engraved on tablets, and set them up for others to live by. Then every time we saw them we could feel comforted, assured that the world is not mysterious or chaotic, that there are essential truths and we know them.

BUT WHAT IF we don't? What if there are no solid, absolute, knowable, incontrovertible truths? Leonard says with conviction:

> Facts, not memories—that's how you investigate.
> Look, memory can change the shape of a room; it
> can change the color of a car. And memories can be
> distorted. They're just an interpretation, they're not
> a record, and they're irrelevant if you have the facts.

But what if "facts" are as subjectively manufactured as memories? Humans have ten toes—that's a fact till you meet someone with nine or eleven. Jews are evil—some people were sure enough of that fact to kill millions of them. The sun revolves around the earth—that was a fact till Galileo revised the picture. The earth revolves around the sun—a fact till Einstein showed that all motion is relative. You're reading this book; what could be surer? But the object you're holding, while it's a book to you, might be a doorstop or kindling or toilet paper to someone else. To my cats it's none of those; if it doesn't sparkle, move, or smell like food, it barely exists.

Here's a rock—*that's* a rock-solid fact. But if we look close enough at it, it breaks down into lots of empty space infrequently punctuated by electrons, which are not even particles of solid matter but chimeras that physicists call probability waves. For that matter, the moment I put the rock behind my back it's just a memory, and therefore suspect, as much a possible dream as Ross's dip in the pool. And anyway, how do I know I'm not dreaming now? I dreamed last night that a friend of mine was in tears because she missed her plane to Paris. It was very moving till I woke up, and even for a while after. True, I can hear you telling me that you're awake and you see the rock too. But am I dreaming *that*? Last night my friend's story was equally persuasive. The longer and harder we look at any allegedly solid fact, the faster it melts down. "Facts" are structures, forms, and as the Heart Sutra says,

Form is no other than emptiness.

That's the core statement of the core text of Mahayana Buddhism—a statement I find so inspiring and reliable, it sort of makes me feel like, well, having it tattooed on my chest. But of course, the moment I do that I'm grasping at yet another "fact," trying to make nonsolidity a new kind of ultrareliable ultrasolidity. Fortunately, the Sutra catches me and short-circuits my little game in the next line:

Emptiness is no other than form.

The rock-solid fact of emptiness is itself just another form—which is empty—which is form—and so on. Whoopee!

Under these dizzying circumstances, about all that can be expected of us is to perform reasonable actions that will hopefully increase happiness and reduce suffering for ourselves and others, and call it a day. But Leonard—like most of the clever people who wind up increasing suffering instead—wants more than that. He wants certainty. As he tells Natalie the barmaid:

> Just because there are things I don't remember doesn't make my actions meaningless. The world doesn't just disappear when you close your eyes, does it?

Well, does it now? The notion that there is a definite, describable, objectively existent universe that objectively justifies our actions is really an article of faith. Any possible "proof" of such a universe, including historical records and scientific measurements, can only be encountered through our subjective experience. As Leonard gradually constructs his ever-more-mazelike diagram, he thinks he's discovering the intricacies of an a priori world, unearthing what was there before he arrived. But as we'll see, he's not discovering it but creating it. That maze is really a picture of his own mind. We are luminous empty awareness that has convoluted itself in endless forms which, on closer examination, prove to be empty. It is we, not some cosmic bad guys, who build the matrix. Then we can wander in it for as long as we like.

As the film goes on, here and there we see little clues indicating that the wretched world in which Leonard wanders is, in fact, of his own making, discrepancies that should shake up his picture of things. But unlike Truman, he ignores the clues. The controlling myth of his life is that he once lived in perfect married bliss, that he now wanders in pain, and that he can return to happiness only through an act of redemptive revenge. But we start to doubt the premise of this story the first few times people call him "Lenny." Visibly annoyed, he tells them that his wife called him that—and he hated it. In a perfect, loving marriage, why would his wife persist in doing something she knew annoyed him? Later we see flashbacks, some of them lasting only a split second, that appear to be suppressed memories of a troubled marriage, bubbling up to the surface of Leonard's consciousness—and in one or two instances, followed immediately by the revised, rosy versions with which he replaces them. Like most of us, Leonard has built himself a purgatory between two false paradises: the golden age of the past (his allegedly idyllic marriage) and the utopia of the future (revenge). If he could see through these two falsehoods, accept that all he has is the present, and relax into it, he would be fine.

This issue is obliquely raised when he explains his memory problem to Burt, the scuzzy motel clerk (who is scamming him by renting him a couple of rooms at a time):

> BURT: What's it like?
> LEONARD: It's like waking. It's like you just woke up.
> BURT: That must suck.

No, as a matter of fact it doesn't suck. It's sublime, if you let it be. "Waking up" is the definition of enlightenment; the literal meaning of Buddha is "awakened one." Leonard is describing a state of perpetually just waking up, in which it's always the present moment and all that allegedly came before and all that allegedly will follow is as insubstantial as a dream. That's almost precisely how enlightened ones describe their own experience.

But this clear cognition of perpetual nowness needn't make us dysfunctional like Leonard. In fact, because the present is where all action is performed, such cognition is essential to doing anything gracefully and effectively. A student of mine once explained this in a paper on the art of tending goal:

> The challenging part comes when, the second
> [the goalie] is scored on, the ball or puck is put back
> into action and could head straight toward the cage
> again. The goalie has to totally forget about what
> happened a second ago and focus on saving the
> next shot.
>
> —MARTA POPIOLEK

The use of the word "forget" here is instructive. Just as we don't want the goalie to literally forget (lose all the mental data from) the game up to this point, or from her previous games and her years of training, so waking up fresh in each moment doesn't require us to develop anterograde amnesia like Leonard. The kind of forgetting that's required is letting go of fixation, letting go of trying to re-inhabit and mend what is unamendable, thus missing the only moment we can ever inhabit. It's the kind of forgetting we're talking about when, here in New Jersey, we say, "Ahh, fuhgeddabouddit."

The same principle applies in meditation. There the critical juncture where we might feel like a scored-on goalie is the moment when we realize we've been engrossed in a thought. The temptation is to suppose there's something we have to do about it. But by the time we *realize* we've been engrossed, we aren't anymore; by definition, when you're engrossed you don't realize it. So while we're engrossed there's nothing we can do because we don't realize it, and when we realize it there's nothing we can do because we're not engrossed. We can try to return to the moment when we had the thought, but since traveling back three seconds is as impossible as traveling back a thousand years, we instead wind up resurrecting the thought in the present so we can knock it down again. For good measure, we might try the added impossibility of traveling forward in time to block new thoughts from coming.

No wonder we feel tied up in knots, like Dark Helmet, the

Darth Vader character in the Mel Brooks *Star Wars* parody *Spaceballs*. He's watching the view screen of his intergalactic Winnebago and sees himself watching himself in *Spaceballs* on the view screen of his intergalactic Winnebago:

> DARK HELMET: What the hell am I looking at? When does this happen in the movie?
> COL. SANDURZ: Now. You're looking at now, sir. Everything that happens now is happening now.
> DARK HELMET: What happened to then?
> COL. SANDURZ: We passed then.
> DARK HELMET: When?
> COL. SANDURZ: Just now. We're at now now.
> DARK HELMET: Go back to then.
> COL. SANDURZ: When?
> DARK HELMET: Now!
> COL. SANDURZ: Now?
> DARK HELMET: Now!
> COL. SANDURZ: I can't.
> DARK HELMET: Why?
> COL. SANDURZ: We missed it.
> DARK HELMET: When?
> COL. SANDURZ: Just now.
> DARK HELMET: When will then be now?
> COL. SANDURZ: Soon.

The untying of our knottedness comes spontaneously when we give up and do nothing, just continue to hang out in the ungovernable present where thoughts, like everything else, come and go on their own. Fuhgeddabouddit.

A good, simple exercise (especially after you've been spinning this mind-bending, time-transcending movie on your DVD player for a while) is this: *In every moment, be just waking up.* Go for a walk, and with each step just wake up, noting the dreamlike not-there-ness of all the previous steps and future steps. Turn your head to the left and wake up in the moment of this new view, where the view of everything to your right is devoid of solid reality. Or, wherever you happen to be, simply take a breath in and out, and at the end of the breath be just waking up. And then the next breath. And then the next breath. Later, as you return to your usual conversation and activities, you'll tend to get engrossed in them and distracted from this waking-up sense, but that's OK: every time you think of it, just wake up again and the whole story of engrossment and distraction also becomes part of the dream of the past.

> You know what time it is. It is time for you to wake
> up from your sleep.
> —ROMANS 13:11

If you persist in this practice, you should notice the dawning of an exhilarating lightness, as the massive (though nonexistent!) weight of past and future is lifted from your shoulders. A man in Leonard's condition should be happy and free of suffering, the benchmark of realization. He suffers instead because he won't *let go* of the past and the future, which he thinks hold the key to his happiness, and which he will never inhabit. Leonard has to not only *be* in the present moment, but *rest* in it—accept its perfect sufficiency without straining ahead or backward for something else. That untattooed spot over his heart will always remain blank.

This business of seeing through time is so central to the enlightenment process that it's worth experimenting with, to see whether you ever really experience time or have just been taking it on faith. For example, hold your arm straight out to the side. Soon your muscles ache more and more until you're compelled to lower the arm. This certainly *feels* (literally) like a very direct experience of passing time. Now raise your arm again, but this time be waking up in each moment. If you observe closely, you'll see how, in each present moment of holding out the arm, the impression of the past moments is just an interpretation of the aching sensations—they're what we could call *traces* of the past, but they're experienced and interpreted in the present. It's only now, and now, and now.

Leonard sees this as a problem. "How can I heal? How am I supposed to heal if I can't feel time?" he asks. The answer is to relax and hang out in timelessness—which is where the most profound healing takes place, as we stand at last in the cool, clear space outside time's drama and trauma. No time means no duration, and no duration means nothing to endure. Check out this no-duration element next time you find yourself in the middle of a five-mile run, a long illness, or a nasty divorce. No duration also means there's no boredom, no occupational tedium, no stale relationships.

In *Memento* those traces of the past take the shape of Leonard's Polaroids. Like us, he interprets his traces and scrawls stories on them; his one-line captions for his people-pictures are based on traces, but usually distorted by spin and generalization. On his picture of Natalie, who goes on to do far worse things to him than spit in his beer, he writes, "She has also lost someone. She will help you out of pity." This is very much the way we often pigeonhole people, creating a dangerously skewed assessment of their present reality, making them good guys and bad guys by interpreting the alleged past. When nations and cultures do the same to each other, the results can be especially dangerous. Also like us, Leonard manages (as we'll see) to get rid of the traces that don't conform to his favorite stories. If a photo doesn't fit in your master diagram, no problem—just burn it and forget it.

AS LEONARD'S POLAROID captions suggest, words are an important part of this whole process; whether spoken or thought, language is the building material we use to structure our matrix of stories. Thus dharma practice makes heavy use of strategies for cutting through language. The simplest is to just give it a rest, taking regular breaks from speaking words and hearing them (walk your dog *without* your iPod). Most meditation retreats are held in partial or total silence, a prospect that causes anxiety in many first-timers, precisely because we're so plugged into constant storytelling as a way of reaffirming our cozy, cracked picture of existence. But taking silence turns out to be deeply refreshing—what a relief! And, with the noise of external language silenced, what an opportunity to hear more clearly all your internal storytelling, and so begin letting go of it. All those fantasy conversations and arguments with the driver in the next lane, your spouse in the next room, the politicians on TV. When you're just sitting on a cushion for several hours a day, so that there's nothing happening, nothing to talk about, and yet all that inner chatter keeps rattling on—well, you finally just have to laugh.

My favorite retreat-time absurdity is one that happens sometimes at the beginning of a group meditation session. The practice leader typically opens the session by striking a bell three times, pausing a few seconds after each stroke. If, in my expert view, she makes the pauses half a second too short, before she gets to the third stroke I'm already telling myself a story about what an unenlightened, hyped-up speed freak she is. If it's a little too long, the story is about how thick she's laying on her ostentatious solemnity.

Trying to silence our stories directly doesn't work because language's capacity to engage the mind is too powerful. But rather than oppose that capacity we can turn it back upon itself. This we do through mantra practice: thinking or intoning sounds that transcend meaning through repetition. Most traditions offer such practices, whether you're doing Hail Marys on your rosary or chanting Hare Krishna on your mala. But here many people miss an important practice principle: When you feel the meaning going away (Oops, I haven't thought about the Blessed Virgin and her wonderful works for the last three minutes), don't clutch at it. Your thoughts, even your most spiritual thoughts, are not spirituality. They're just thoughts. They're just stories, and because you're the one who's telling them, they're limited by the boundaries of your conceptual mind.

Instead, let go of meaning and marinate in the pure, meaningless dimension of sound. (Buddhist practice sometimes skips a step and goes directly to that dimension by using such potently meaning-free sounds as OM AH HUNG.) Let the sound resonate in your bones, your blood, your DNA, the whole room, the whole universe, till it opens into the dimension of empty radiance beyond sound, beyond everything, which is the *reality*, the essence of the Blessed Virgin, which is the essence of existence and of ourselves. There, you can continue to intone the mantra or just sit and bask ("meditate"); at that point there's not much difference.

Also note that if you do mantra practice in a spirit of plodding through your prescribed repetitions (Whew, 887 Hare Krishnas down, 121 to go!), you're just further embroiling yourself in the illusion of time and duration. In no-time, there's no repetition. Jesus warns against praying with "vain repetitions," and he's right: if it's experienced as repetition, it's in vain. Instead, practice with relaxed but vivid attention on *this* instance of the mantra, the present instance, as all the reality there is, sandwiched between the twin insubstantialities of past and future. (In fact, as your attention becomes more finely tuned, there's only this syllable of the mantra, or even this phoneme of the syllable.) Then the practice liberates you into the dimension beyond time and language.

I'm especially fond of the mantra of transcendental wisdom, presented at the climax of the Heart Sutra:

GATE GATE PARAGATE PARASAMGATE BODHI SVAHA!
(gah-tay gah-tay pah-rah-gah-tay pah-rah-sahng-gah-tay bo-dhee swah-hah!)
Gone beyond, gone beyond, gone supremely
beyond, gone supremely and totally beyond,
awakened—how wonderful!

Part of the brilliant power of this mantra, in addition to its sublimely catchy sound, is the way its meaning merges seamlessly with meaninglessness, its iterations melt into timelessness, so that every time we bob up at the surface the words pull us down again into the transcendental depths. GATE GATE—gone, gone, beyond your previous thought, beyond the previous instance of this mantra, beyond all fabrication of past and future, beyond the illusion that there's anywhere to go. The present moment is the only game in town, and the GATE mantra is a power tool of consciousness for boring through the illusory structures of time to reveal the underlying effulgent emptiness.

This transcendence of time is consistent with the Buddhist assertion of "no creator God." If there's no "In the beginning" in an inaccessible past, there's no Other as an inaccessible power, no supreme auteur pre-scripting our movie. The beginning is every instant, and the auteur is this present awareness, projecting away. Existence is a do-it-yourself project. We think we live in time, but time, like everything else, lives in us. Our backstory is a story indeed, one that we tell and retell, make and continually remake as we pulse through the present. We have all the time in the world to elaborate the past, but no time to live in it.

I'M NOT POSITIVE I've pieced together exactly what happens in *Memento*, but after repeated viewings I think I've got most of it. The major revelations come, as they must in a mystery, at the end of the film, which in this case is in the middle of the chronology—in the last scene, where the end of the forward-running black-and-white sequence flows into the beginning of the backward-running color sequence. Teddy, who is in fact a police detective and the one who has been talking with Leonard on the phone in the black-and-white scenes, sends him to a rusted-out, abandoned industrial shack, where Leonard kills the man Teddy has told him is his wife's murderer, a drug dealer named Jimmy Grantz. But before dying, Jimmy breathes the name "Sammy," and Leonard starts to doubt.

Teddy shows up and, under pressure from Leonard, reveals the truth: Teddy, who was assigned to Leonard's wife's case and felt sympathetic toward him, helped him find and kill the real attacker over a year ago. But Leonard's vengeance, like everything else, slipped away into the void of forgetfulness and gave him no satisfaction. So Teddy has been leading him from vengeance to vengeance, setting him up to whack one low-life after another, in a weird symbiosis that provides Leonard with a fleeting sense of resolution and Teddy with ready cash. (Outside the shack, in the trunk of Jimmy Grantz's little Jaguar, is $200,000 in drug money.) Desperate to prove him wrong, Leonard rifles through his pockets for Polaroids but comes up with a blood-stained shot of himself, Adam-naked, bathed in blood, grinning broadly as he points to the blank spot over his heart. "*I* took that picture," says Teddy, "just when you did it. Look how happy you are."

Then comes an even more stunning revelation. Leonard's wife survived her assault. But she was a diabetic. It was Leonard, not Sammy Jankis, who killed his own wife with an insulin overdose—Sammy didn't have a wife. (And although Teddy doesn't spell this part out, there are hints elsewhere that Leonard is an escapee from a psychiatric hospital, placed there after killing her.) This should all be upsetting news, but Leonard is resourceful. He has already, as Teddy explains, destroyed the twelve pages of the police report that would have told him all this. Why? "To create a puzzle you could never solve," says Teddy. Now Leonard goes outside and takes the Jag, but first pauses to burn the bloodstained Polaroid and write on Teddy's photo, DON'T BELIEVE HIS LIES. Then he drives off to have Fact 6 about the killer—Teddy's license plate number—tattooed on his thigh. The End.

Or the beginning. The real end, of course, we saw at the beginning, when Leonard returns to the shack to shoot Teddy, whose lies are, after all, not to be believed, and whose license plate number matches Leonard's tattoo—proof positive of his guilt. Here is the film's final and most shocking enlightenment teaching. We think the present flows out of the past, but the past flows continuously out of the present. It is in the perpetual present that we construct our ever-more-intricate mythology of pain and pleasure, loss and redemption, which we call the past. Thus the culprit we're seeking, the one responsible for our suffering, is ourself: not someone in our story who injured us back then, but the one who's telling the story right now. "Well, maybe you should start investigating yourself," Teddy advises Leonard, but Teddy winds up dead—a not unprecedented fate for messengers of truth whose message strikes too close to home. Leonard means "lionlike," and having silenced the annoying prophet, Leonard is now the undisputed king of his own little jungle; Leonard Shelby can be in his own little shell. With no one left to question his carefully crafted tale, he can indulge his masochistic quest without end, suspended forever between his bogus golden past and his bogus utopian future.

If *we're* crafty enough and masochistic enough—as billions apparently are—we can do the same. When our future paradise is deferred long enough, we get pissed, and our vision of that paradise becomes one of blood vengeance, a final elimination of those responsible for the ancient injury that displaced us from our ancestral home or our holy land or our ideal romance. The Jews or the Arabs, the Catholics or the Protestants, the parent who messed you up, the spouse or lover who did you wrong . . . once you get him or her or them, everything will be fine. *But you've already gotten them.* As this film so brilliantly demonstrates with its very structure, what we think is our future is our past, and it didn't help. *Gornisht helfen,* as they say in Yiddish: "Nothing helps." I've read interviews with family members of murder victims who waited years for the killer to be executed so they could achieve "closure," but then found they didn't feel different. We're stuck (we've stuck ourselves) on a treadmill of reprisal, going the same fool's errand again and again. We've been there time after time, slain the Evil One in various guises over and over, and it never satisfied us, and it never will.

> TEDDY: So I helped you start looking again— looking for the guy you already killed.

On that endless quest, even our under-the-skin credos may be lies. REMEMBER SAMMY JANKIS turns out to be as trumped up as REMEMBER THE MAINE; the telltale license plate number is as much a mirage as Saddam Hussein's weapons of mass destruction.

It's déjà vu all over again all over again. Only the names and the details change. As long as we've cut ourselves off from the astonishing richness of existence, we'll have an aching sense of loss and we'll find someone else to blame it on. In such a world, it's momentous when any one person elects to take himself out of the cycle, to release himself from the bloody myths and— GATE GATE—into the skylike clarity of present awareness. In a small (but cumulative) way, that changes the world.

For all the intricate precision of this film, it has, as far as I can see, one logical contradiction: If Leonard has been unable to form new memories since his injury, how could he remember that he has a memory problem? He should just be very confused. (In fact, that's how Sammy is depicted.) If the film had shown him in *that* boat, he'd be really hopeless. But then he'd be in *our* boat. How can we know we're ignorant when we're ignorant? An exchange that Beckett would have enjoyed hints at that vicious circle:

> TEDDY: Where you staying?
> LEONARD [consulting a Polaroid]: The Discount Inn.
> I don't know what room. I don't have my key.
> TEDDY: You probably left it in your room.

If he could find his key he could get into his room; if he could get into his room he could find his key. If we weren't so blinded by ignorance, we could see our way to enlightenment. Under those circumstances, it's a miracle that anyone ever takes up dharma practice. And with your own personal myths of loss and blame and those of resentful ethnic groups and warring nations pounding in your ears, it's a double miracle. If you've somehow nevertheless stumbled into that impossible, miraculous situation, it's best to take full advantage of it.

I BELIEVE IN AMERICA

He is Father. Even more, God is Mother,
who does not want to harm us.
— POPE JOHN PAUL I

PRESIDENT JED BARTLET [addressing God]:
Have I displeased you, you feckless thug?
— *THE WEST WING*

IN MY PARENTS' HOUSE THERE WAS NO RELIGION. I WAS introduced to the deity in kindergarten, which I entered in 1954, the same year the words "under God" entered the Pledge of Allegiance. We had started out in September learning to put our right hand (the one next to the window, kids) over our heart and say "one nation, indivisible." When the teacher announced the change, of course she didn't explain that we were thick in the McCarthy era and Congress had added the phrase to flush out godless Communists who might be using the pledge to pass for good Americans—starting, apparently, at the age of five. So I came up with my own explanation. I thought, Oh, like so many things in school, they're teaching this to us a little at a time. They're going to keep adding bits, and by the time I get out of college this thing will take two hours to say. Well, OK.

At the time I didn't give much thought to who or what God

might be, or how we had come to be under him. The pledge was just a thing you recited and felt good about getting right, like the alphabet. We were under God because large people in positions of authority said we were, and we were certainly under them. It made no more or less sense than incomprehensible words like "allegiance" and "indivisible."

Later I heard the phrase "God the Father," which gave me some kind of handle on the concept. I thought of my own father, who provided for my brothers and me, answered my questions about the world, was unseen for long stretches of the day or evening, but then reappeared. He had a thick leather army belt from his years in the war, with which he spanked us. When we'd been bad, the three of us ran to hide the belt, but he always found it. He was an oboe player, and when we attended performances my proudest, most thrilling moment was when the conductor walked on in a spotlight and pointed his baton at my father, who played the A to which the other musicians tuned. (I can still hear that A.) As A began the alphabet, Daddy's A began the symphony; he made it all happen.

Then we got older and the '60s happened. Traditional institutions like family and religion were shaken. The religion part was no big deal for me, since I had never had any—if anything, I was going in the opposite direction, looking into spirituality for the first time. When *The Godfather* opened in 1972, the magazines were full of essays about how Francis Ford Coppola's national home movie reaffirmed the value of the family, showing it weathering all kinds of crises and corruption. But the film also addresses the other shaken institution. While salvaging the family, it also tries—heroically, against all odds—to salvage the patriarchal deity who mercifully provides for his children, justly spanks them when they're bad, answers all questions, and makes everything happen: the Godfather is God the Father.

As we've seen, the Jews forbade graven images of God; their temple had an empty sanctum at its center. But luminous emptiness is an elusive experience, a subtle thing to try to organize a people around. So they also produced eloquent poetry in which they glorified God as a great king and, later, as a stern but loving father. When I teach literature, I try to make sure my students understand what metaphors are, so that when they read "My love is like a red red rose" they don't expect the girl to show up with petals and thorns. But because God is seen less often than women, religious metaphor is often taken too literally.

> O Lord, pardon my three sins:
> I have in contemplation clothed in form
>   Thee who art formless!
> I have in praise described Thee who art ineffable!
> And in visiting shrines I have ignored Thine
>   omnipresence.
>   —SHANKARA

Clothing the formless in personal form makes it accessible and intimate, but at a price. To impose a face or name on the infinite is to make it finite; to ascribe to the One a personality that wills some things and abhors others is to plunge into dualism. This confusion is the root of much grief.

IF THERE'S ONE MOVIE that's indelibly impressed in people's consciousness, scene by scene and line by line, this may be it. If there's a perfect movie this may be it: an almost Shakespearean marriage of popular entertainment and classical form, a universally readable cinematic poem with every part unimprovably in place. There's scarcely a gesture, a face, a word of the terse Coppola–Mario Puzo script, a note of the tragic Nino Rota score, that can be changed without injuring the whole, and the young Coppola had to fight bitterly to keep the studio from changing most of it. His casting choices are inspired, with some of them—the unknown Al Pacino, the unpredictable

Marlon Brando—the result of his thankless struggle against Paramount's corporate wisdom, which kept producing such alarming suggestions as Ryan O'Neal or Robert Redford for the role of Michael.

The violence, though abundant, never becomes soul-numbing, prefab movie violence; like everything else in the film, it is gorgeous and exact. Each violent scene has a precise narrative value and emotional weight and, as a kind of psychological punctuation mark, some unexpected detail that makes it unique and thus real: the knife sticking Luca Brasi's hand to the bar, the bullet through the lens of Moe Greene's glasses, the fire hydrant spraying wildly as Sonny beats Carlo, McCluskey's puzzled look and awkward clutching at his throat when Michael shoots him, Sollozzo's head snapping back in a pink mist of brains and blood—these last two so strangely like JFK nine years earlier in the Zapruder film, America's other tragic home movie.

We see the deliberate, stately rhythm of Coppola's cinematic poetry in the opening scene. First, black. Out of the black, a man's Italian-inflected voice saying, "I believe in America." Then a quick fade-in to the face of the speaker, the undertaker Bonasera who is telling the tale of how his beloved daughter defended her honor against two boys who beat and disfigured her, and how they laughed when they were set free by the American courts. All the while, the camera very slowly pulls back, revealing Bonasera at full length in his tuxedo, the darkened office in which he sits, and, seated with his back to the camera and bathed in shadow, a listening figure—Marlon Brando as the Godfather, Don Vito Corleone, on the day of his daughter's wedding, when no Sicilian can refuse a favor.

As his first name implies, he embodies the principle of vitality. He is the giver of life and potentially its withholder. (In a scene that was cut, his dying former consigliere Genco begs Vito to use his power to turn back death.) His last name, which means "lion-heart," suggests the king of beasts reigning in the wild jungle, ferocious by Darwinian necessity. It also suggests some questions the film will try to answer: What is the heart, the core, of kingship, or leadership? Is authority derived purely from might, enforced strictly through intimidation? And in spiritual terms, does this mean worship must center on a mighty father figure? Must worshippers be God-*fearing*?

These questions are quietly insinuated as Don Corleone plays placidly with a gray and white cat (which Coppola happened to find on the set and dropped without warning in Brando's lap). Gently stroking the cat, scratching its neck, he provides a silent counterpoint to the conversation, revealing its true power dynamics as the cat submits to him, lying stretched on its back with its belly exposed, like a pack animal showing its submission to the alpha male. At any moment Don Vito could bite that belly or twist that neck; we see genuine warmth but also latent violence, held in check for the moment by a kind of noblesse oblige. What Coppola has given us here is something much closer to the ancient idea of God the Father than what we would derive from our modern relationships with our own fathers. Stephen Mitchell makes this clear in his indispensable book *The Gospel According to Jesus:*

> Few of us . . . can feel the intensity of what Jesus
> meant when he said *abba* [Aramaic for "father"].
> Actually, we don't have a word for . . . the reality
> a first-century Jewish father had for his children:
> a position of absolute power, for both good and evil,
> which commanded a fear or a respect that we can
> barely conceive of.

In these opening moments, the film's fundamental transaction is set forth. Bonasera, whose name means "good evening," has presumed that the sun has set on the traditional Old World system in which an all-powerful, godlike *padrino*, in exchange for "respect" and "friendship," offers protection and justice. Under that system, Don Corleone explains, "If by chance an honest man like yourself should make enemies, then they would become my enemies—and then they would fear you," much as the Old Testament God promises to strike fear in the hearts of the enemies of the Hebrew people he has adopted as his own. Instead, Bonasera has embraced the American vision of a secular society, where divine power and justice are replaced by a rational mechanism that promises equal protection to all. As Don Corleone mockingly puts it, "I understand. You found paradise in America."

But now that promise of a democratic, secular paradise has proved empty. Begging that the boys be punished, Bonasera bows his head, kisses the don's ring, asks him, "Be my friend," and then adds the respectful title he has till now withheld: "Godfather." It doesn't matter that he nearly chokes on the word. By acknowledging our fealty to God the Father, we seal the deal. We renounce our presumption of mastering our own fate, of creating our own earthly paradise, and place our hopes in his hand. "Good," says the don, and clearly the air in the room has changed. Bonasera has entered into the covenant— the formality of the procedure is as clear and straightforward as in any ritual of the Church.

Now, with his arm heavily around the undertaker's shoulder as he walks him to the door, Don Corleone says that someday *he* may ask a favor. And as his consigliere Tom Hagen tells Jack Woltz later in Hollywood, "Mr. Corleone never asks a second favor once he's refused the first. Understand?" Those who refuse the first are liable to wind up with a horse's head in their bed. Here's the fine print on the contract. Once you ally yourself with the benevolent despot, you're beholden. Lyndon Johnson, one of the last old-fashioned godfathers of American politics, once said, "I never trust a man unless I've got his

pecker in my pocket." To this day, Jews—the first people to accept this God's protection—offer a piece of that organ as a
sign of their devotion.

Don Corleone has already shown us some other important
Old Testament qualities. His sense of justice is finely calibrated;
he refuses to order the deaths of the two boys, who did not,
after all, kill Bonasera's daughter.

> [T]hou shalt give life for life, eye for eye,
> tooth for tooth, hand for hand, foot for foot,
> burning for burning, wound for wound,
> stripe for stripe.
> —EXODUS 21:23–25

This "eye for eye" principle is often misunderstood as indiscriminately ruthless, but the point is precisely that God doesn't sanc-
tion lopsided retribution. Don Corleone is not arbitrary; he will
"make them suffer as she suffers" and is careful to assign the job
to "people that aren't going to get carried away." Everything
about him is measured. Like the Israelites in Babylon, he is
surrounded by sensualists and fornicators but maintains self-
control, dignity, and rectitude, signaled by his quiet, husky voice
and the erect carriage of his head (both expertly reproduced by
Robert De Niro as the young Vito in *The Godfather Part II*).

As the Godfather continues to receive supplicants, the film
cuts back and forth between his dark office and the brilliantly
sunlit wedding party in progress, as if contrasting the fes-
tive, sunny, communal, public face of theistic religion with its
darker, private side, the solemn, solitary confrontation with a
God who makes you an offer you can't refuse. Outside at the
party, young Michael, fresh from the war and handsome in his
army uniform—he believes in America too—introduces Kay
Adams to the concept of nonrefusable demands and to the nature of his family by telling a story about how his father, with

the help of the hulking Luca Brasi, coerced a signature on a contract. He is clearly courting her, seeking an uncoerced contract of his own with this American girl whose last name carries echoes of Anglo founding fathers as well as Edenic innocence, and as he does so he gently explains what she's getting into.

His explanation and courtship are also addressed to us; the film doesn't work unless we're drawn into an intimate relationship with Michael. Thus we identify with Kay, the white chick (she appears to have been powdered to exaggerate the contrast with the olive-skinned Italians), who is saved from tedious blandness by Diane Keaton's loopy rhythms. The film's only major character who lacks gangster exoticism, she's easily overlooked, but as the dubious, fascinated, emotionally torn outsider, she's us—she's our way into the film. With her we are drawn into the Corleones' world by Michael's gentle honesty, the basis of *their* transaction. Should he ever violate this honesty, that would rupture his bond with her and with us.

IF THE GODFATHER is God the Father, Sonny is the Son. As the eldest of the three boys, he is the heir apparent to the family business, the Christ in whose name the Church is perpetuated. Sonny is the only character to conspicuously wear a large cross, and with his tall frame and his broad, exceptionally square shoulders, James Caan goes through the film looking like he's already nailed up on one. We'll assume that his initials are just a happy coincidence.

But there are really two Christs in the Gospels: the kind, forgiving Good Shepherd, and the vengeful smiter of men, the embodiment of his Old Testament Father's most thuggish tendencies. Mitchell makes a persuasive case that the first is the authentic, enlightened Christ and the second the invention of revisionist scribes and self-righteous churchmen. He calls the two Jesus and "Jesus."

Jesus teaches us, in his sayings and by his actions,
not to judge (in the sense of not to condemn), but
to keep our hearts open to all people; the later
"Jesus" is the archetypal judge, who will float down
terribly on the clouds for the world's final rewards
and condemnations. Jesus cautions against anger
and teaches the love of enemies; "Jesus" calls his
enemies "children of the Devil" and attacks them
with the utmost vituperation and contempt. Jesus
talks of God as a loving father, even to the wicked;
"Jesus" preaches a god who will cast the disobedient
into everlasting flames. Jesus includes all people
when he calls God "your Father in heaven"; "Jesus"
says "*my* Father in heaven." Jesus teaches that all
those who make peace, and all those who love their
enemies, are sons of God; "Jesus" refers to himself
as "*the* Son of God." Jesus isn't interested in
defining who he is (except for one passing reference
to himself as a prophet); "Jesus" talks on and on
about himself. Jesus teaches God's absolute
forgiveness; "Jesus" utters the horrifying statement
that "whoever blasphemes against the Holy Spirit
never has forgiveness but is guilty of an eternal sin."

Sonny is "Jesus," not Jesus. Caan, who hung out with some
real mob guys to pick up their speech patterns and body language, plays him as a violent, antagonizing force right from the
opening minutes of the wedding scene, where he confronts the
feds who've dropped by to jot down license plate numbers.
("Goddamn FBI don't respect nothin'.") Later, when he becomes
head of the family, we see the film's real struggle to come
to terms with the church's history, its slide from Jesus to
"Jesus." *The Godfather* presents this slide in terms of the
Catholic Church. But every religion has compassionate, tolerant,

open-hearted people and narrow, self-righteous, potentially violent people. Both groups can quote scripture to justify their
views; the history of most religions consists largely of the struggle between the fascists and the flower children, and the fascists usually have an edge.

Why is that? First, because institutionalizing spirituality, like
personifying the spirit, is giving form to the formless. By nature
it's already a kind of contradiction, like organizing a party. Yet
to have a party you need to do some organizing. Running a
church is a tricky, delicate business that requires at the very
least that you're aware of the dangers; it's much easier to ignore
the paradox and pretend you're just operating a corporation.
And second, because people who are already overly fond of
form and hierarchy and dogma (the fascists) are naturally attracted to positions of power within the institution. Those who
just want to hang out, do loving works, and open themselves to
the amazing spirit within (the flower children) are happy to let
someone else run things.

As the Church evolved into an institution concerned with
perpetuating itself into successive generations, it emphasized
the distinction between believers and nonbelievers, with no one
allowed to be neutral. (Clemenza deliberately leaves Michael's
gun loud to scare off any "pain-in-the-ass innocent bystanders.")
You either were a member of the club or you weren't, and the
community of the faithful was besieged by hordes of unbeliev-
ers; pagans and heretics had to be converted, at the point of the
sword or with the aid of the rack if necessary. Thus every don in
the *Godfather* saga (and, later in the lineage, in *The Sopranos*)
justifies his aggression as necessary to preserve the legacy for
his children.

But just as the Church reached its greatest strength, the rise
of science and the first stirrings of democracy began to weaken
the idea of God as a supernatural king. Galileo and Newton
began the process that gradually revealed a vast, elegantly self-

evolving 13.7-billion-year-old universe that made God's little six-day affair look like a rather shabby backyard handyman project; and every overthrow of some worldly king further eroded the reverence for divine authority that kept God on his throne. Still around but wounded, God went into semi-retirement, just as Vito does, sapped of his vitality after he is wounded in an assassination attempt (at the fruit stand—as he goes sprawling, the film's only bird's-eye shot shows the fruit spilling into the street, suggesting that the bounty of his works has been spilled). This clears the decks for the hot-headed Sonny to declare war on the other families—"go to the mattresses"—the Church Militant fully engaged in its darkest struggles (the Crusades, the Inquisition) against its perceived enemies.

The fulcrum of that struggle is the Crucifixion—Sonny's slaughter at the tollbooth, which is portrayed as no ordinary murder but an act of transcendent, earth-shaking significance.* For this scene Coppola's crew rigged Caan with a record 147 explosive squibs. Sonny is gunned down as he pays the toll, an almost punning allusion to Jesus paying for our sins. Sonny's helpless vulnerability, his writhing body, his reeking wounds recall the whole tradition of Passion paintings, plays, and now movies. (At the beginning of every *Sopranos* episode, Tony drives through a tollbooth on the New Jersey Turnpike and pulls his ticket out of the machine with a defiant snap, as if to say, Hey, I'm still livin'.) The squad of faceless, fedora-hatted men who fire at Sonny suggests the universality of those who participate in Christ's death. The scheme of Christian theology requires that he be cut down so that he can be raised up.

---

* Its global impact is subtly underscored by an anachronism. Although the ambush takes place in 1948, as Sonny approaches he is listening to the legendary Dodgers–Giants playoff game of October 3, 1951, and he dies half an inning before Bobby Thomson's "Shot Heard 'Round the World"— a crucifixion from which Brooklyn fans never recovered.

Historical arguments about who was complicit are beside the point. Believers nail him up with every crucifix they erect, imploring and employing him again and again to save them with his blood.

And it is now that the Godfather calls upon Bonasera for that favor, to tend to Sonny's bullet-riddled body. In the Christian view, accepting the benevolence of God the Father obligates us to deal with the crucified Son. "I want you to use all your powers and all your skill. I don't want his mother to see him this way," says Vito. We are asked to dress him up, to remake him whole. Just as it is within our own consciousness that we crucify him, it is there that we must resurrect him.

WITH SONNY'S DEATH comes the question of succession. Fredo, the middle son, is a 'fraidy-cat, who fumbles his gun and dissolves in tears when his father is shot. The only son who is unmarried and childless, he is the barren branch of this evolutionary tree, the nonrecipient of the inheritance. Perhaps he is a stand-in for the Jews. He fits the nervous, nonmacho stereotype—in *Take the Money and Run* all Woody Allen has to do is put a gun in his hand and it's already funny. Fredo specifically fits the Church's view of the Jews, the people who blew their chance to receive the new covenant. In fact, it's hanging out in Vegas with the Jewish Moe Greene (who stereotypically offends by grubbing too passionately for mo' green) that leads Fredo to "take sides against the family" and eventually, in *Part II*, to become an out-and-out traitor.

Thus the mantle passes to Michael. His name, which in Hebrew means "Who is like God?," poses the question with which he struggles throughout the film. Is he like his father? Has he inherited the gifts and duties of a don? But the name also contains the answer, in its allusion to St. Michael the Archangel. The Bible's two main books of prophecy present him as a kind of messiah of the future (like Maitreya, the future Buddha, or Kalki, the future avatar of Vishnu), who, wielding a mighty sword, will come forth at the critical moment in cosmic history to lead the righteous in a triumphant struggle, much like Michael Corleone's climactic struggle with the Five Families:

> And at that time shall Michael stand up, the great
> prince which standeth for the children of thy
> people: and there shall be a time of trouble, such
> as never was since there was a nation even to that
> same time: and at that time thy people shall be
> delivered, every one that shall be found written in
> the book.
> —DANIEL 12:1

> And there was war in heaven: Michael and his
> angels fought against the dragon; and the dragon
> fought and his angels, and prevailed not; neither
> was their place found any more in heaven.
> —REVELATION 12:7–8

This apparently foreordained destiny is in tension with the way Michael has been groomed to be the squeaky-clean son, the Americanized college boy who has been kept clear of the family business. For Coppola, a member of the Woodstock generation who in 1972 was still immersed in its experimental spirit, Michael clearly represents the bright hope of the new generation, suddenly and miraculously free from the deadly momentum of the old ways. Gentle and reasonable, he holds out the hope of being a Jesus rather than a "Jesus," but that hope keeps being tested. When the corrupt cop Captain McCluskey breaks Michael's jaw, it's an almost literal staging of one of Jesus' parables:

> But I say unto you that ye resist not evil; but
> whosoever shall smite thee on thy right cheek,
> turn to him the other also.
> —MATTHEW 5:39

Michael doesn't turn the other cheek. With the justification that "it's not personal . . . it's strictly business," he kills McCluskey, and his drug-pushing patron Sollozzo for good measure.

But Michael's subsequent exile in Sicily is an idyllic sojourn, a return to a green, sunlit Mediterranean Eden where a fresh start seems possible. Like a new Adam, he dwells there with no name or history, and as with any '60s youth his hair is, for the only time in the film, tousled and longish. (In the Sicilian wedding sequence he looks oddly like Bobby Kennedy.) His Eve, Apollonia, is named for the solar god of truth who dispensed wisdom centuries before the ritual bloodlettings of Christianity were devised. She is described as "a type more Greek than Italian," also harking back to the great pagan philosophers who predated the rise of the Roman Church.

Apollonia's being a female form of Apollo hints that the essence of that ancient wisdom is female—receptive. In the anatomy of copulation the male asserts, the female receives. In the field of spirit, the male approach asserts (we could say erects) doctrines, images, buildings, institutions, empires, and, when empires inevitably clash, warfare, as typified here by Sonny. The female opens to receive what is.

As it happened, at the exact moment that this film was released I was on Mallorca, another sunny Mediterranean island, on a long retreat led by a meditation master from India and attended by some 2,000 people, most of them young Americans, absorbing his Apollonian wisdom. Since the mid '60s, many of my and Coppola's generation had been studying with gurus in

India or lamas in Katmandu, and back home various forms of this ancient wisdom, which was also excitingly fresh and new, were spreading through bookstores, meditation centers, and eventually yoga classes at the Y. What we were learning (at best) was the simple, essentially female act of opening to pure being, a spirituality that transcended the old assertive male approach with its dogma and institutions.

This spirit of undogmatic openness had touched the Catholic Church as well, with priests running "rap sessions" in coffeehouses, bishops committing themselves to striving for racial and economic justice, and the monk Thomas Merton traveling to Asia to compare notes on meditation with the Dalai Lama. The tone was set by John XXIII, probably the most progressive, inclusive pope of modern times. According to one lovely story, when it was announced that Protestants would be invited to observe the Second Vatican Council, a conservative cardinal sputtered indignantly, "But Your Holiness, Protestants are heretics!"

"Do not say 'heretics,' my son," replied the pope. "Say 'separated brethren.' "

"But they are in league with the devil!"

"Do not say 'devil,' my son. Say 'separated angel.' "

But John died in 1963, and with him much of that open spirit left the institutional Church. In 1978 John Paul I, the Smiling Pope, offered a glimmer of hope, with his love of God the Mother and his humble spirit (at his coronation he refused to be carried on the traditional sedan chair or to wear the jeweled tiara). But he died after a month on the throne, sparking conspiracy theories to this day. And as time wore on, many of those who had embraced the fresh, ancient wisdom of nondogmatism in various exotic outposts encountered the difficulties of bringing it back home. As Apollonia tries to drive Michael's car to show what a good American wife she is going to make him, she is killed by an assassin's bomb, as if the attempt at reintegration is fatal. The old blood feud reaches its long arm even into this Eden, and the medieval mind-set takes hold again.

But Apollonia has a successor. We have seen the Father and a few versions of the Son, but not the Holy Spirit, the third and most mysterious person of the Trinity. As the one aspect of Christian divinity without a distinctly male persona, it is identified by some with the *anima,* the female aspect of existence and of our own consciousness. To many churchgoers it appears to be something rather vague, abstract, and colorless. Here we may connect it with Kay, the most colorless, vague member of the family. Having lost Apollonia and returned to the States, Michael renews and intensifies his courtship of Kay. Their marriage poses the question whether the Church can finally incorporate the feminine wisdom of openness and compassion into its traditional structure. Will St. Michael the Archangel lead the Church into a more benign, humanistic incarnation? Will Michael Corleone, who promises Kay that within five years all the family business will be legit, be a Jesus or just another "Jesus"?

Of course the dark, brooding tones of Gordon Willis's cinematography have tipped us off to the pessimistic answer from the very first scene. After Sonny dies and Michael takes over, he gradually morphs into just the kind of strong-armed don his father was. His transformation is signaled by his hair, which goes from '70s dry look to '40s retro; prophetically enough, that slicked-back style also anticipates the corporate '80s, when so many former seekers, now fitted out with Armani suits, suspenders, and cigars, exchanged their pursuit of truth for pursuit of mergers and leveraged buyouts.

Only at the film's climax does the Church, whose invisible presence has been felt all along, become visible. Coppola saves it for the scene where Michael assumes full, ruthless power—raises the mighty sword—as he stands godfather to his sister

Connie's son. The baby is also named Michael, a dire hint that the violent legacy will go on and on, endlessly through the generations. The parallel cutting is thrilling as we alternate between Michael's ritual embrace of the tenets of the Church and the equally ritualistic preparations for several assassinations, while the tension is ratcheted up to an almost unbearable level by the baby's insistent crying and the organ's upward spiraling climb in a minor-key Bach fugue. Then the killings are consummated in an orgiastic bloodletting, and all who have dared oppose Michael's will—Barzini and his allies, "the dragon and his angels"—are destroyed, while Michael stands calmly in the house of God, *his* house, detached, unmoving, a fearsome deity whose hand is unseen but is at once everywhere, working mighty deeds.

A little later, after Michael has Connie's husband Carlo killed for setting up Sonny, we see proof that the tragic transformation is complete. Our own feelings are painfully ambivalent. We love Michael and naturally root for him against his enemies, but we are shocked and disillusioned by what he has become. Kay, our emotional stand-in, must test him. When he looks her in the eye and lies to her, reassuring her that he didn't order Carlo's death, she hugs him with relief, but we know that his honesty, the basis of his transaction with her, has been forfeited, their bond broken. He has cut himself off from the Holy Spirit. Caught up in the male need to assert itself against its enemies, the institutional Church finally retreats from the female wisdom of openness. Kay steps out of his office to pour some drinks, then looks back through the door to see that three mobsters have somehow appeared, kissing Michael's ring and calling him "Don Corleone." They are like dark angels summoned out of nowhere, a sign that her husband now commands great and strange powers from which she is excluded, as the door closes on her and the picture ends as it began, in darkness.

HERMANN GÖRING IS SUPPOSED to have said, "Whenever I hear the word 'culture' I reach for my revolver." I'm starting to feel that way about the phrase "God's will." *The Godfather* begins with Bonasera, in a deal to have a request granted, submitting his own will to a higher authority. That's roughly how most religious people, at least in the West, think of their prayerful relationship with God. But maybe that's backward. If we pray for any particular thing, whether it's a winning lottery ticket or world peace, we're trying to bend God to *our* will. (As I write this, a famous televangelist is conducting a "prayer offensive" to induce God to knock three ailing justices off the Supreme Court and replace them with new ones who will be tougher on sodomites.) Once in the habit of attributing our desires to him, we may take the next step and start announcing God's will to the world.

> I believe God wants me to be president.
> —GEORGE W. BUSH, 1999

The scriptures, on the other hand, are very clear in busting us at this little game:

> For my thoughts are not your thoughts,
> nor are your ways my ways, says the Lord.
> As the heavens are higher than the earth,
> so are my ways higher than your ways
> and my thoughts than your thoughts.
> —ISAIAH 55:8–9

Nevertheless, God keeps being pressed into service as the rationale for our agenda. Our crusade or our jihad is not only sanctioned but sanctified. By ascribing our violence to a God who allegedly made us an offer we couldn't refuse, we can be complicit without being culpable. Our "humility before God" is really cosmic egotism. If we've kissed the ring and convinced ourselves that the hand wearing it belongs to the ultimate Godfather, the *capo di tutti capi*, then it follows that ours is the ultimate gang, which must prevail over all others. Get two or more gangs going with this concept, throw in a little technology we didn't have in the Middle Ages, and once we go to the mattresses we've got a recipe for world destruction.

It's pretty easy to see how dangerous "God's will" is in the hands of a bin Laden or a Bush. What's harder to accept is that the danger can start with a Gandhi or a Dr. King. If you say God tells you to treat others with decency and compassion, why can't I say God tells me to fly planes into buildings? Who's going to adjudicate, who's going to listen to both of our answering machines and decide who got the right message? That's why *I* believe in America. Not so much America as a place, but the America of the mind, the place within us (no matter where we live) where we don't have to bend the knee to anyone's invented king, whether on the earth or in the sky, where we treat others with decency and compassion because that's what we freely choose—and where Tom Paine and Chuck Berry, Walt Whitman and Susan B. Anthony, Emily Dickinson and Henry Thoreau, Frederick Douglass and Alfred E. Neuman, Mae West and Lenny Bruce all teach us in various ways to shake our booty for freedom.

Despite *The Godfather*'s dark pessimism, one scene leaves us with this kind of hope: the death of Don Vito. As Michael has morphed into his slicked-back, corporate look, the retired Vito has gone in the other direction. Carelessly dressed in rough cotton peasants' clothing, his hair unkempt and long, he's become a bit of a flower child in his old age.

> **VITO:** I like to drink wine more than I used to.
> **MICHAEL:** It's good for you, Pop.
> **VITO:** Anyway, I'm drinking more.

Having perpetrated and survived the grisliest kinds of violence, Vito now passes a sunny afternoon playing with his grandson in his tomato garden—another little Eden, wild, primordial and pre-institutional in contrast to the urban streets of Vito's career. Having given his final advice to Michael and let go of the family business, he is at last without an agenda.

This extraordinary scene gains much of its power from the fact that the little boy at first wouldn't play with Brando. After several unsuccessful takes, Coppola was ready to call it quits when Brando, asking for one more try, conceived a wonderful bit of improvisation. Shoving a section of orange peel into his mouth, Vito becomes a comic monster, chasing little Anthony, who wavers between fear and laughter, about the garden. Has the wrathful God been a game all along? Is the one that men have feared, defied, loved, and railed at for all these centuries merely a let's-pretend? Or is he, at most, a kindly cosmic grandpop, made fearsome and imposing in our imagination as grown-ups can be in the eyes of a child?

It is in this softened, indeterminate state that Vito collapses and dies. In a spine-tingling moment, the boy runs laughing to the body and stands over it, burbling something that sounds like "Uh-uh-uh-uh-uh-uh-uh-uh-ouch!," shooting Vito triumphantly with an old-fashioned spray-pump that could contain either fertilizer or insecticide (birth or death—here in Eden, it's all the same). The big bad Father God, whom the big men could not kill with their real guns, is killed by a child with a mock gun who sees that God is a mock monster. It's as if we're being shown that all our deadly serious struggles to know the truth or to come to terms with the infinite—to discern God's will—only conjured it into more oppressive forms. The personified God, like all constructs, must finally deconstruct.

Here, in this garden of the retired, agendaless deity, the phrase "God's will" has no meaning. The infinite doesn't will: it just *is*. We harmonize with it—we realize ourselves as it—

when *we* don't will but just be. And we can enter into the garden, into the kingdom of heaven, by being like Anthony, like a little child, by having the same playful, spontaneous relationship with the infinite that a child has with everything. Don't take God so goddamn seriously—*he* doesn't. And don't blame God for the dogmatism and unkindness with which we've hardened our hearts. As Vito tells Michael in their last conversation, "I never wanted this for you." He wanted him, he says, to be a governor or senator. At the last, even God does not believe in God. He believes in America.

When I was in the first grade, my family moved to the suburbs of Los Angeles. We wound up in a new tract home with a swimming pool in the San Fernando Valley. One day my little brother Eric asked a bare-chested poolside guest about the cross around his neck, something unfamiliar in our godless household. The man explained that he was a Catholic, that Catholics wore crosses, Jews wore the Star of David, and so forth. Eric considered this for a few moments, then responded brightly, "But us Americans don't have to wear anything!"

DIVINE HEAVINESS

LESLIE BENEDICT [Elizabeth Taylor]: Money isn't all, you
know, Jett.
JETT RINK [James Dean]: Not when you got it.
— *GIANT*

HOW COOL IS JAMES BOND? THE QUESTION ANSWERS
itself. He's as cool as cool gets. He's the essence of coolness, the
ultimate in coolitude, the embodiment of coolosity. When you
look up "cool" in the dictionary, there's a picture of him there.
He's so cool he uses Frosty the Snowman for a campfire. With
his double-oh designation, he's licensed to chill.*

And even more than cool, he's smooth. Life is sort of like the
greater New York–New Jersey area. There are a lot of toll roads
and bridges, and everybody has to pass through every tollbooth, pay their dues, take care of business. But if, Velcroed to
the inside of your windshield, you have a little white electronic
wafer called an E-ZPass, you can zip right through the tollbooth
without stopping and the toll is automatically charged to your
credit card. That's how Bond handles the difficult missions he
undertakes and the dangers he faces, flowing through them

---

* Albert R. ("Cubby") Broccoli, who, along with Harry Saltzman, was the
original producer of the Bond series, was also the grandson of the man
who introduced broccoli to the United States. So one family gave our culture both that which is the essence of racy, rule-breaking coolness and
that which is the essence of dull, sensible virtue. Weird.

with friction-free smoothness. It's something we so admire and envy that we've sustained the series through some twenty films, despite the silly, formulaic comic book plots, the nonchalant sadism, and the leering sexism that have had social critics predicting the imminent end of the Bond craze for over forty years. In 007 we recognize the smooth operators we'd like to be, and the cool, effective, enlightened way in which we'd like to face our own dangers and accomplish our own missions.

There are, however, two ways that Bond films can go wrong. One is to make him a superman—a constant temptation as each film tries to top the last. The other is to make him too vulnerably human, the George Lazenby–Timothy Dalton problem. Bond's appeal depends on maintaining that tricky in-between status, neither super nor ordinary but the ordinary discovering its potential to rise to the super. This parallels the story of Shakyamuni. Noting his blissful radiance, people asked whether he was a god. "No," he replied. Then he must be just an ordinary human? "Not that either." Then what was he? "I am awake," he replied, using the Sanskrit word *buddha,* by which we have known him since. To be Buddha is to be neither god nor ordinary, but human at the highest level, a human who is fully awake.

Bond is a budding Buddha. His role as a secret agent resembles that of the film noir detective, but surpasses it. A detective is an investigator, one who looks into a situation and (especially in noir) is often stung when he tries to do more. An agent, as the word implies, does things, transforms the situation. Thus Philip Marlowe represents the spiritual seeker; Bond represents the deeper commitment and more developed proficiency of the spiritual practitioner. His transcendental aspiration is indicated by the Bond family motto: THE WORLD IS NOT ENOUGH. If we practice with commitment, the element of growing enlightenment infiltrates our lives just as Bond infiltrates the various exotic locales of SPECTRE's evil operations ("as a thief in the night"). His usual cover is as a representative of an outfit called Universal Export, and enlightenment is indeed the one good that can be universally and beneficially exported to every situation and problem.

Bond's adversaries represent various obstacles to growing enlightenment, obscurations of our true nature. As we've already seen, the real obscurations are internal, our own patterns of thought and resultant behavior. Dr. No, as his name and his chilly personality suggest, could be the negativity with which we isolate ourselves from others, just as he has isolated himself to lord over his little island, and which keeps us from reaching out and touching others, as if we too had black-gloved mechanical hands. Kananga (aka Mr. Big) of *Live and Let Die*, with his plan to hook millions of Americans on free heroin and then jack up the price, could be our lazy, addictive, get-lost-in-substances-or-TV-or-video-games-today-and-pay-the-consequences-tomorrow side. And Auric Goldfinger is greed, or, to use the more clinical, less moralistic-sounding Buddhist term, attachment. His character reveals the nature of our own greed, and his nefarious plot to raid Fort Knox reveals how greed threatens to keep us mired in ignorance, while Bond's supercool methods of quashing him show how greed can be overcome.

GOLDFINGER, WHICH MANY 007 buffs regard as the ultimate Bond film, was a huge hit when it opened in 1964. It set a record as the fastest-grossing film of all time, and its title song, sung by Shirley Bassey, was heard everywhere, crowding the Beatles off the top of the charts.* *Goldfinger* gave birth to the age of movie-product merchandising as a major industry, with 007 trading cards, action figures, puzzles, walkie-talkies, clothing,

---

* Before that, the last movie theme to be so successful was *Breakfast at Tiffany's* "Moon River" three years earlier. Oddly enough, although its mood is quite opposite it opens with exactly the same three-note hook.

swimming trunks, board games, dress shoes, lunchboxes, and, of course, model Aston Martins. Our conviction that some sleek iGizmo will make *us* cool is probably traceable to the moment in this film when Bond first visits Q's weapons lab.

This is the third Bond film but the first with all the elements of the formula in place. The first film in the series, *Dr. No*, shows Bond receiving his orders from the ever-huffy M, traveling to an exotic locale to take on a colorful, villainous megalomaniac, casually killing a lot of bad guys, and dallying with a lot of sexy babes along the way. (Many of the babes start off working for the opposition, but once they're sufficiently charmed they invariably help lead 007 to his goal. In this they resemble the *dakinis* of Vajrayana Buddhism, sexy wisdom angels that can appear malevolent but turn out to be powerful enlightenment guides.) *Goldfinger* retains all these ingredients, as well as Sean Connery, the definitive Bond, but also marks the debut of the fabulously customized Aston Martin DB-5, the straitlaced Q issuing Bond hilariously lethal gadgets, and the pre-title sequence that, having no connection to the film's plot, becomes a sort of appetizer, a minimovie in itself.

Here the pre-title sequence provides the first hints of the elements that make Bond a dharma hero. It begins at night, in Mexico, with a rather greasy, bedraggled-looking duck swimming through murky waters. As it reaches the shore it rises to reveal that it's a stuffed bird, mounted on Bond's head to conceal his snorkel, which he now discards. In a few minutes Bond will strip off his wetsuit, under which, immaculately groomed as ever, he wears an elegant white dinner jacket. Then he'll complete his ensemble by sticking a red carnation in his lapel, recalling the lotus flower, which traditionally symbolizes enlightenment by sinking its roots into the muck at the bottom of the murkiest waters yet emerging to unfold its immaculate blossom at their surface.

But first Bond breaks into an ordinary-but-impregnable-looking oil refinery tank, in which an elaborate drug-processing operation is hidden, and sets a bomb with a timer. This is the job of the dharma agent, to break through the apparently impregnable ordinariness of outer existence, find its surprising inner content, and set off some kind of explosive transformation. Then, strolling sans wetsuit into a nearby cantina, Bond checks his watch and lights his cigarette just as the bomb goes off. It rocks the building, and all the panicked revelers flee for the door as he moves in the opposite direction, coolly approaching the bar. This is precisely how a seasoned spiritual practitioner carries himself, heading placidly upstream from the agitated crowd, unruffled even as seemingly unchangeable, fortresslike structures (whether external or internal) come tumbling down. No matter how much things are shaken, he's never stirred.

Having shown us what he's all about, Bond flies to Miami to see what his adversary is all about, and the movie proper begins. He first spots Goldfinger beside the deluxe hotel swimming pool, bilking another guest in a crooked card game. Gert Frobe is wonderfully cast here, probably the best of the Bond villains. Never a mustache-twirling, hand-rubbing caricature, he is completely convincing as a fellow driven by insatiable craving, a fat man whose supposed natural jollity is spoiled by a perpetual, gnawing hunger. A little later in the film, Colonel Smithers, a Bank of England patriarch, explains just what Goldfinger hungers after:

> Gold, gentleman, which can be melted down and recast, is virtually untraceable, which makes it, unlike diamonds, ideal for smuggling, attracting the biggest and most ingenious criminals.

Gold's untraceability and malleability are almost mystical properties. As a single, radiant, supremely valuable substance that can take countless forms, it edges close to the definition of the formless infinite. And this suggests Goldfinger's fundamental confusion. What he really wants—what we all really want, whether we know it or not—is the infinite, the spirit. The curse and the blessing of being human, what separates us from other species, is a kind of limitless hunger, which can only be fulfilled by the limitless itself. Lacking that, we pursue whatever seems to resemble it most closely.

And money, which is usually dismissed in theory (but rarely in practice) as the grossest, most material of substances, is in fact so close to the nature of spirit that the confusion is understandable.

> [N]othing is less material than money, inasmuch as any coin whatsoever (a twenty-centavo piece, let us say) is, strictly speaking, a repertory of possible futures. . . . It can be an evening in the suburbs, it can be the music of Brahms, it can be maps, it can be chess, it can be coffee, it can be the words of Epictetus teaching us to despise gold.
> —JORGE LUIS BORGES,
>   "The Zahir"

Yeah yeah, money can't buy happiness, blah blah blah—during the Depression, rich studio executives produced a lot of movies to remind poor moviegoers of this. But money used intelligently, as a means rather than an end, can buy a whole lot of freedom.

> A feast is made for laughter, and wine maketh merry: but money answereth all things.
> —ECCLESIASTES 10:19

They say that time is money, but money is time. It buys the luxury of deciding to write your novel at a café in Venice instead of flipping burgers at a Mickey D's in Bayonne. The next time you hear someone spouting off about how base and demeaning money is, please ask him to send his to me.

But when money becomes an end in itself, that's an illness that can be fatal. Later, Goldfinger himself describes some of the symptoms:

> This is gold, Mr. Bond. All my life I've been in love with its color, its brilliance, its divine heaviness. I welcome any enterprise that will increase my stock— which is considerable.

That "divine heaviness" is especially interesting. In seeking that which has gravitas, that which sits solidly at the bottom-most level of life when all else floats away, we're really seeking the infinite. Any substitute—even a pretty good substitute like money or gold—will fail to yield the infinite satisfaction that it promises, so that, no matter how considerable our stock, we always want to increase it. This roiling dissatisfaction is what drives our economy. Whether it's for Miller beer or Disney World, every commercial that sells the sizzle, not the steak, is really selling the golden radiance of ultimate fulfillment. And when the product turns out to be not as advertised—when half an hour later we're hungry again—the advertisers are happy to sell us something else. No problem.

This idea of ultimate fulfillment is closely tied to that of ultimate value. To say that a medical procedure or anything else is indisputably the best, we call it "the gold standard," but the notion that a certain soft, yellow metal has ultimate value is, considered objectively, absurd. Its value, of course, is merely imputed by consensus, like that of the flimsiest paper money. J. S. G. Boggs is an artist who specializes in showing how we make up value. A superb draftsman, he has been known to walk into a restaurant, order a fine meal, and then, over coffee and dessert, open his little backpack, take out a nearly finished, hyperrealistic, life-size drawing of a $100 bill (with a few sly modifications such as the motto IN US WE TRUST), and start adding the finishing touches. Typically, the waiter is soon looking over Boggs's shoulder and making admiring comments. "I'm glad you like it," Boggs will respond. "This is a work of art whose value I have set at $100. I plan to pay for my meal with it—and naturally I expect change."

WHAT AURIC GOLDFINGER really wants is not only to *have* gold but to merge with it, to become it. The good news, if he had ears to hear, is that he already *is* it. The ultimate value that we hungrily seek is none other than our own nature, as we can experience by leaving off seeking and, instead, just being. Hindu scriptures sometimes even call this inner dimension "the realms of gold." The hint should be the gold color of our villain's hair, along with his first name, Auric, which means "golden." But having failed to recognize his own inner goldenness, he seeks it on the outside (starting with the gold fabrics in his clothes), and that's dangerous. As the film's theme song reminds us, "He's the man, the man with the Midas touch." King Midas of legend suffered the misfortune of having the god Dionysus grant his wish that everything he touched should turn to gold. To his horror, he could no longer eat—his food became gold as he raised it to his lips. When, in his grief, he embraced his daughter, she became a golden statue.

This is precisely our (and Goldfinger's) situation. The desire to see the golden radiance of the infinite everywhere, to feel its divine heaviness in everything, is the highest of impulses—it's the impulse to enlightenment. But when we try to *make* it radiant from the outside, by gilding our lives with ever more wealth and ever finer stuff rather than by perceiving the inner value that's always already there, we turn our lives into something as pretty but as rigid and dead as Midas' daughter. Thus the film's most memorable image follows Goldfinger's discovery that his blond hired girlfriend has tipped off Bond to the poolside gambling scam and wound up in Bond's bed. After being knocked unconscious by Goldfinger's enforcer Oddjob, Bond awakes to discover the girl lying dead of "skin suffocation," covered head-to-toe in gold paint. Her fate is a powerful symbol of what Goldfinger is doing to himself. Even his last name suggests that too much greedy fondling of gold has already begun the lethal process: today the gold finger, tomorrow the arm . . . once he gets started, he can't stop. He's like turkeys, which, unlike chickens, must be brought in out of the rain; otherwise they become so hypnotized that they keep looking skyward till their throats fill with water and they drown.

Does this mean that to live an enlightened life we must renounce all wealth and go about with a loincloth and a begging bowl? Fortunately, no. Now back in London headquarters, 007 gives M a delightfully pseudoscientific explanation of the girl's suffocation, noting that she would have survived if a small patch down at the base of her spine had been left unpainted. All we need is some such breathing patch. We can lead busy, complex lives in which we're well compensated for our busy-ness and still avoid spiritual suffocation, as long as deep down, at the base level of our awareness, we see our accomplishments and acquisitions as empty, as things of only relative value and temporary endurance. Through regular meditative practice we can keep that space open.

Here in London, 007 does his obligatory teasing flirtation with the lovelorn Miss Moneypenny and is briefed by M and Q, the nonidentical twin grumpy old men. As his venerable preceptors, they're a reminder of the importance of tradition in perpetuating enlightenment teachings. Since everyone seeking enlightenment is by definition ignorant, we never really know what we're doing till we don't have to do it anymore. So we rely on traditional teachings, even if, as agents in the field, we must sometimes improvise within their context, just as a Bird or a Coltrane can blow his way into the stratosphere by improvising within the harmonic context of traditional standards.

The dharma tradition, here embodied by these two august lineage masters, always answers our two key questions: where are we going (nirvana, enlightenment) and what do we need to get there (upaya, skillful means). M delineates Bond's mission and Q issues the equipment to carry it out. Our dharma mission is to clear away the obstacles to enlightenment, while our upaya comprises such specific methodologies as breath work, mantra, meditation, and visualization. Here M gives the assignment, to assess and foil Auric Goldfinger's evil designs on the world gold supply, and Q provides several cool gadgets.

The supreme gadget is the Aston Martin, which in itself neatly sums up several important characteristics of upaya. When we think of this fabulous car we usually focus on its secret weapons and exotic features, just as we tend to focus on the most exotic aspects of dharma practice. But in both cases, what's most important and most often overlooked is what's *not* there. This is a sports car, not a tank. Its sleek, aerodynamic lines suggest the elegant simplicity of just being, abiding in the natural state—"meditation," as we are obliged to call it. Both meditation and sports cars work by being streamlined, coming as close as possible to being nothing at all. Every moment the mind spends resting in the just-being state, it's discovering that quality of "just," so that, when we return to action, walking becomes just walking, running a corporation becomes just running a corporation, without all the fussing and fumbling, blame or self-doubt or ego-tripping that often attach to action. In other words, we're training to be 007 cool.

Of course, the car *is* tricked out with all sorts of gadgets, but they're hidden—they emerge, as it were, from its unbroken sleekness just as all the skillful tricks of dharma practice (and of effective action) emerge from the simplicity of just being. The car's bulletproof shield evokes the protective quality of set practices such as mantras or prayers. In fact, the word *mantra* literally means "mind protector," and traditional texts often describe the mantras that are resonated either vocally or mentally as "vehicles" for safely traversing unfamiliar regions of consciousness, which can be wondrous but sometimes disorienting or even frightening. Staying strapped into the mantra (with all hands and feet inside the car, please) allows one to pass safely through to the far side.

The smokescreens and oil slicks that the car shoots out of its taillights to repel attackers suggest two important tactics for protecting our dharma mission. It's advisable not to be a showoff with your spiritual life. Don't cast your pearls before swine, says Jesus. Don't pray ostentatiously, don't announce loudly that it's time for your meditation break and plop yourself down in the lotus pose in the middle of the lobby. Better to be discreet, to shoot a little smoke out the back of your practice. If people want to know about it, they'll ask you. And when it's time to get up and jump back into the fray, a bit of Bond's slick, oil-smooth style of interacting can keep us from getting awkwardly entangled.

The revolving license plate, which prevents Bond's enemies from identifying him, suggests the need for a fluid sense of self, not rigidly identified with any one conventional persona. Many traditions give practitioners new names when they enter into a life of serious spiritual commitment, to help loosen their identification with the old self. 007 is such a name, one that reminds Bond that he is essentially empty; two-thirds of him is zero. As with any enlightened warrior, his license to kill, to judiciously terminate the existence of others, is rooted in the cognition of the emptiness of his own existence. But out of that emptiness emerges seven, the number of prodigious achievement—crossing the seven seas, spanning the seven continents, building the seven wonders, playing like Mickey

Mantle, opening all the chakras, lighting all the lights—the fullest *expression* of our emptiness. I got *plenty* of nothin'.

Vajrayana Buddhism goes even further by offering techniques for imaginatively identifying with a "meditational deity." Through the use of elaborate visualization and the deity's special mantra, the practitioner steeps in the sense of being, say, Tara, the compassionate female buddha, or Garuda, the soaring space eagle. The session usually ends by exploding the visualization into pure, empty awareness-space, the point being not so much to become the deity as to realize that you're not, in any absolute sense, you.

One modification of the Aston Martin that's never mentioned is that the car's sun visors have been removed. This is done for strictly cinematic purposes, to give the camera a clear view of Bond's face from all angles, but it also suggests that spiritual practice requires a basic attitude of openness, to let in life, to let in the light. That's balanced, however, by the red button hidden in the gearshift knob, which activates the passenger-side ejector seat. Bond uses it later in the film to dispose of an armed hijacker, just as we need to eject anything that threatens to hijack our vehicle of dharma and sway us from reaching our goal.

On first being apprised of this feature, Bond exclaims, "Ejector seat? You're joking," prompting Q's defining line: "I never joke about my work, 007." The old lineage masters are all business. They don't fool around with the dharma and are often not amused by jokesters (like me) who present it in a more playful light, or by practitioners who find that the realities of modern life require some adaptation of the practices. For example, there are techniques for expanding our love throughout the universe that start by dwelling upon the simple, unquestioning love that everyone has for their mother—or at least had, in medieval Tibet. In our culture, where people's feelings about their mothers are often more complicated, we may have to modify the practice. But even when they disapprove, such straitlaced guardians of the dharma deserve our gratitude and respect. Somebody has to be the grown-up in charge. Somebody has to be orthodox so that those of us who are a little heterodox have reliable reference points. Q being Q allows Bond to be Bond.

> Q [handing Bond a tiny electronic tracking device]: And incidentally, we'd appreciate its return, along with all your other equipment—intact for once— when you return from the field.
> BOND: You'd be surprised at all the wear and tear that goes on out there in the field.

ONCE HE'S BEEN BRIEFED, Bond declares, "I think it's time Mr. Goldfinger and I met—socially, of course." Of course. Bond's style of genteel, ultracivilized social intercourse with his upper-crust villains, where everyone shares cigars and serves Dom Pérignon '53, trading witty repartee and calling each other "Mister," demonstrates the most effective way to deal with the obscurations to our enlightenment: gently and obliquely. An aggressive, head-on approach will just get them riled up. If we decided, say, that from this moment on we will root out all our greed or lust or anger, we would probably generate a powerful blowback. The annals of spiritual exploration are full of stories of earnest young people taking impulsive vows of celibacy—till they just as impulsively plunge into making-up-for-lost-time promiscuity. Bond, as the skillful practitioner, does not confront Goldfinger with guns blazing but challenges him to a friendly game of golf at Stoke Poges, where he gets under his skin with some subtle cheating involving deft switching of balls.

He also makes Goldfinger miss a putt by dropping a distracting gold bar at his feet, telling him he has more to sell. This luring of the obscurations with bait is a time-honored technique. When spiritual teachers speak of the nirvanic or heavenly state

in terms of celestial cities or gardens full of maidens, or even as
states of bliss rather than the transcendence of all states—or,
for that matter, when they use terms such as "goal" and "transformation" and "enlightenment" as if what's involved is a matter
of becoming rather than being—they're practicing bait-and-
switch. But it's a benign bait-and-switch. No one ever asks for a
refund. The teachers appeal to our attachment by speaking of
the "goal" in terms of those things to which we are attached. A
related approach, common nowadays especially in the West, is
to tout meditative practice for its worldly benefits: better job
performance, better athletic performance, better sexual performance, lower blood pressure, higher grade-point average. . . .
As it happens, all these benefits and many more do accrue, but
by that time we've tasted enough of the deeper result of practice
that they fade in significance. Those worldly benefits are, as a
traditional metaphor puts it, like the milder sweets that the
tongue can barely taste when it is subjected to the intense
sweetness of honey.

Playing it cool and civilized with our attachments may not
seem too difficult as long as they play by the same rules. But
sometimes they get riled up—when someone else takes the last
piece of cake or outbids you on eBay or outsells your book—
and then hunger turns to aggression. The genteel Goldfinger
resorts to the services of his manservant and alter ego, the hulking Oddjob. The thing about Oddjob, like our lurking aggression, is that you can dress him up but you can't take him
anywhere. He's decked out like a gentleman's gentleman, but
his thick-necked, 284-pound wrestler's body always looks like
it's ready to burst out of his tuxedo shirt like the Incredible
Hulk, and whenever his master figuratively flips his lid Oddjob
flips his literally, flinging his lead bowler hat at his hapless victims like a killer Frisbee.

By the time things reach this point, a different, simpler tac-
tic, which 007 demonstrates several times, is required: duck.

When the Oddjob in us or in others is fully aroused, there's no reasoning with him. (Oddjob speaks no English, and he specializes in destroying wisdom—in this film his odd jobs include knocking off two dakinis.) As one of my teachers used to say, when the cyclone hits, lie low. If we just recognize this aggression for what it is (don't be fooled by the elegant ways we dress it up) and stay out of its way, it will burn itself out, just as, near the film's climax, Bond dodges the hat several times till it lands in an electrified grate and Oddjob makes the mistake of grabbing it. He goes out in a blaze of fireworks, but he goes out.

This happens during Operation Grand Slam, Goldfinger's complicated assault on Fort Knox. To grab the American government's entire gold supply would be a grand slam indeed, the mother of all heists. We can see it as greed's ultimate attempt to swallow up the infinite in one big gulp. Since the building's real-life interior is a closely guarded secret, production designer Ken Adam was free to imagine it as a magnificent temple of gold, an appropriate sanctum for the source, the essence, of divine heaviness. But as Bond points out earlier, it would take twelve days for Goldfinger's crew to carry the loot out—it's *too* heavy, *too* divine.

Here is greed's supreme frustration: confronting at last the true object of its desire, it finds that it's not an object at all and so can't be carried into the outside material world. Its nature is transcendental, invisible. It gives value to all that is visible by remaining out of sight, just as our gold reserves underpin our monetary system by staying in reserve. But Goldfinger knows that. His real plan, it turns out, is to detonate a bomb (genteelly referred to as "an atomic device") that will render the Fort Knox gold radioactive for fifty-eight years and thus drive up the value of his own. When greed realizes it can't swallow or own the infinite, it tries to pollute it, devalue it, deny it.

The Bible is full of stories of arrogant kings who do this, persecuting the faithful so their own claims to supremacy will be unrivaled. And they are always struck down. As Goldfinger explains Operation Grand Slam to some mobsters who are in collusion with him, he grandly pushes buttons and twists dials to produce aerial photos on screens and a giant scale model of the fort and its surroundings. "My plan is foolproof, gentlemen," he boasts, but at just that moment we zoom in to see Bond's eye looking out through the window of the model fort. He has escaped from the cell where Goldfinger has been holding him and sneaked into the model to learn and ultimately sabotage the plan. And it's the 007 in *our* fort that subverts our own kingly, foolproof plans. The ghost in the machine, the fly in the ointment, is really the growing influence of enlightenment in our lives, our bond with our spiritual destiny, which will not let us stay confused and distracted by lesser destinies forever.

Bond's eye in the window is a strangely striking image, recalling the all-seeing eye of God floating above the unfinished pyramid on the Great Seal (look on the back of a dollar bill). And Fort Knox has, roughly, an unfinished-pyramid shape. Because the grand pyramids of our ambitious projects are really intended to reach the sky of boundlessness, they're always incomplete. Only the eye of awareness, abiding in the sky that is its natural home, can confer the sense of great completeness that we crave. (The Tibetan term for the innately enlightened nature of existence is *dzogchen,* a contraction of *dzogpa chenpo,* literally "great natural completeness." It's the only true completeness, without which we feel something's missing, no matter how much we accumulate or achieve.) When our projects fall apart, when our best-laid plans gang aglee, it's actually a blessing. Appreciating this is often easier said than done, but at that moment of "failure," if we pay attention rather than bury our heads in recrimination and self-pity, we'll see that our broken dreams are opportunities to wake up to that which is beyond all dreaming, beyond all breaking.

Bond's unexpected collaborator in foiling the heist is Goldfinger's personal pilot, Pussy Galore. (After all these pages of trying to make clever interpretations, at last a gimme!) Miss Galore's role in the plan is to deploy her squadron of equally babelicious assistants, Pussy Galore's Flying Circus, in spraying invisible Delta-9 gas to knock out the 41,000 troops that guard the fort. Indeed, the babes (or hunks) of rampant sexuality are legion, ever-ready to knock us off our feet. But after a roll in the hay (literally) with Bond, this dakini, per the usual pattern, switches sides and becomes an ally of the enlightenment project, spraying fake gas instead. (In a typical plot absurdity, the troops feign sleep and wait till Goldfinger and his henchmen get inside the fort before taking them on. Why?) And in fact, sex does have that potential to switch sides: it can put us to sleep or help wake us up. Like money, it's often considered the antithesis of the spirit. But sex makes us not acquire but strip, get down, get basic. If we *pay attention to the actual experience* of sex, instead of the usual fantasies, seduction strategies, and performance anxieties, it can give us some vivid previews of the self-sufficient, don't-need-nothin' reality that undermines all greed.

And as it turns out, 007 needs all the allies he can get. He will eventually facilitate Goldfinger's being sucked out the window of a jet (falling from great heights being the obligatory end for overreaching villains), but first he must thwart Operation Grand Slam. He winds up in Fort Knox, locked inside with the nuke, which is in a heavy steel case some nine feet long, as the government troops battle Goldfinger's men outside. After dispatching Oddjob, Bond opens the case to face a dizzying profusion of revolving gears and cogs and tangled wires, an infernal machine driven by the obligatory countdown clock with only seconds left till annihilation. As the heavily perspiring 007 tries to figure out how to shut the thing down, he is, for once, at a loss. Just as he's about to pull apart two wires as a desperate guess, the troops fight their way in and a silent, bespectacled

atomic expert reaches in his hand and—apparently—turns off
a simple switch. We must say "apparently" because, in a weirdly
sloppy departure from the crystal-clear, lead-the-viewer-from-
Point-A-to-Point-B kind of filmmaking that we've been seeing
up till now, the switch is never shown. It's beneath the bottom
of the screen, invisible to us, and the hand reaches out of the
frame to operate it.

What's going on here? I think we're getting a final, dramatic
lesson in the dharma wisdom and the dharma skill that our enlightenment mission requires. The bomb we're trying to defuse
is our own life. The complex, relentlessly churning gears resemble life's outer circumstances, with so many constantly
changing and interconnected complications of work, family,
money, health, that it can seem as if one explosive catastrophe
or another is always just a few ticks away. At first Bond gingerly
lays a hand on a gear or two, but he quickly sees that they're
controlled by the machine's wiring, just as our outer lives are
controlled by our mental wiring, a network of concepts and
perceptions, memories and delusions, impulses and emotions
as hopelessly complex and tangled as the wires he now takes in
hand. And indeed it is the mind that has the power to either ra-
dioactively contaminate the vision of life's golden essence or
allow it to shine forth. Yet underlying all our thinking, just as
thinking underlies all our doing, is the invisible area just outside the frame: endless, frameless, silent being, which, if we let
it, brings the problematic quality of life to an instant stop.

Once you know where that switch is, flipping it is easy. The
surprise, and the lovely joke here, is that the real dharma expert
brushes right past all the outer and inner complexity. The anti-
dote to complexity is not more complexity but simplicity. The
way of peace keeps being overlooked exactly because it's so
simple. Don't get more deeply enmeshed in the tangle of circumstances; you've already tried that and it didn't work. Don't
get involved in analyzing your tangle of thoughts, or in trying to

silence them, or trying not to try, or trying not to try not to try. Just relax in place, right where you are, right in their midst. For Bond, the lesson hits home when the countdown timer stops— on 007. Tag, you're it, James! You've been searching for the answer, the solution to life's dangers and the mind's unease, and the answer turns out to be the one who was asking. It's you, this very awareness, just as it is, in any given moment.*

In other words, Bond must finally learn for himself precisely the wisdom that Goldfinger lacks. Don't seek outside yourself. The essence of dharma expertise is to stop leaning forward to have or to do; just lean back and be. Not only in our formal meditation sessions but in the way we pulse through every moment of the day, even when engaged in the most demanding activities, we can keep making this liberating adjustment. It's so subtle that others won't see what we're doing (the switch being invisible, out of the frame), but the result, which others *will* sense, is that the feeling of impending disaster dissolves. We keep doing what we have to do, but all our doing becomes cool and smooth, Bond-like, E-ZPass–like, and beneath it all we know, with growing certainty, that everything's OK.

IN ADDITION TO SUBVERTING our greed from the inside through meditative practice, we can also subvert it from the outside through another simple technique: giving. We've already discussed dana, first of the transcendental virtues, but here it's worth raising again in the light of an issue we discussed in the *Truman Show* chapter. The reason I'm so reluctant to give stuff away—the reason I feel such a tug at the prospect—is that I know the stuff brings so much enjoyment *to*

---

* There's a confusing line a moment later, when Bond says, "Three more ticks and Mr. Goldfinger would have hit the jackpot." As the scene was originally shot, the timer stopped at 003. Shortly before the film's release, producer Harry Saltzman realized how much more fun 007 would be, but the dialogue was never updated to match the new shot.

me. But if, through practices such as exchanging self and other, I become less tightly caught up in the sense of me, I can then consider that the stuff will bring as much enjoyment to someone else. It doesn't much matter who's doing the enjoying. Otherwise, even memories of past enjoyment can keep us prisoners of our own accumulation, locked in our own little Fort Knox in some closet or other.

Last year, our kids having grown up, Maggy and I moved from the big Victorian we'd lived in for twenty years to a cozy Tudor cottage. One Sunday I helped my daughter fill up a truck with the last of her possessions, including everything from books and furniture to her trove of high-school love letters and the E.T. doll she had cuddled at age three. We moved it all to her apartment in Brooklyn, where she then began the bittersweet process of sorting through all the dollies and stuffed animals for which she has no room. We had a good talk about it. As she packed them up to be donated, she just kept reminding herself of how much more they would be enjoyed by other children. Of course she kept a few favorites. I'm sure that's all right.

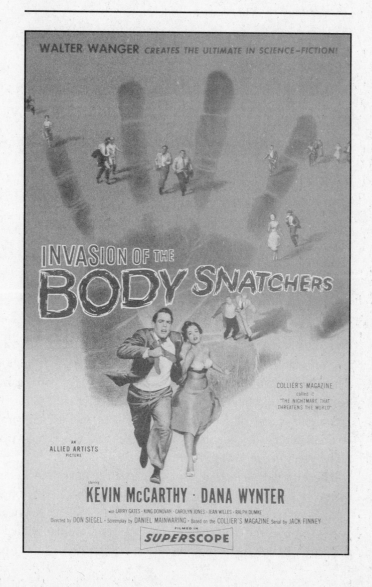

THE LIES OF THE ENLIGHTENED

Jesus asked his disciples: Make a comparison; what am I
like? . . . Thomas replied: Teacher, I cannot possibly say
what you are like. Jesus said to Thomas: I am not your
teacher; you have drunk from and become intoxicated
from the bubbling water that I poured out.
> —THE GOSPEL OF THOMAS

Don't follow leaders,
Watch the parking meters.
> —BOB DYLAN,
> *"Subterranean Homesick Blues"*

I'VE BEEN THINKING A LOT LATELY ABOUT J. EDGAR
Hoover's lawn. The old FBI chief owned a house in Washington
where he had all the grass ripped out and replaced with Astro-
Turf. It was, of course, perfectly uniform in length, perfectly
green year-round, perfectly maintenance-free. Aside from being
soulless and dead, aside from being a lawn that wasn't a lawn, it
was perfect in every way.

There's a part of us that wants to do that to ourselves. In our
quest for a life free from messiness and pain, there's a temptation to try to become humans that aren't human. If we're imagi-
native enough, we may even dream up grand utopian systems
that include others in our messless, friction-free state. And

since spirituality generally begins by addressing the problem of human pain and culminates in some sort of paradise, it has always been a fertile field for utopian dreamers and dehumanizers. Sometimes this utopianism is so clumsy and obvious it's laughable. Sometimes, especially when it's our own, it seems pretty reasonable. Either way it's a wolf in sheep's clothing, the enemy of liberating dharma disguised as dharma itself.

All utopian schemes, even atheistic Communism, are attempts to manifest the kingdom of heaven on earth. But trying to mold a model of nirvana out of the substance of samsara violates what we could call the vertical code, mixing up two levels of existence that have two different sets of rules. *Utopia* means "noplace"; it abides beyond time and space, in the realm of nirvana. In their frustration at trying to make utopia happen someplace, and to impose it on stubbornly imperfect humans, utopians sooner or later either give up or become totalitarians.

> They won't have mankind developing along some
> *living* historical path to the end, turning finally
> of itself into a normal society; but on the contrary,
> a social system emerging from some kind of
> mathematical brain that's going to reconstruct
> mankind and make it in one moment righteous
> and sinless. . . . A *living* soul isn't called for . . .
> [but something that is] servile and won't rebel.
> —DOSTOYEVSKY,
>   *The Brothers Karamazov*

One of the most powerful teachings on this topic is contained in a black-and-white grade-B horror film, shot in nineteen days for $300,000 in the era of B's like *Godzilla* and *Creature from the Black Lagoon* that are heavy on cheap special effects, guys in rubber monster suits, and ray guns that look like they came out of Cracker Jack boxes. But *Invasion of the Body*

Snatchers has none of that. It deals in horror of the mind, where the monsters are our perfectly normal-looking friends and neighbors.*

THE STORY IS SIMPLE. A family doctor in a wholesome, all-American small town gradually discovers that alien seedpods are being sneaked into people's homes, where they substitute emotionless, conformist replicants for little Jimmy and Uncle Ira and ultimately everybody.

> **DR. KAUFFMAN:** Out of the sky came a solu-
> tion. . . . Your new bodies are growing in there.
> They're taking you over cell for cell, atom for atom.
> There's no pain. Suddenly, while you're asleep,
> they'll absorb your minds, your memories, and
> you're reborn into an untroubled world. . . . Love,
> desire, ambition, faith—without them life's so sim-
> ple, believe me.

By the film's end, pods are being carted out of town by the truckful, clearly headed for world domination. This vegetative nightmare has invited a number of interpretations, especially political ones. When the film was released in 1956, right-wingers assumed that the body snatchers were commies; left-wingers thought they were McCarthyites. But Jack Finney, author of the magazine serial on which the film was based and cowriter of the screenplay, disclaimed any political intent, and the director, Don Siegel, was too pure a storyteller to weigh down his films with messages. Of course this won't deter us from finding spiritual messages aplenty.

---

* There's also an excellent, truly scary 1978 remake starring Donald Sutherland, and a truly stupid 1993 version called simply *The Body Snatchers.*

My favorite line occurs late in the film, when the doctor, Miles Bennell (played by Kevin McCarthy), and his love interest, Becky Driscoll (Dana Wynter), realize that the whole town has been taken over and their only hope is to escape by passing for pod people themselves. Miles tells Becky, "Keep your eyes a little wide and blank. Show no interest or excitement." I've seen that look on the faces of so many spiritual aspirants who think that enlightenment means curbing their enthusiasms, suppressing their emotions and individuality. I've seen whole spiritual organizations cultivate that vacuous mind-set in their ranks, and, like Miles and Becky, I've had to run like hell to avoid getting trapped in it myself.

What is the source of this folly? It's a reasonable misunderstanding. Holy books are full of exhortations to be "unmoved in loss and gain," "free from joy and sorrow," "steady as a candle flame in a windless place." It's easy to forget that these are descriptions of enlightenment's *features*, its symptoms rather than the means of attaining it. Trying to gain realization by being free from joy and sorrow is like trying to catch a cold by sneezing. Such striving can only produce a sort of strained emotional flatness, so different from the authentic experience of pure, steady, unclouded, skylike awareness as the background to the incessant changes of the relative world, including one's own changing emotions.

Genuine meditative practice doesn't turn you into a zombie, despite some spiritual seekers' best attempts at self-zombification. If anything, by establishing us in the perpetual silence of being, meditation makes it safe to throw ourselves into the rowdy noise of feeling, with total, Zorba-like abandon. That's what the most enlightened people I've known have been like. They laugh, they cry, they feel. It's *before* enlightenment that we're afraid to feel our feelings all the way down to our toes. And out of that fear we project the ideal of pseudo-enlightenment as a spiritually ordained state of repression.

We can also use spirituality to club our intellects as well as our hearts. This is generally done in the name of "faith," which is taken to mean replacing all one's own thoughts and doubts with the unexamined teachings of the guru or the doctrines of the scriptures. This may have worked for people in cultures where one's father and king were believed and obeyed without question. But here in the West, where we had the Renaissance and the scientific revolution, and especially here in America, where the first thing we did was to fire our kings, we're wired differently. Our mantra is QUESTION AUTHORITY, and the freedom to question is not incompatible with the vaster freedom of enlightenment—in fact, it helps prepare us for it. An open mind leads ultimately to that which is infinite openness and infinite mind.

The accumulated wisdom of traditional spiritual teachings is precious, no doubt—without the traditions we wouldn't know where to start. But they also contain superstitions and cultural baggage that are irrelevant or even detrimental to our process of realization, and separating baby from bathwater can be a delicate process. Our Western legacy of skepticism is actually very close to the Buddha's spirit of clear-headed, starting-from-zero inquiry. He didn't speak of "Buddhism" at all but of dharma, which, coming from a Sanskrit verb meaning "to hold," is usually translated as "that which is upheld." But it also implies "that which holds up." After all the shifting sands of theories and beliefs and all the squishy mud of neurotic fears and wishful fantasies have been washed away by the surging tide of actual experience, what solid rock is left? What holds up? The Buddha was a challenger of orthodoxies; his genius was the application of scientific method to ultimate questions. When he attracted followers, he urged them to take the same approach:

> Do not believe a thing because many repeat it.
> Do not accept a thing on the authority of one or
> another of the Sages of old, nor on the ground

that a statement is found in the books. . . . Believe
nothing merely on the authority of your teachers or
of the priests. After examination, believe that which
you have tested for yourselves. . . .
                —KALAMA SUTRA

If anything, repressing your doubts reflects a *lack* of faith.
Real faith—the wordless intuition, deeper than any dogma,
that existence is ultimately OK and that somehow we're on our
way to living that OK-ness—makes it OK to have doubts.
Thomas Merton expresses this kind of faith eloquently (and
theistically) in his "Prayer of Surrender":

> My Lord God,
>   I have no idea where I am going. I do not see the
> road ahead of me. I cannot know for certain where
> it will end. Nor do I really know myself, and the fact
> that I think that I am following Your will does not
> mean that I am actually doing so.
>   But I believe that the desire to please You does in
> fact please You. And I hope I have that desire in all
> that I am doing. I hope that I will never do anything
> apart from that desire. And I know that if I do this,
> You will lead me through the right road though I
> may know nothing about it.
>   Therefore, I will trust You always though I may
> seem to be lost and in the shadow of death. I will
> not fear, for You are ever with me, and You will
> never leave me to face my peril alone.

This kind of affirmative uncertainty spurs us to look deep into
whatever traditional teachings are presented to us, and into
ourselves, to find the sticking places and work them loose.
Only that way can we make the teachings our own.

That's a job. If we want to duck the job, one convenient way is to ape the teacher unthinkingly. Anyone who has spent time hanging around spiritual venues has probably seen this. On a Buddhist retreat I once attended, one of the teachers had back problems resulting from a car crash some months before. Without saying anything about it, she led meditation sessions sitting in a chair rather than on a cushion. Every once in a while she stood up to relieve the pressure on her back, meditated standing up for a few minutes, then sat back down again. Darned if after a few days several sincere retreatants weren't dutifully standing up and sitting down right along with her.

Clearly, such slavishness can't be blamed on the teacher. Good teachers are always exhorting us toward freedom, but if we're determined enough we can turn even these exhortations into their opposite, like the adoring multitude in Monty Python's *Life of Brian* who have decided that the hapless schlemiel Brian is the messiah:

> BRIAN: Look, you've got it all wrong. You don't need to follow me. You don't need to follow anybody. You've got to think for yourselves. You're all individuals.
> THE MULTITUDE [chanting in robotic unison]: Yes! We're all individuals!
> BRIAN: You're all different.
> THE MULTITUDE: Yes! We're all different!

The fact is that we're offered boundless freedom all the time, not only by teachers but by life itself. But we're like Keiko the killer whale, star of the *Free Willy* movies. Despite the millions of dollars spent trying to return him to the freedom of the ocean where he could hunt and sport with his fellow whales, Keiko preferred the familiarity of a tank and the acquired taste of dead fish. His body was finally found butting up against a pier, as if trying to return to dry land. Perhaps fittingly, he was buried in the ground.

AN ALERT TEACHER who doesn't succumb to the flattery of adoring disciples will find ways to subvert it. Chögyam Trungpa, the first Tibetan lama to teach extensively in the United States, noted that most of his students here were devoutly nonsmoking, vegetarian types, who saw their health-conscious lifestyle as the obvious choice of all the more enlightened folk. So one day Trungpa started smoking. This discombobulated his students at first, but then many of them decided that the enlightened choice after all was not to be such prudes, and they took up smoking themselves. As soon as enough of them had made the switch, Trungpa suddenly stopped. Eek! Now what? This kind of creative mischief, which short-circuits the student's most strenuous attempts to identify spirituality with a specific belief or lifestyle or person, is part of the teacher's job description.

When I was little, I read a story about a man who follows a rainbow into the woods and finds a leprechaun's pot of gold. It's too heavy to carry, so he buries it at the foot of a tree and goes off for a wheelbarrow. First, though, he ties a ribbon around the tree so he can tell it from the thousands of others, and makes the leprechaun promise not to take the ribbon off. When he returns, he finds that the leprechaun has kept his promise—but has tied ribbons around all the other trees. The teacher is that sort of trickster, except that his trickery forces us to keep digging till we discover that the treasure of enlightenment is buried under *every* tree. OM MANI PADME HUNG, the jewel is in the lotus, says the mantra of transcendental wisdom: existence, in its infinite variety, is like a profusion of blooming lotuses, each one containing the precious jewel of boundless happiness. The treasure we sought over here or over there is everywhere. Pay attention.

Body Snatchers offers several shrewd insights into this drama of conformity, repression, and freedom. The replicant bodies, when they first emerge from the seedpods, are perfectly smooth, with "no details, no character, no lines," not even fingerprints. This smoothness suggests our intuitive feeling that there *should* be some such process of being born again, of entering the kingdom of heaven by re-creating ourselves with the tabula rasa innocence of little children. The appeal of cults and creeds that promise such a rebirth by wiping out our personalities is understandable. In fact, as we gradually gain clearer cognition of the simplicity of just being, we *are* born again . . . and again and again, in the pristine freshness of each moment. What we *are*—changeless, formless being, sublime emptiness—is perpetually blank and innocent, infinitely smooth. (This is represented in the descriptions of such deities as Lord Rama, one of the most popular Hindu incarnations of our ultimate identity, who is depicted in the *Ramayana* as having cool, soft skin "so smooth even dust would not cling to him.")

At the same time, the manifest *expression* of what we are— the changing realm of form, which includes all action and reaction, history and personality—will always be full of bumps and wrinkles. But that's fine. We can scribble as wildly as we like on the tabula, and it remains rasa underneath. There's no need to reduce life, or ourselves, to sterile AstroTurf regularity. In its crazy, messy imperfection, it's already perfect. In its fierce asymmetry, life is all Chartres Cathedral, with its accidentally, gloriously mismatched spires.

> There is a crack in everything
> That's how the light gets in.
> —LEONARD COHEN,
> "Anthem"

This applies to our teachers as well. After I developed some mild dyslexia in my mid-forties, I became a better English teacher, more understanding of what my students were struggling with, more compassionate. By extrapolation, I suspect that the very greatest, most compassionate teachers, the Buddhas and Christs, were not superperfect but had flaws that helped them understand and connect with the humans they taught.

The potential for confusion about these matters increases the moment we become involved with any "spiritual organization"—which, like "jumbo shrimp," is an oxymoron. While authentic spiritual experience opens us to the untrammeled freedom and autonomy of our own awareness, organizations require rules and doctrines to hold themselves together—a tricky balancing act. A joke making the round of spiritual organizations goes like this: One day God and the Devil are walking down a road, when God stops in his tracks, bends over, and picks up a brilliant, gemlike object. "My God!" he says (or words to that effect). "That's the most beautiful thing I've ever seen!"

"What is it?" asks the Devil.

"It's Truth," says God.

"Oh, good," says the Devil. "Give me that—I'll organize it."

I have a theory that every spiritual organization, no matter what the time or place, has the same standard cast of characters. Somebody has to be Jesus, the charismatic, visionary storyteller. Somebody, usually many people, have to be Peter, who compensates for his doubt and wavering commitment by becoming a stalwart, rocklike soldier for the cause. Somebody is always Mary Magdalene, the would-be guru-groupie.* And somebody has to be Paul, the brilliant, tormented organizer and

---

* Yes, I know, this is not historically accurate—Mary got a bum rap—but it's psychologically accurate.

PR man, who takes the message global while the senior disciples complain that, in doing so, he has fatally distorted it, turning the founder's living visions into calcified doctrines and systems. Because most visionaries are notoriously lacking in administrative skills, over time Paul prevails.

Body Snatchers reflects how organizations, at their worst, enforce conformity and repression, keeping their members on the program. Dr. Kauffman, the skeptical psychiatrist whom Miles calls in for advice when he first starts to add up the evidence that people are vegging out, eventually ends up (of course) being a shill for the pod people. Through most of the film he smugly explains it all away, convincing Miles to distrust what he's seen with his own eyes. One of my first spiritual teachers told me, "Never let anyone talk you out of your own experience." But spiritual organizations frequently employ commissars of explanation who do just that, whether it's the nuns in Catholic school explaining that all the sincere, unselfish non-Catholics you see are bad enough to go to hell, or meditation teachers explaining that any doubts you might have about the guru's doctrine are "just some unstressing."

The film also shows how the sense of uncertainty and dislocation that frequently draws people to spiritual practice in the first place can also make them prey to manipulation. Both Miles and Becky are divorced, which in 1950s mid-America makes them outsiders, self-doubting and guilt-ridden over their neglect of conventional family and social roles. Becky starts to suspect that her father is a replicant, but, recently returned from some vaguely racy adventuring in England, she says, "I felt something was wrong, but I thought it was me because I'd been away for so long." And because spiritual booms usually take place in eras of disorienting change (the crumbling of the elaborate Vedic system of caste and sacrifice in the Buddha's time, the industrialization and commercialization of America in the early nineteenth century, the political and cultural upheaval of the 1960s), it's hard to know what to believe:

BECKY: Where do they [the pods] come from?
MILES: So much has been discovered these past few years, anything is possible.

But the film is at its spookiest in its depiction of the evangelistic impulse. Everyone must follow the Way, including one's own children. Eavesdropping on a nighttime cell meeting in a suburban living room, Miles hears: "Is the baby asleep yet, Sally?" "Not yet, but she will be soon, and there'll be no more tears." Why must the pod people convert everyone? Why can't they coexist with a minority of skeptics? (Why can't we all just get along?) It's an unspoken assumption that they can't. The answer, I think, lies in the psychology of evangelism. When you've found something you consider sublimely good, there's nothing inherently evil about wanting to share it. But with just a subtle twist, evangelism becomes a form of aggression meant to shore up your own shaky faith, and every unconverted infidel is a threat.

You've probably seen the Mormon missionaries who canvass neighborhoods in, apparently, every town in the world; there's always a pair of them, on foot, always male and about nineteen years old, in slacks and short-sleeved white shirts with plain dark ties, sometimes with a bicycle or a little backpack. They're doing mandatory service. Church officials acknowledge that, while these young men rarely convert anyone, that's beside the point—what they're doing is converting themselves.

I KNOW A LITTLE about this.

Early in my spiritual career I got involved in Transcendental Meditation, which was energetically propagated throughout the world by Maharishi Mahesh Yogi, the tiny, long-haired, white-robed teacher from India who became a cultural fixture when the Beatles took up with him. TM gained a big following because it worked. It's a simple, easily learned technique that in most people quickly induces a deep state of inner tranquillity, the vital first element in awareness training. It's not so strong on cultivating the second element, the perception of the essential nondifference of the tranquil inner and the changing outer. My friend Bob recently visited me; he had just finished a TM session and was basking in mellowness when a particularly loud, jarring telephone went off just behind his head. "There goes my meditation," he grumbled. He has not yet seen that the ringing phone *is* his meditation. (In some forms of Buddhist practice the teacher will occasionally give a loud, unexpected shout in the middle of a session so that no one gets to cling to such one-sided quietism.)

But for me as for many young people in the late '60s, Maharishi provided the bridge from the psychedelic phase of the journey to the meditative phase; the rite of passage was a mandatory fifteen-day drying-out period. Many of us became so enthusiastic that we cut our hair and went on months-long residential programs to become TM teachers.

Maharishi had a very distinctive way of speaking. When beginning a lecture or moving on to a new topic, he usually started with "So . . . ," followed by a pregnant pause and a smile of glowing anticipation. As he spoke, his hands moved in graceful and almost constant illustration of his thoughts, and when he wanted to express the idea of "et cetera" he would wave one hand in a sort of rolling motion from the wrist and say "like that, like that." Soon young TM teachers everywhere were starting lectures with a grinning "So" and waving their hands "like that, like that" whenever they were at a loss for words.

But it's easy to fall into that sort of thing with a charismatic guru. The first time I saw Maharishi, onstage in an auditorium in Squaw Valley, California, in 1968, the thought that immediately flashed across my mind was, "He's not real. He's a hologram—he's made out of light." In fact, as I found out in auditorium after auditorium over the next several years in the U.S., Spain, Italy, and Switzerland, he filled the whole room with an intense white light that bathed everything and everyone in the place. And somehow, rather than falling off as the square of the distance like physical light, this light seemed only to grow more intense in bigger rooms with more people. Meanwhile, up front—usually sitting on a gold couch, surrounded by elaborate flower arrangements, under a picture of his guru—Maharishi would be giving a lecture that was witty, charming, and, in its analysis of the nature and process of enlightenment, profound.

But over time I began to find certain elements of Maharishi's lectures troubling. I began to note how shockingly provincial some of his comments were, as when he expressed surprise that a group of Africans he had met with turned out to be intelligent, when "they don't *look* to be intelligent." And I found that what he had done most brilliantly in his early days—laying out the enlightenment path in simple, commonsense, nonsectarian language—was gradually giving way to a jargon concocted of Hindu doctrine and dubious interpretations of modern science. Eventually he started placing incomprehensible full-page ads in national magazines, using superstring physics to demonstrate why TM was "one solution to all problems."

This "one solution" idea was particularly dicey. For some people it became license to ignore glaring personal problems. I remember Maharishi lecturing on how TM creates "perfect health," frequently interrupted by his hacking bronchial cough. None of the earnest acolytes in the audience, me included, inquired about the contradiction. In part this was because the atmosphere was being set by a contingent of transcendental pod people—"bliss ninnies," some of us called them. They never lost their faint smile, they spoke very softly with the sort of raised-eyebrow inflection and air of mild amusement that implied that they *knew*, they were constantly standing up in the lecture hall to read their flowery poems of praise for the guru, and there always seemed to be a gaggle of them, female, who managed to elbow their way (smiling blissfully the whole time) into the front row, where they sat and *cooed* rapturously at everything Maharishi said.

There was also a kind of spiritual smugness that, to some degree, infected most of us. I remember being in L.A. one night in the early '70s with my friend Ginzburg. We were fresh from a retreat with Maharishi in Italy, glowing with transcendental self-assurance, and we met a girl who was involved in a different spiritual practice. She asked if we had ever heard of it. "No," said Ginzburg, "but if you'll describe it I can tell you what's wrong with it." I wouldn't have put it so bluntly, but that's pretty much the way I felt.

Maharishi, by then, had hatched a grand evangelistic vision, something he called the World Plan, complete with elaborate maps and posters in his favorite pastel-and-gold color scheme, showing how 350 meditation centers would be established, spinning off x many sub-centers and training y many meditators, so that in a few years the atmosphere of the whole world would be shifted, ushering in an age of global peace and prosperity. I think he was that rarity, Jesus and Paul, the visionary and the PR huckster, rolled into one.

What made these pleasant dreams so appealing is that, in essence, Maharishi had it right. The world *does* need enlightenment. The intractable outer problems of war and poverty *do* have their roots in inner ignorance. But the grander Maharishi's schemes became, the more they tended to collapse under their own weight. Even at that starry-eyed time, I could see that the phrase "World Plan," with its Third Reich overtones, was going to be a turnoff. And as the organization grew, it required ever bigger infusions of cash to keep it alive; by the time I quit, the instruction fee had risen from $35 to a couple of thousand, and Maharishi had surrounded himself with yes men and bliss ninnies, purging his inner circle of anyone who might point out that this marketing strategy was doomed.

One night, in a hotel conference room in Weggis, Switzerland, I sat in on a meeting Maharishi was having with some of his staff, drafting some new TM literature. When he dictated a sentence that was patently false, someone protested. Maharishi chuckled: "The lies of the enlightened are pearls of wisdom for the ignorant." What did that mean? That there are many levels of reality? That the dazzling light of realization washes away a lot of quibbling details? Or that once again, for the billionth time in history, spiritual hubris was justifying amorality? What other things had he lied about? On the other hand, maybe Maharishi was just messing with our heads, which is also part of the teacher's job description—shaking up the rigid concepts that keep the students bound. What did it mean? I chewed on that one for a long time, and I'm still chewing.

Maharishi's way of generating teachers for his World Plan was similarly double-edged, both inspired and hopeless. As he went from training dozens of teachers to thousands, the instructional methods became more tightly regulated. Eventually the trainees did nothing but memorize scripts, for every lecture or teaching they would ever give. Some procedures had doses of meditation timed to the second, with numbered and lettered responses to recite for any experience the meditator might report, like an elaborate flow chart. In the short run this was brilliant. It enabled Maharishi to take a bunch of hippies like me off the street, give us haircuts and neckties till we looked not unlike Mormon missionaries, and turn us into an army of meditation teachers that brought a life-changing technique to thousands of people. But in the long run, the public kept hearing the same script with the same robotic delivery and found it scary. They had the sense to recognize pod people when they saw them. Even worse was what this did to the deliverers of the lines, making them afraid to think their own thoughts, to generate their own sentences out of the freshness of their own experience.

THE LAST TWENTY MINUTES of *Invasion of the Body Snatchers* is about running. With the pods controlling the whole town, including the police and the phone lines, Miles and Becky literally run for the hills, pursued by a mob of emotionless replicants, and take shelter in an abandoned mine. In a particularly exciting shot, they huddle together in a hole in the floor of the mine, which is covered loosely by a couple of boards. The camera looks up through the crack between the boards as the mob runs across them, just inches above the protagonists' heads.

My own running episode took place in Seelisberg, Switzerland, at the TM movement's then international headquarters, an isolated resort hotel overlooking Lake Lucerne. My friend Stephen and I had been recruited there to help with a project in the publications department. We had been in the middle of a course with Maharishi in Interlaken, and Stephen, who had just gotten engaged, was especially reluctant to leave his fiancée. Nevertheless, we got into the car that had come for us from Seelisberg and passed a very pleasant couple of weeks there, meditating, editing copy, and walking beside the glorious vista of the mountains and the lake. We ate in the dining room along with the international staff, who were very serious customers. This was the land of the zombies. Not that we minded—it was kind of fun egging these guys on. We would spend lunchtime singing doo-wop over our rice and zucchini, trying to get the pod people, many of whom were Germans, to help us fill in the harmonies. They were not amused. (I suspect that the low-protein diet helps keep disciples passive; they don't have the energy to rebel.)

One day, though, sitting in our little office, we realized that the copy coming across our desks was no longer for our project but for other TM publications. We asked the chief editor, who acknowledged that the project was done, but we were doing such nice work that it had been assumed that we wouldn't mind staying on. . . . That's when we realized that if we didn't get right out of there we would turn into lifers, Stephen would never marry his fiancée, and we'd live out our days staring blankly at a plate of zucchini. There was one car going back to Interlaken that day, and it was leaving in fifteen minutes. We threw our stuff into our suitcases and literally ran to catch the car as it was pulling out of the hotel driveway. Right at our ankles were four or five zomboid staffers, urging us to stay on.

I taught TM for several more years, but all that time I was, in a sense, running to catch the car. Maharishi's style was growing steadily more grandiose. He claimed to teach people to levitate, started an Age of Enlightenment TV station with guys in white silk suits expressionlessly reading good news only, and spent several years trying to build an enlightenment theme park. He declared that he could create heaven on earth and then bitterly denounced the heads of state who wouldn't give him the millions of dollars he needed to do it. At the same time, his organization grew even more regimented. At one point he issued a statement to all TM teachers, saying that his work was being undermined by doubters and anyone who had doubts should quit. Well, I have doubts about everything, including whether I'm sitting here typing these words. I finally took Maharishi at his word and bailed.

A few years ago I came across a box in my basement. I sat at the foot of the stairs in the front foyer, opened it up, and found notebooks, filled with near-verbatim notes from all the retreats and courses I had ever attended with Maharishi, on everything from Vedic literature to teaching procedures to superstring physics. Notebook after notebook, in my most careful handwriting, far neater than anything I'm capable of today, with an occasional ecstatic little poem of joy and devotion scribbled in the margins. When my wife walked into the room she found me crying. I looked up and said, "I was a good disciple."

WHAT'S THE MORAL of the story? I guess it's "Stay awake." That's what Jesus tells the disciples at Gethsemane the night before the Crucifixion, but they can't do it—staying awake is hard. It's also what Miles tells Becky in the mine. They've been up all night, knowing the pod people will snatch their bodies the moment they fall asleep. All legitimate spiritual practices, teachers, books, organizations, like that, like that, have the purpose of helping us wake into the clarity and simplicity and freedom of existence itself. But, again, with just a subtle twist the very means of awakening can become something that puts us more deeply to sleep. Even out of sheer familiarity and repetition, the text or prayer or mantra that was once a clarion call to realization makes our eyes glaze over.

We can't really blame it on the church or the guru; we choose it ourselves. Freedom is scary, or at least it *looks* scary, so when dharma comes into our lives and threatens us with freedom, we find ways to turn it into another form of bondage. Usually it happens incrementally, as in the old saw about cooking live frogs—if you put them in hot water they jump out of the pot, but if you use cool water and turn the heat up gradually they relax and go right along with the program. As Miles tells Becky:

> In my practice I've seen how people have allowed their humanity to drain away. Only it happened slowly instead of all at once. They didn't seem to mind. . . . Only when we have to fight to stay

human do we realize how precious it is to us, how dear.

Indirectly, I think Maharishi taught me about humanness by making me fight for it.

Miles leaves the cave to find the source of what sounds like hopeful, spiritual music coming from somewhere over the next hill, but it turns out to be the radio of a truck picking up seedpods en masse from a huge greenhouse. When he returns he kisses Becky, and in that terrifying moment he feels the deadness of her kiss and knows that she has fallen asleep. "He's in here! He's in here! Get him! Get him!" she yells, and the mob again takes up the chase.

The end of the film—as Siegel shot it—is truly disturbing. As night falls, Miles escapes to the highway, where, looking by now like a crazy, disheveled prophet, he bangs on car windows, trying to stop the drivers and warn them of the invasion. He jumps onto the back of an interstate truck but sees, to his horror, that it's full of pods. In the final shot he yells into the camera, "They're here already! You're next! You're next! You're next!" This was too much for test audiences, and the studio tacked on a lame wraparound plot in which Miles is hauled into a hospital as a mental case and tells the whole story in a flashback. When a sympathetic doctor finally believes him and mobilizes the cops, everything's supposed to be okeydokey. Of course this undercuts the film's delicious paranoia; in the very last, supposedly reassuring, line, the doctor calls the FBI— headed, remember, by Hoover of the AstroTurf lawn. He probably *was* a replicant.

I'm not here as a wild-eyed prophet, yelling that you're next, although there are plenty of supposed spiritual leaders out there who have done far more harm and far less good to their sleepwalking acolytes than Maharishi, from sociopathic self-styled gurus to child-molesting priests. The spiritual path, like any path of adventure, is risky, but there are other ways to turn yourself into a vegetable, some as easy as clicking on the TV or listening uncritically to politicians, and *they* don't offer even the possibility of enlightenment. Body snatchers are everywhere. They're very active in high school, for instance, where the most important subject everyone takes, the one not listed in the curriculum guide, is Socialization 101. That's where we learn how heartily to laugh, how openly to display our fears and lusts, and how far from the norm our thoughts may stray before we're unacceptably weird. We learn secondhand feelings from one another and from TV till we wouldn't recognize a spontaneous feeling if it jumped us in an alleyway.

Although it's been a couple of decades since I've seen Maharishi, I'm still learning things from him, whether or not they're lessons he intended. I'm still faithful to the ideal that first drew me to him—that of bringing simple tools of enlightenment, in straightforward language and without a lot of cultural baggage, to large numbers of people. I think it's him that moved, not me. But perspective in these matters is tricky. Anytime you try to evaluate the awareness or integrity of another, you're doing it through the lens of your own awareness and integrity, which is relative—there's no solid ground to stand on.

I also think that ultimately you follow the inner teacher, which is the *non*relative aspect of your awareness, its skylike nature, of which all outer teachers are projections, approximations. When you decide some outer teacher has enlightened qualities, or if later you revise your view, what are you comparing him to but the quality of enlightenment you recognize within yourself? This is what's called, in Tibetan tradition, the Vajra Guru: the pure, clear, brilliant, indestructible, diamond-like teacher that is beyond all qualities and whose mantra is OM AH HUNG BENZA GURU PEMA SIDDHI HUNG—diamond teacher residing in the lotus of my heart, enlighten me!

These days there are a handful of teachers whose pictures I

keep on the small shrine in my meditation room, Maharishi's included. Not wanting to become, as Ram Dass puts it, a collector of clay feet, I don't focus on their foibles. I feel deep gratitude and love for them all, but I suspect that the intense kind of relationship I had with Maharishi happens only once in a lifetime, and I've used mine up. One of the valuable things I gained from the experience is a high level of sales resistance. I'm not bowled over by every guy who comes along with a jim-dandy spiritual flashlight—I was with a guy who was a million-candlepower floodlight and I walked away.

I still believe that my first impression was right, that he was made out of light. We all are, the universe is, but some people, by being *consciously* so, may manifest that luminosity in an extravivid way that can inspire others to find it in themselves. I'm pretty sure he was one such. But how can someone so luminous also be so flawed? Perhaps that's his final lesson to me. The blazing, omniradiant light of enlightenment, unlike physical light, isn't limited to straight lines; it can travel even through twisted vessels like him, like me, like you. Despite our best efforts to make ourselves and our teachers smoothed-out super-beings, pod people without any fingerprints, we're only human.

FISTFUL OF DOLLARS
(1964)

SPAGHETTI SAMURAI

A soft answer turneth away wrath.

—PROVERBS 15:1

JIMMY: So, this Joe, is he cool?
PINKY: My motherfucker is so cool, when he goes to bed, sheep count him.

—*HEIST*

I ONCE SPENT A DAY BIKING THROUGH THE COUNTRYSIDE just north of Amsterdam. The Dutch call it Waterland, and it's a storybook-lovely region of dikes and canals, houseboats and villages, spongy green fields and grazing cows, all bathed in moist, hazy sunlight. On the banks of the narrow canals that edge the fields, I noticed an occasional blue heron on patrol, standing perfectly still, its gaze fixed calmly on the water, waiting for dinner to surface. Without an ounce of perceptible tension, these birds, it appeared, could stand that way forever—thin and long-legged, they looked like impassive sticks of wood planted in the ground. They outwaited me. I never saw one catch anything, but had to imagine the suddenness with which its long neck would dart out and the fish would disappear into its beak.

Young Clint Eastwood in *Fistful of Dollars* reminds me of those herons, with his lanky, almost gawky build, his plume of hair (which vaguely resembles their crests), but especially his unblinking stillness. He seems equally content to stand motionless all day or to suddenly draw his gun and, without any apparent change in heart rate, pick off four men as they're still struggling to get theirs out of their holsters. The simplest explanation is that he's a sociopath, a cold-blooded killer, and films that fetishize the exploits of such people are merely a pornography of violence.

There's some truth to that. But this character, and the genre to which this film gave rise, resonate too powerfully in our consciousness for that to be the whole story. We respond to the promise of coolness in the heat of conflict. We face large and small conflicts every day, and we long not only to prevail but to prevail through the elegant skill that arises from undisturbed inner tranquillity—stillness in action. If we must do battle, we want to be enlightened warriors. The Eastwood persona, and the spaghetti westerns in which it was born, can show us how.

THE FIRST OF SERGIO LEONE'S stylized, cut-rate westerns (shot for $200,000 in Spain by Italians, with an American star and a pan-European cast), *Fistful of Dollars* features Eastwood as a gunman-for-hire who kicks off the action by provoking that confrontation with the four men, knowing he can outdraw them. (As he strides toward them down the dusty main street of the Mexican desert town, he pauses before the coffin maker's workshop to lightheartedly order their coffins. Big fun.) From there things only get more grisly, with murder by arson, ambush, crushing, machine gun massacre, and more. In keeping with the cinematic practice of the time, the killings are weirdly antiseptic, with no limbs flying and no blood splattering, yet they paved the way for *The Wild Bunch*, the film that finally gave us the explicit gore from which there was no turning back.

When *Dollars* was shot in 1963–64, the western was essentially dead. Leone revived it by taking a revisionist approach, steeped in a European's love-hate relationship with America. He felt deep ambivalence toward the naive heroism of the earlier westerns, where unreflective good guys dispatched Indians and bad guys as if earning merit badges. Leone's West has no such Boy Scouts, but men driven by greed, lust, revenge, and casual sadism. (Women are incidental except as objects of lust.) Using the traditional elements, he took a new angle, even literally: noting how westerns had usually shown horses in noble, photogenic profile, he made a point of shooting them from behind, "up their asses" as he put it.

In need of a story that blurred the categories of good and bad guys, Leone borrowed—actually ripped off—his plot from Akira Kurosawa's action comedy *Yojimbo*, about a lone, unemployed samurai (the great Toshiro Mifune) who wanders into a town overrun by two rival gangs of gamblers and deftly plays them off against each other. Disdaining the buckaroo optimism of the usual western music, Leone collaborated with composer Ennio Morricone, whose haunting themes suffuse the action with a stark fatalism. And Leone shunned the frenzy of accelerating action, the rumbling stagecoaches and whooping, war-painted Indians that had brought the traditional western to its climax. Instead, Leone froze time. Taking his cue from Rembrandt's psychologically probing portraits, he suspended action at its height, in extreme close-ups. The images we retain from his films are not long shots of fights and chases but Eastwood's or Lee Van Cleef's narrowed eyes, spread gigantically across the screen.

The spaghetti western became part of the culture wars of the '60s, widely condemned as brutal and sadistic. But for all its stylization, it's more honest and humanistic than the "clean" westerns that now crowd the Family Channel's schedule, where, when a man is shot, he clutches his breast, says a few wise words, and peacefully goes to sleep. Leone makes us witness the real pain that violence inflicts on real people, even the ones we've judged as bad. We see this at the end of *Dollars*, when Eastwood's character shoots his nemesis, Ramón Rojo, who staggers and reels, blood (finally) streaming from his mouth, the desert sun spinning as we see through his eyes. A few moments earlier, as the two face off, Morricone plays a solemn Mexican trumpet dirge rather than a triumphal theme, again inducing us to empathize with the doomed victim.

> [The Master] enters a battle gravely,
> with sorrow and with great compassion,
> as if he were attending a funeral.
> —TAO TE CHING*

THIS REINVENTED WESTERN needed a reinvented hero. The figure of the *ronin*, the wandering, masterless samurai of *Yojimbo*, gave Leone the ambivalent protagonist he required, The Man with No Name, who, like us, is cut adrift from the old authority structure. Here The Man is still slightly unripe; in later films, Eastwood's silence seems deeper and realer, less in need of being propped up by Leone's melodramatic style. Leone overstates his hero's understatement. Kurosawa understates it; he shows that being no one is no big deal—there's nothing to it. It's there in Mifune's weightless, catlike walk, in his gentle amusement with himself and everyone else. Kurosawa's style is Japanese haiku, Leone's is Italian grand opera meets American comic book. (A certain adolescent silliness clings to the proceedings.) There's a Zen story about a monk whose state of enlightenment is so dazzling that, wherever he goes, flower blossoms rain down out of the heavens. One day he meets a master who sees this marvel and scolds him for it. The monk goes back to the woods for a few more years of meditation, then

---

* All Tao Te Ching quotations in this chapter are from Stephen Mitchell, *Tao Te Ching*, Harper & Row, 1988.

returns without the blossoms. "Good," says the master. "Your enlightenment was sticking out like a sore-thumb." Here Leone gives us the sore-thumb version of the enlightened warrior, but that's probably what we needed in 1964.

Fistful of Dollars also gave birth to the Eastwood icon, and its many later incarnations as Dirty Harry, Josey Wales, Will Munny, and the rest. With its powerful impact on our sense of how to carry oneself skillfully in a dangerous, uncertain world, that icon is, at root, transplanted samurai energy. After the scrubbed and shaven, immaculately outfitted, white-hatted traditional western heroes, Eastwood—with his black jeans, scruffy beard, rough poncho worn at a haphazard angle, battered brown hat (not black, not white), and cigarillo clenched in his teeth—was something new.*

His ambivalent appearance underscored his moral ambivalence. With lucky timing, a plagiarism lawsuit filed by Kurosawa delayed the film's release till 1967, when the Vietnam War had shattered our Cold War moral clarity and left us wondering whether we were still good guys—and, if not, how we could at least find an honorable path through the wreckage. No longer squeaky-clean John Waynes, we looked to the scruffy Clint to see whether redemption was still possible. The not entirely convincing answer is yes. Amid the amoral gang warfare and profiteering, The Man with No Name finds a moral cause, eventually freeing Ramón's sex slave Marisol and reuniting her with her husband and child.

Eastwood's outsider stance and his spare minimalism of voice and gesture also echo the cool California jazz that was

---

* He is said to have assembled the outfit himself by browsing L.A. shops, but the image also owes much to *Yojimbo*. The poncho appears to have been suggested by Toshiro Mifune's kimono, and the cigarillo derives from a toothpick Mifune chews in an early scene. Mifune's character is also the source of Eastwood's stubbly chin and his habit of scratching it in droll thoughtfulness.

making its way through the nightclubs during his early days playing piano in Oakland. When he speaks his few words, his clear, understated tenor is the vocal equivalent of a pared-down, vibratoless Chet Baker trumpet solo; like the best musicians, Eastwood finds as much intensity in *pianissimo* as others do in *fortissimo*. That coolness, so well-suited to the eye-of-the-storm placidity of the Zen warrior, is enhanced by another lucky accident. Because Leone, along with most of his cast and crew, didn't speak English, Eastwood seems isolated, disconnected from everyone else—which, in fact, he was throughout the shoot. He's detached from the action, in the film's world but not of it.

As The Man with No Name, Eastwood suggests anatta, the state of no-self. (The only person in town who thinks he knows The Man's name—he has somehow decided it's Joe—is the film's personification of death, the crinkly old troll of a coffin maker, whose business is booming. Even if you're a fearsome samurai, death ultimately has your number: he knows you're just another Joe.) With no history or connections—The Man has no fixed enemies or friends, no sidekicks or sweethearts—he's a walking embodiment of transcendence.

There's a joke in Buddhist circles: "Don't just do something, stand there!" Don Siegel, who later directed Eastwood in five films, once observed that people underestimate him because they don't realize that what he does best—nothing—is the hardest thing in the world to do, especially on camera. In 1963 Eastwood was a second-string TV actor who, Leone worried, was too "light" for the role; he hired him only after more macho types like Charles Bronson had passed. But Eastwood, who took the job for $15,000, turned out to be the right man for Leone's emerging style, with its merciless close-ups. In these long moments of silence, like a heron on the bank of a canal, he's doing nothing and *he's OK* with doing nothing. That's a very precise definition of meditation, and bringing the quality of meditative nonaction to films of action may be Eastwood's most important achievement. It could only have been done by someone for whom this quality is authentic.

> In real life, Clint is slow, calm, rather like a cat.
> During the shooting he does what he has to do,
> then sits down in a corner and goes to sleep
> immediately, until he is needed again.
> —SERGIO LEONE

In fact, following his natural proclivity, Eastwood received formal meditation training a few years after shooting *Dollars*, and at last report still practices faithfully.

THE FILM'S MICROCOSM of a damaged world is the pueblo of San Miguel. As The Man with No Name rides in on his mule (again, a deliberate step funkier than the horse of the '50s western hero), the dusty streets are deserted, with cowering townspeople peeking out through shuttered windows and doors—the result, he soon learns, of ongoing warfare between the Rojos and the Baxters, two rival gangs that traffic in guns and liquor. At last another rider comes the other way, but with his eyes closed—dead, we suddenly realize, as we see the ADIOS, AMIGO sign pinned to his back. (In *Yojimbo*, the corresponding omen is a dog, happily trotting along with a human hand in its jaws.) The town bell ringer cheerfully explains that here in San Miguel everyone winds up either rich or dead. Rich aggressor or dead victim, Rojo gang or Baxter gang—there seems to be no middle path through the violence.

Yet the middle is where The Man goes, first befriending the proprietor of the local cantina and then ascending with him to an upper balcony to survey the situation, explaining, "Things always look different from higher up." This is a basic rule of enlightened coping in an unenlightened world: to avoid getting caught up in black/white, either/or polarization, ascend to a higher level of awareness and gain a clearer, more dispassionate view. We can see people trapped in polarization everywhere, from Iraq to our own office politics and family dynamics. When two kids squabble over a toy, each thinks that he's absolutely right and the conflict is insoluble. An adult, looking at things from higher up, can show them how the problem can be solved by sharing the toy or taking turns. But who will show *us*? We need to work out our own methods of getting higher: having drinks with the business rival, laughing in the face of disaster. From higher up, things are more smoothed out; big hills are not so big, insurmountable obstacles have ways around them.

Wayne Gretzky, generally considered the greatest player in the history of ice hockey, was, like Eastwood, slender and cool in a world of sweating, hulking thugs. When a team of doctors examined him, looking for clues to his extraordinary talent, they discovered that, even under stress, his heart rate remained unusually low: his coolness had a physiological reality. And he could coolly dodge his way through the thugs without getting hit, almost magically placing himself where the puck was instead of where they were. He developed that ability by adopting a view "from higher up": as a young fan, he had watched game after game on TV, charting the puck's motion on a piece of paper, studying the places where it tended to come to rest under various circumstances.

The Man's walk up the stairs suggests that recourse to the vertical plane always opens up new, liberative, unpolarized possibilities. He looks down from the balcony and, with the tavern keeper as his guide, sees members of the two gangs busy with horses and contraband at opposite ends of the town's main street. Laying out the film's basic geometry, The Man says, "Baxters over there, Rojos there, me right in the middle." And for the next hour and a half he works that geometry, hiring himself out first to one gang, then the other, piling up dollars as he plays the two polarized ends against one another and dodges the crossfire.

In taking on both gangs single-handed, he must turn his adversaries' coarse violence against itself. His tactics recall those of aikido, the Japanese martial art whose name literally means "the way of harmonizing with energy": that is, harmonizing with the aggressor's force and using it to neutralize him. Because of its radically nonconfrontational nature, aikido was not accepted as a true martial art when it was introduced in Japan in the 1940s. Eventually it gained respect, and its founder, Morihei Ueshiba (known as O Sensei, "Great Teacher"), came to be regarded as the premier martial artist of his era. Like this film, aikido has roots in the samurai tradition. It derives many of its techniques from the movement of the sword; and the *hakama*, the dark split skirt that hid the samurai's footwork, is worn by present-day *aikidoka*, creating a graceful swirling effect that emphasizes the circularity of their movements. I've had the good fortune to practice aikido for some years under Rick Stickles Sensei, a no-nonsense Jersey guy who, like me, came up in the '60s, but was studying intensely with O Sensei's direct students while I was hanging out with yogis and lamas.

Aikido has one fundamental principle: *Blend.* Don't oppose— join the direction of the attack. Thus The Man never directly confronts either of the gangs but joins, quits, and rejoins them, subtly redirecting their trajectories till they destroy themselves. This tenet is so important that most aikido classes start with practice of *tenkan,* a simple but powerful exercise in which the student's wrist is grabbed by an attacker. This grab represents all aggressive encounters, from kitchen spats to world wars. The untrained reaction would be to counterattack or try to run away. Tenkan introduces a third possibility: simply pivot to stand beside the attacker, facing the same direction, blending with him.

Tenkan is the basis of all other aikido techniques, so that, for example, when a punch is thrown I can pivot to avoid being hit, join the direction of the punch, and use its energy to help the attacker throw himself. This blending principle has many real-life applications. Once while chatting in the dressing room with my friend Mike, we discovered that we both had the same trick for successful marriage: take a walk together every day. But Mike pointed out *how* it works. As you walk along and discuss whatever's on your mind, you're facing the same way: everything gets hashed out in a context that's literally non-confrontational. Nonconfrontation is especially effective when you're dealing with people who are convinced they're right—when, for example, you're in a committee meeting and an excited consensus is growing around some really dumb idea. If you frontally oppose it, everyone will dig in for a fight. Instead, you can Yes them: jump on the bandwagon and, once aboard, start subtly *leaning* till it safely derails itself somewhere off in the woods.

AFTER SEEING SOME of The Man's fancy work with a pistol, the film's baddest bad guy sets us up for another aikido lesson by stating the conventional might-makes-right view:

> RAMÓN: When a man with a .45 meets a man with a rifle, the man with the pistol will be a dead man. That's an old Mexican proverb, and it's true.

In aikido, right makes might. *The one who is attacked can always neutralize the attacker, regardless of size.* I've attacked ninety-five-pound women who have sent me sailing across the room. (O Sensei himself was just 5'2".) This is because every act of aggression places the aggressor in an intrinsically unstable position by creating a local disturbance in the equilibrium of the universe. So the one who is attacked, we might say, has the universe on his side. He merely needs to enlist its power, as manifested in the laws of physics, to defeat the attacker with his own force. The best offense is a good defense.

Yet another important principle is *Move from the center.* As a novice aikidoka, I kept struggling to execute throws, pushing or pulling with all my might, but if the attacker outsized me I couldn't budge him. The problem was precisely that I was pushing and pulling, trying to do it with my arms and upper body strength. Stickles Sensei would come around, gently place his hands on my straining shoulders, and say, "Drop your energy to the center." The moment I relaxed my shoulders and let the throw come from the *hara* (upper abdomen), it became almost effortless and the attacker went sailing. An indispensable convention of westerns is shooting from the hip. Despite being wildly unrealistic (no one can aim a gun that way), it looks really cool. But *why* should we find that cool? Because the action comes from the hara, which we intuitively recognize as the point of origin for calm, powerful, grounded action. Again, the onscreen epitome is Mifune in *Yojimbo,* where he's so centered that everything he does is completely cool, even, in one scene, casually picking his nose.

Without necessarily learning a martial art, you can practice this centeredness in ordinary activity. Think of the body as being something like a submarine, cruising through the waters of daily experience. The head, where we're usually convinced we live, is merely the periscope, a structure for collecting sensory information through the eyes, ears, nose, and tongue.

- Stand quietly with eyes open.

- Gently drop your sense of self from the head to the upper abdomen. Hear from the center, see from the center, feel from the center, as if the hara were one big multifunctional sense organ.

- Continue standing this way for a little while. You'll probably notice a subtle sense of balance and groundedness, a
  less constricted sense of being, almost a warm glow.

- Now walk around a bit, maintaining this centeredness.
  When we're in the head we tend to walk leaning forward,
  with shoulders slightly hunched. Instead, drop the shoulders, lean back a little, and walk from your center, as if
  you're being pulled along by an invisible string attached
  to your belt, letting everything else trail loosely behind.

- As you go through your day, drop your awareness to the
  center whenever you think of it. See, hear, feel, smell, taste
  your food, think your thoughts, experience your emotions
  from the center, and have a sense that your speech and actions originate from there as well.

- When you have to do something you find stressful—say,
  speaking before an audience—start by reestablishing this
  centeredness. Take a moment to breathe out, drop the
  sense of self to the hara, and fill the whole room with
  centered awareness. Then, within the context of that
  awareness, start to speak.

The sense of operating from the hara does have a physiological reality. Researchers have discovered that the digestive tract
contains what they call a "second brain"—the enteric nervous
system, two nexuses of some 100 billion brain cells (more than
are found in the spinal cord) that appear to mediate a certain
amount of experience and behavior without the participation of
the head brain. So when we talk about our "gut feeling" or "gut
reaction," that's not just an expression.

Of course, dropping the sense of self to the center is merely a
transitional phase on the way to dropping it completely, but it's

a big first step. This is one reason why it's common to start a meditation with some very full, deliberate breathing, exaggerating the pressure in the abdomen. Here's a meditative technique for segueing from the first step to the second in an even more direct way:

- Sit with eyes closed in a meditative position. Take a minute or two to let things settle naturally.

- Have a sense of the body as being something like a pyramid-shaped candle, with your head as the apex. Then imagine that the wick has been lit and the candle is melting down into itself, so that your head is gently dissolving into your center.

- When you feel as if your head is gone, allow the center to gradually melt outward into space, as if the candle itself is evaporating. When you feel as if the candle is gone, just rest in the space that remains.

BEING COOL AND CENTERED facilitates learning yet another principle: *Fall fluidly.*

> The hard and stiff will be broken.
> The soft and supple will prevail.
> —TAO TE CHING

In aikido, being thrown is actually a lot of fun. We humans have a heavy emotional investment in maintaining our two-footed verticality. But once you've learned to fall safely by going soft and relaxed rather than rigid, being thrown is a letting go into exhilarating freedom. For an instant, you're flying.

In life, falling is inevitable. We get comfortably planted and emotionally invested in our jobs, our relationships, our positions of power, our good health and youthful appearance, our opinions and beliefs. But, as the Buddha taught, it's all *anitya*, impermanence. Back in the committee meeting, the art of falling might entail recognizing that this time *your* ideas are the misguided ones, and gracefully giving in. Sooner or later we fall from all our cozy positions. At the time of death, we fall all at once from any we haven't lost already. But if we can relax and fall softly, we can minimize the damage and even enjoy the freedom of flight, the release from the narrow confines of the known into the wide expanse of the unknown.

This principle is dramatized near the end of the film, in The Man with No Name's final face-off with Ramón. Appearing in an extreme long shot at the far end of the town's wide main street (emerging like a phantom, in fact, from a dramatically swirling cloud of dynamite smoke), bareheaded and empty-handed, he goads Ramón to shoot at him with his cherished Winchester, reminding him of his earlier words, spoken while using a suit of armor for target practice: "When you want to kill a man you must shoot for his heart." Ramón shoots him, knocking him backward off his feet. But, in a film full of loud, violent impacts, The Man's dusty landing seems soft and strangely silent. A moment later he is back on his feet, slowly advancing on Ramón in a disconcerting zigzag path, prodding him again and again to shoot him in the heart, and getting up each time— till finally he throws back his poncho to reveal his armor, the homemade breastplate that has been deflecting the bullets.

Once more, the film's theme is expressed in its geometry, with Ramón standing upright, holding his ground and clutching his rifle, backed up by his four henchmen, while The Man advances toward him with his contrastingly fluid motion and his repeated falls. Here is the contest between our rigid adherence to our position (backed up, after all, by our friends) and our willingness to be fluid, to be repeatedly knocked out of our position and change course. Here also is the contest between the large and the small. Now within pistol range, The Man reminds the thoroughly unnerved Ramón, "When a man with a .45 meets a man with a rifle, you said the man with the pistol's a dead man. Let's see if that's true." Drawing his .45, he picks off all Ramón's henchmen and finally Ramón himself.

Nimble egg-eating mammals survive the lumbering dinosaurs; Drake and his smaller, more maneuverable flotilla whip the Spanish Armada; leaner, meaner corporations beat the corporate giants to market. Being smaller than your attacker can be an advantage. The principle is *Stay low*. The physics of aikido is largely based on keeping your knees bent and your hara lower than your attacker's. From that position you can stabilize your own position and control his. (This also works in wrestling, rugby, or any other sport where you take people down.) Earlier in the film, when The Man escapes from the clutches of the Rojo gang, who have discovered his stratagems and savagely beaten him, they run frantically through the town looking for him. He evades them by crouching under the wooden sidewalk, beneath their very footsteps. Our usual impulse in any confrontation is to try to dominate by somehow being bigger, taller, higher, than the others. This obtains not only in the human world: when a male dog pees he lifts his leg as high as he can to mark the rock or tree with a signal that says, This is a *big* dog's territory—back off. But, as we learn through life experience, carrying ourselves high also makes us a wobbly and conspicuous target.

> He who stands on tiptoe
> doesn't stand firm.
> —TAO TE CHING

In the committee meeting, this principle has many applications. By understanding that everyone else is marking the trees and trying to be the big dog, and by relinquishing your own need to do so, you gain tremendous power. When you're pretty sure you have the solution to the problem under discussion, never speak first. Let others elbow each other aside as they clamor to make the first and loudest noises. They're like bombastic politicians at a political convention; I once heard a news correspondent say, as the speeches droned on and on, "At this point everything has been said, but not everybody has said it yet." You have to give the blowhards room to blow hard. Once they've run out of steam (and perhaps had a chance to quietly notice the weaknesses of their own arguments), they're ready to hear your suggestion. This gives fresh meaning to Jesus' saying, "The first shall be last and the last shall be first." And when you make your statement, of course, do it modestly and respectfully, so as not to reignite any smoldering egos. In fact, having heard the others' statements, you may be able to join the direction of the attack and subtly redirect it by echoing some of their language and presenting your position as if it were just an elaboration of theirs.

> When the Master governs, the people
> are hardly aware that he exists. . . .
> When his work is done,
> the people say, "Amazing:
> we did it, all by ourselves!"
> —TAO TE CHING

MY SINGLE MOST profound aikido lesson consisted of one sentence, spoken from a staircase. I was in the *dojo* (practice hall), working on my *randori* (response to multiple attackers). As my three opponents rushed in, each trying to grab and immobilize me, I moved around the mat, pivoting and throwing them one after another. At least that's what I was trying to do. Instead, I kept getting stalled, hung up in grappling with each attacker. Stickles Sensei happened to be on his way up the stairs to the men's dressing room, and had paused to watch. He called out to me:
    "Relax at the moment of contact."

I hadn't noticed that I was physically and mentally tensing up each time I was grabbed. (Catch-22 here: we're too frozen to notice we're frozen.) But Stickles Sensei, with his trained teacher's eye, could see it from across the room. Mine was a natural reaction, just as it's natural for us to tense up at *any* moment of confrontation: with a work emergency, with a health problem, with an upset romantic partner, with the cop who pulls us over, with the drink or the drug we know we shouldn't take. But, natural as it may be, tension doesn't help. Ever. In fact, the more we tense up, the more rigid and clumsy our response becomes—like my randori.

As the next attacker grabbed me, I relaxed. No longer working against myself, I could threw him with a fraction of my previous effort. Suddenly, what had been hard became frictionlessly, hilariously easy. A few seconds later the next attacker was on me and my longtime habit of tensing reasserted itself, but again and again, as each attack came, Stickles Sensei called from the stairs, "Relax at the moment of contact," and I kept dropping back into that zone of fluidity and ease.

For most people, it takes years of practice to get to where your aikido—or, better yet, your life—all takes place within that zone, but it can be done.

> He who in action sees inaction and in inaction sees
> action is wise among men. He is united, he has
> accomplished all actions.
> —BHAGAVAD GITA 4:18

The equivalency of action and inaction may sound like abstract metaphysics, but an O Sensei—or a Willie Mays or Joe Montana, or a Fred Astaire or Allegra Kent, or an Emily Dickinson or Frank Sinatra—makes it visible. They make it look so easy. It took a lot of work to get there (as they say in aikido, "You have to go through the hard to get to the soft"), but at that highest level it *is* easy. For Louis Armstrong, it got so easy that he would scrunch up his face and bug out his eyes to make it look hard, so the audience felt they were getting their money's worth. Eastwood also, at his best, makes the equivalency of action and inaction visible, in the silence that suffuses even the most vigorous action. He prevails by relaxing at the moment of contact, while his enemies strut, sweat, and finally destroy themselves. "He is united"—he's got it together.

LOOKING DEEPER INTO the matter, we discover *why* relaxation is the most effective way to deal with conflict. In reality, there never *is* a conflict. Ultimately aikido is not really attainment of harmony by neutralizing the attack. It's perception of the larger harmony that is there all along—before, during, and after the attack. In moments of practice when you're in that zone, you perceive that you're not just the person who's throwing or the person being thrown. You are the whole process, the whole environment, whose components happen to include both of those persons. This nonduality is the highest level of nonviolence, because no violent act can be perpetrated where there is no duality of aggressor and victim. In our usual dualistic state we're like a hand that thinks another hand is violently striking it. One day we expand our view and realize that we're something larger— a person—whose components include two hands coming together in what we call clapping. (And yes, the transcendence of duality and violence calls for applause.)

This broadening of perspective is cultivated by another aikido principle: *Widen your gaze.* Part of the training is learning to allow the gaze to relax into an open, panoramic view that effortlessly takes in the whole room. This frees us from the usual tunnel vision that limits us to seeing the attacker's body, or the four inches of our wrist that have been grabbed. Wayne Gretzky was reputed to have uncommonly wide peripheral vision, but he said he was just paying attention. We all have wider vision than we realize, if we'll just use it. A good classroom teacher does this instinctively, so that as she's calling on one student or responding to another's question, she's gauging the reaction of the class as a whole and shading or elaborating her answer accordingly. Moms and elementary school teachers are famous for having eyes in the backs of their heads.

Here's an exercise.

- Sit easily, gazing (not staring) straight ahead.

- Stick your hands straight out in front of you and wiggle your fingers; then, continuing to wiggle, move your hands slowly out to your sides.

- Notice how wide your visual range is, how far the panorama extends beyond the small central area on which you usually focus.

- Now, as you go through the day, every time you think of it relax out of that constricted way of seeing.

- Later, try connecting this habit of wider vision with the habit of functioning from the center. As you learn to relax into the center and see from there, note how vision becomes panoramic.

The psychological equivalent of tunnel vision is what's called *fixation*, which, centuries before Freud, Buddhist investigators identified as a fundamental obstacle to a happy, progressive life. Perversely, we fix our attention on the, let's say, five percent of our experience that is problematic, blocking out the 95 percent that's just fine, like the Short Hills matron who once told my wife, "Today has been my worst nightmare!" "My God," Maggy said. "What happened?" She thought someone in the family must have been stricken with some terrible accident or disease. Gesturing toward her beautifully furnished, meticulously landscaped multimillion-dollar house, the woman answered, "I've been waiting *all morning* for the man to come and fix the electric garage-door opener." Growing enlightenment includes growth out of such blinding fixation.

Leone conveys a sense of the unfixated, panoramic gaze with his trademark time-freezing wide shots, often showing a tableau of men eyeing one another in the protracted moment just before their guns start blazing, their bodies arranged on the screen in a subtle, asymmetrical, yet cohesive rhythm. (You must see the film in widescreen format to appreciate this.) His usual sequence is then to cut to Eastwood's narrowed eyes and back again to the group. Paradoxically, the narrowing of the eyes draws us into the widened, panoramic gaze.

A few days after my expedition through the Waterland, I found myself in the Rijksmuseum in Amsterdam, viewing one of Vermeer's most sublime paintings: *Het Straatje*, "The Little Street." It also is a tableau: a couple of brick row houses, seen head-on, populated by four small human figures. There's a woman cleaning an alleyway, another woman seated in a doorway sewing, and two children crouched on the sidewalk, playing under a wooden bench, all faceless, all unaware of each other except the children, yet all together in an unconscious, irregular, but perfect harmony. As individuals they are intent on their diverse activities, but as a group they are united in a shared silence. They don't see the grouping, the composition; they *are* the composition.

Everything—every situation or environment we'll ever be in, the entire universe—is Vermeer's little street. We're all in a subtle harmony with everything and everyone else, including those we've never seen. No parts without the whole, no whole without the parts. Sufficiently deep practice of aikido, meditation, painting, or anything else yields glimpses of it. This is the harmony people are seeking when they play easy-listening music

("*I* don't find it easy to listen to," says my friend Steve) or buy those terrible, mawkish Thomas Kinkade prints, thinking they must retreat into a fairyland of false sentiment to find it. What's sublime about Leone's murderous tableaux is that they reveal this harmony in the most unsentimental situations imaginable. If I can see it there, I'll see it everywhere.

ENGAGE, NEUTRALIZE, DISENGAGE—that's the rhythm of aikido. The attack brings two people together, they interact, and then, the conflict resolved, they part. *Fistful of Dollars* ends with The Man riding out of San Miguel, in the same state of equilibrium and nonattachment in which he entered. By destroying both gangs he has changed the town, but it has not changed him. (He's like the catalyst in a chemical reaction.) By keeping his hands off beautiful Marisol and reuniting her with her family, he has found a moral path through the amoral violence. Giving her the money he has amassed, he washes his hands of the dubious karma that produced it and leaves as unencumbered as he came. He is as relaxed about getting paid as he is about getting shot; he is caught up in neither attachment nor aversion.

> Therefore the Master takes action
> by letting things take their course.
> He remains as calm
> at the end as at the beginning.
> He has nothing,
> thus has nothing to lose.
> —TAO TE CHING

Having passed between the horns of the bell ringer's prophecy, The Man with No Name is neither rich nor dead—he is free. The film is finally not about a fistful of dollars. Fists grasp or hit. When a fist opens to give, to relax, to let go, it is no longer a fist.

JAILHOUSE ROCK
(1957)

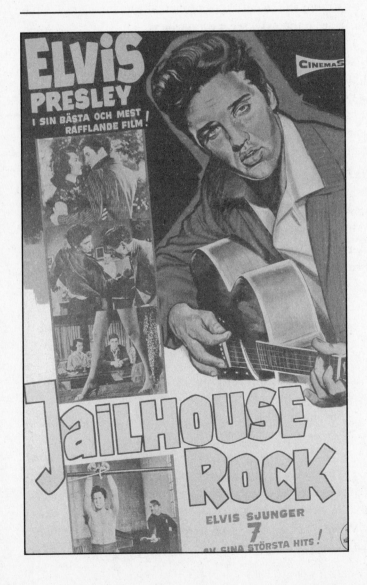

NIX, NIX

Today I am released from Central Jail forever.
—NEEM KAROLI BABA
(on the day of his death)

THIS COUNTRY HAS HAD MANY PRESIDENTS, BUT ONLY
one King. In the parched summer of 1998, my wife and I visited
his shrine. . . .

We're driving through the South on a book tour, in an old
yellow Cadillac with a cranky air conditioner, limping down
blazing highways from one motel pool to the next. Peach stands
and fireworks stands. LIVESTOCK ROAD . . . TIPTOE ROAD . . .
WILLIE MCCAINE ROAD . . . FLOWERY BRANCH ROAD. I've a feeling
we're not in New Jersey anymore. We pass sprawling forests of
parasitic kudzu, the shapes of the smothered trees smoothed
into mysterious green humps, and I fantasize aloud about writing a screenplay for a sort of Dixie horror film: killer kudzu,
embodying the tormented soul of the conquered South, creeps
northward, gradually destroying the arrogant Yankee empire: In
the climactic scene it scales the Trump Tower, its prehensile
tendrils reaching through windows to strangle complacent cap-
italists and socialites who are too rich *and* too thin.

Man, it's hot!

We drive through towns with two hundred residents and
three Baptist churches—many of them offering homey marquee wisdom and stark admonitions in stick-on capital letters.
CLEAN YOUR FINGERS BEFORE YOU POINT AT ANY SPOT . . . BE

HUMBLE OR YOU WILL TUMBLE . . . WARNING: PREPARE TO MEET GOD . . . GOD IS SUCH A GOOD GOD—DETAILS INSIDE . . . COME FOLLOW THE SON . . . TIRED OF SIN? COME ON IN , . . YOU THINK IT'S HOT HERE? CONSIDER ETERNITY! Hopeful little homes on the highway, with un-ironic pink lawn flamingos. USE-IT-AGAIN FURNITURE . . . WHOAH! BILLY'S RESTAURANT—GOOD OL' HOME COOKING—BUFFALO BURGERS . . . PEACHES FIREWORKS EXIT NOW . . . BIBLE FACTORY OUTLET. Double-wides in tow, a flatbed truck carrying a reclining white church steeple. ALWAYS REMEMBER TENNESSEE-ALABAMA FIREWORKS—40% OFF LOWEST PRICE IN THE SOUTH—DON'T GET RIPPED OFF ELSEWHERE.

In sweltering Memphis we check into our motel, only to be informed that the swimming pool is closed for repairs. Wearily we haul our bags back into the car and wind up downtown at the elegant old Peabody Hotel, where crowds gather in the lobby every morning at ten to watch as the famous Peabody Ducks, to the scratchy strains of a piped-in Sousa march, parade out of the elevator and along a red carpet to the ornately carved Italian marble fountain, where they swim all day with cool disregard for the small children who harass them, then reverse the process at five in the afternoon. Twice a day, busloads of flashbulbing tourists jostle for a glimpse of this fleeting spectacle, famous for being famous. Every guest towel and menu in the place is emblazoned with duck icons. Is this how religions start?

Four blocks away is Beale Street, with its blues clubs and barbecue joints. We hit it on a Saturday night, when it's closed to traffic and becomes a wall-to-wall pedestrian party, fueled by lots of open containers—jumbo plastic cups of beer, wacky tourist drinks in bright colors and Dr. Seuss shapes, with long, twisty-spiraling plastic straws, the beverage equivalent of Funny Cars. On one block, black kids stripped to the waist perform spectacular running flips and handsprings in the middle of the street, then collect change from the crowd of applauding spectators. Maggy and I sit on a curb to people-watch. Behind us, a young man tells his friend, "I don't think you understand the concept of a whore." Maggy tells me, "There are just too many people to have opinions about all of them."

The next day we visit Graceland (pronounced "Gracel'nd" by the locals). 24 HOUR ELVIS MOVIES GUITAR SHAPED POOL promises the marquee on the local Days Inn. As we cross the little footbridge from the parking lot to the Elvis museum, we notice that someone, perhaps some white-trash ghost haunting Elvis's glory beyond the grave, has dumped an old vacuum cleaner into the stream. Graceland is unexpectedly moving. The famous front gate, with its wrought-iron music staff, is flanked by a brick wall crammed with reverent chalked-on graffiti: outpourings of undying love and unhealed grief, hopeful greetings, heartfelt thanks, commemorations of wedding-day pilgrimages and journeys from distant lands. Aside from the Vietnam Veterans Memorial, what other place in this country affects people like this? Mount Vernon? Monticello? Who *cares* who's buried in Grant's tomb?

Behind the gate, the house—surprisingly modest by today's superstar standards—is a sincere country boy's somewhat tacky dream of opulence, heavy on the velour and zebra stripes. The museum displays furlongs of framed gold records, many of them for songs I've never heard of, and a plaque memorializing Elvis's many charities: Mile O'Dimes, Cynthia Milk Club, Duration Club Inc., Lawo Man-for-Boy Club, Home for Incurables, Hospital for Crippled Adults. Finally, the gravesite, with its circular walkway and the copyright notice at the bottom of the epitaph: commercial considerations also have followed Elvis into eternity. Still, this is clearly the power spot. Moved to respond and commune in some way, Maggy begins to circumambulate the King's grave and I join her, both quietly chanting OM MANI PADME HUNG, the mantra of great compassion.

OUR KING IS a tragic king. But as with all great tragedies, from within its depths the hero's spirit, ever fresh and clear, rocks on. Elvis's fall seems to me both passion play and dharma teaching. The flesh is crucified, but the soul is resurrected. Samsara is birth, old age, disease, and death, but nirvana is sublime transcendence.

I find most of Elvis's movies—the post-army, Technicolor ones—painful to watch. The songs are dumb, the stories dumber, and Elvis knows it. He's a god in chains. His raw animality and pouting vulnerability are gradually entombed in pancake makeup and embarrassing costumes as he goes through the motions of being a racecar driver or circus barker, mincing about in silly dance numbers with the likes of Ann-Margret. (*Viva Las Vegas* is the cruelest title of all, celebrating the city whose crass values finally killed him.)

Jailhouse Rock is different, sort of. Probably Elvis's best film, it's no *Citizen Kane*, but it's a modest, even charming, black-and-white production with flashes of spooky honesty. (Elvis, however, could never bear to watch it because his costar, Judy Tyler, died in a car crash two weeks after shooting wrapped.) Released in 1957, barely a year into Elvis's national stardom, it captures him near the peak of his power and beauty. The story is a thinly fictionalized account of his rise from truck driver (in the first scene he pulls up on a backhoe) to pop star. His character here is called Vince Everett, a hint at his conquest of the Mount Everest of show business. Aside from a detour through prison, it follows Elvis's trajectory pretty closely, from crooning in local clubs to cutting records for a small local label to the triumphs on radio, on TV, in Vegas, and finally in Hollywood. The uncanny part is how prophetically it shows the simultaneous descent into drink, fast women, outbursts of violent temper, and breakups with old friends and musical partners—all of which lay ahead in the next twenty years.

What's most haunting is the alternate ending this peppy

little film provides to Elvis's tragedy, much as the "improved" versions of Shakespeare's plays popular in the nineteenth century had Hamlet survive to ascend the throne of Denmark or Romeo and Juliet live happily ever after as man and wife. As stardom goes to Vince's head, he throws away the two most precious things he has: true love, embodied by a wholesome, girl-next-door record promoter (Tyler), and musical authenticity, represented by Hunk Houghton (Mickey Shaughnessy), the old-timer cellmate who gives him guitar lessons and gets him started in prison talent shows. But our hero comes to his senses in time, reconciles with the girl and the mentor, and throws off the self-destructive habits of his flashy showbiz lifestyle. If only.

The record promoter is pretty much the standard-issue '50s good-girl ingénue, but the old-timer is interesting. His cell is plastered with pictures of Hank Williams and other country music stars, and when Elvis/Vince makes his network TV debut, he brings Hunk along, in a dopey-looking country outfit, to do his own song. The producers kill the act, deriding it as "hillbilly music," a parallel to the way Elvis's rural roots were cut under the pressures of commercial success. But Hunk's "country" song tells yet another story. If you close your eyes and imagine a slightly more soulful delivery than his four-square, plunkety-plunk, cracker-barrel style, you realize it's actually a delta work song, a black man's lament about laboring "like a slave till the day is done" and hoping that "glory waits for me at the end of the road." At least as important as Elvis's country roots were his black roots. He grew up sneaking into black Memphis after-hours clubs, where he picked up his wailing sound and his hip-twisting moves; he bought his sharp clothes in stores that catered to blacks. It was the marriage of black blues and white country within Elvis (abetted by the innovative guitarist Scotty Moore and the other young guns at Sun Records) that effectively gave birth to rock 'n' roll. In abandoning

Hunk, he symbolically cuts himself loose from his most important sources, both white and black, musical and personal.*

Like Vince, we scale dangerous heights of hubris when we forget our legacy and start to believe we are wholly self-made—when we devalue our sources, be they our family, culture, teachers, artistic predecessors, or professional mentors. (One of Hinduism's most charming teachings on this point is the story in which the elephant-headed god Lord Ganesh is asked to run three laps around the world in a race with his brother. Being fat and slow, Ganesh offers up a prayer and circumambulates his parents' throne three times. He's declared the winner.) In the spiritual realm it's good not to disparage our old gurus if we move on to new ones, but to regard them as, say, the esteemed kindergarten teachers who prepared us for graduate school. Ultimately, the source of all we are and all we accomplish is the infinite. Cut off from that, we're isolated egos that are eventually helpless. Like Vince, we learn that narrow, ego-bound success, in refusing to acknowledge its source, eventually undercuts itself by cutting the fundamental connectedness that makes love and authenticity possible.

In one of the pleasant time-machine fantasies I occasionally indulge in, I show up in Elvis's kitchen during one of his long, sleepless nights in the dissipated '70s, sit down with him at the table, explain all this to him (as he downs a fried peanut butter, banana, and bacon sandwich), give him a meditation lesson or two (and perhaps a few diet tips), and put him on the path to salvaging his life. The King, who still brings so much joy to his subjects, deserves that much. But that happy ending is only in the movies.

---

* Unlike Elvis, Vince does at least stick with Scotty and the rest of the early band members—they keep magically reappearing to back him up, everywhere from the southern prison to a Hollywood pool party.

THE JUICIEST THREE MINUTES of the film is the sequence where Vince, in mock prison stripes and denim, performs the "Jailhouse Rock" number for the NBC cameras, dancing his way around a stylized two-story prison set (with a fireman's pole, for no logical reason except to allow him to do some hot pole dancing), flanked by a chorus of some sixteen male dancers in the same getup, all echoing his bumps and grinds. The first in a long succession of choreographed musical numbers, this is a crucial moment in Elvis's history, perhaps the very synapse between his rise and fall. As he wails the opening line, it's clear that he's still fully charged with the raw Dionysian power that is the reason why, decades after his death, Elvis lives. Yet, as the chorus of dancers—the original Elvis impersonators— transform his primal writhings into a choreographed routine, he has stepped into a Hollywood hall of mirrors. He's already becoming a reproducible commodity and a cheesy self-parody.

But not without a struggle. Choreographer Alex Romero, a Gene Kelly protégé and veteran of musicals like *On the Town* and *An American in Paris,* had to contend with Elvis's reluctance to do full-out MGM-style hoofing. What wound up on the screen is a compromise between Romero's polished concept and Elvis's more elemental moves. Apparently Elvis was starting to feel that enough was enough. He had just had his hair dyed, his nose fixed, and his teeth capped. As if his body were resisting all this processing, rejecting the transplant as it were, one of the caps shook loose while he was shimmying his way through this number. It wound up lodged in his lung and he had to be rushed to the hospital.

The song itself was penned by Jerry Leiber and Mike Stoller, the rock 'n' roll geniuses whose credits also include "Hound Dog" (and several other Elvis tunes), "Spanish Harlem," "Stand by Me," "On Broadway," "Poison Ivy," "Yakety Yak," "Charlie Brown," "I'm a Woman," "Love Potion Number Nine," and

"Kansas City." Minus the big band intro and ending, and the chorus's cornball unison shouts of "Go, go, go!" and "Lay it on me, daddy-o" (heard in the sound track version only), it's one of Elvis's most exciting recordings. Leiber and Stoller were, like him, two young white guys who fell in love with black music, then combined it with another legacy—in their case the sophistication of the (usually Jewish) Tin Pan Alley songsmith—to make rock 'n' roll. "Jailhouse Rock" combines Stoller's rhythmic exuberance, Leiber's image-rich, hipster-inflected narrative, and something rare in the rock world: a literate sense of humor.

Not surprisingly for a work so charged with creative energy, the song fairly oozes with spontaneous enlightenment teachings. *Our* jailhouse is samsara: ignorance, unenlightenment. When we escape from that prison, we break into the all-surrounding, all-pervading open space of nirvana. The archetype of the great escapee is the Buddha, at the moment when his years of meditation reach their fruition:

> [He] felt as though a prison which had confined
> him for thousands of lifetimes had broken open.
> Ignorance had been the jailkeeper. . . . [T]he mind
> had falsely divided reality into subject and object,
> self and others, existence and non-existence, birth
> and death. . . . The suffering of birth, old age,
> sickness, and death only made the prison walls
> thicker. The only thing to do was to seize the
> jailkeeper and see his true face. . . . Once the
> jailkeeper was gone, the jail would disappear and
> never be rebuilt again.
> —THICH NHAT HANH

In ignorance, this finite world, even at its most delightful, even when we're privileged and healthy and lucky, is a world of boundaries, and our innate hunger for boundlessness makes us chafe against the bars. But just as Elvis rocked within the jailhouse of his own tragedy, within the strictures of samsara we can all do the joyous, rockin' dance of liberation. Since form, as the Heart Sutra tells us, is no other than emptiness, when we gaze with sufficient clarity at the things that bind us, their solidity melts away. Form—the limitations of the body, of situations, of time and space—is the jailhouse, emptiness is boundless freedom, and, by experiencing the miraculous equivalency of the two in each moment, we rock.

COPYRIGHT LAW PREVENTS me from reproducing Leiber's lyrics here in full, but you can reach for your nearest computer and Google them up in a few seconds. The first verse sets the scene, with the prison band wailing and the joint swinging. The idea that the Warden throws a party for the inmates is redemptively delightful. In a world of plagues and holocausts, apparently whoever or whatever runs this joint, whether it's God or chance or ignorance, may not be all-merciful but at least has a soft side. We're condemned to a term of confinement (a life sentence in the Judeo-Christian-Islamic scheme of things, innumerable lives in the Hindu-Buddhist view), but our confinement is never absolute. No matter how bad things get, there's always some slack, some built-in possibility of partying on, of seeing our way through to joy.

The second verse, as it names the members of the band, stresses an essential element of this joy-seeing: harmony in diversity. The slack that the Warden of this universe has left us is such that our happiness depends largely on how we get along with one another. The list of players implies a multiplicity of species (Spider Murphy on tenor saxophone), sizes (Little Joe on slide trombone), places (the drummer boy from Illinois), and colors (the Purple Gang). We revel in our separate identities, but if we get caught up in the clash of those differences we intensify the torments of confinement for everyone: we all wind up doing hard time. If, though, we can each find our niche and allow plenty of room for others to do the same—you play trombone, I play sax—we can band together, harmonize, and make it a free-swinging party. It's probably not a coincidence that America, the nation that had to accommodate such a vast array of regions, languages, and experiences, gave birth to jazz, in which players improvise musical conversations, making statements of bold individuality yet somehow negotiating a way for it all to fit together.

But for our banding together to be an enlightenment project, it must be at the highest level. This is suggested by the reference to the rhythm section: the Purple Gang (historically, a Detroit-based, Prohibition-era syndicate of vicious Russian-Jewish mobsters). Of all the colors in the spectrum of visible light, purple has the highest frequency. Mystical systems usually associate it with the highest, finest, most enlightened vibrational frequencies of human energy. In earlier cultures, when "noble" qualities were considered the exclusive property of the nobility, the wearing of purple was often reserved to the royalty. But now we must all find those highest, noblest frequencies within ourselves, then find them in others, then let that common nobility (no longer an oxymoron) set the beat of all we do.

The third verse, where Number Forty-seven calls Number Three the cutest jailbird he's ever seen and proposes they do the Jailhouse Rock together, may well be the first rock allusion to gay romance. At this point in the choreography, two "prisoners" underscore the idea by pairing up in a coy, flirtatious little couple's dance. (But to keep it all safely on the level of a joke, they're the two oldest, ugliest guys in the chorus.) The hooking up that takes place in prisons, as a matter of convenience rather than preference, is a striking metaphor for the situation of us samsara dwellers. What we really crave, consciously or not, is enlightenment, ecstatic union with the one-ness beyond our prison walls; failing that, we embrace our cell-mates as stand-ins. Desiring to merge with the infinite, we settle for merging with each other.

In this sense, all sex, gay or straight, is a preview of coming attractions. The usual emphasis on sex as physical sensation, or even as emotional communion, overlooks a profound third component. The escalating intensity of sensation and emo-tion powerfully concentrates the mind, and, at the instant of release, that concentration momentarily opens out into transcendence—no time, no space, no limits. Thus Tibetan iconography is full of buddhas seated in meditative pose while coupling with their consorts, who personify the other half, the missing piece as it were, of enlightened awareness. And the Song of Solomon evokes God as the supreme paramour:

> A bundle of myrrh is my well-beloved unto me;
> he shall lie all night between my breasts.
> —SONG OF SOLOMON 1:13

The chief difference between full enlightenment and that brief glimpse of liberation during sex is that enlightenment lasts longer. Because it doesn't depend on any sensation or emotion or anything else, it never ends.

Verse four, then, goes on to show that we can have that ec-stasy even without a worldly consort. Here we see the predica-ment of the Sad Sack, who sits alone weeping, a wallflower at the party. The Warden encourages him to make skillful use of the materials at hand, to dance with a wooden chair if he can't find a partner. The most serious spiritual adventurers are, in fact, usually to some degree outsiders, wallflowers at the party of life, with a deep sense of the sadness that pervades it. Both Christ's and Buddha's wisdom came out of the crucible of soli-tude and wandering; Buddha's teaching begins with suffering and ends with compassion, and Christ is suffering and compassion embodied. But you don't have to be a Christ or Buddha, or a celibate for that matter, to sooner or later realize that even though sex is, fleetingly, a pretty good substitute for enlightenment, it's still only a substitute. It doesn't solve the basic problem of human unhappiness, and it doesn't provide ultimate, permanent freedom.

Then you find that your most reliable partner is the wooden chair that the Warden recommends, or a meditation cushion—anything you can sit on to settle down and dissolve into transcendence. By so doing, you start to realize the truth of the Warden's other advice in this verse, not to be a "square." What really confines us is not the square walls of our prison, or of our particular cells—our achy breaky bodies, our sometimes frustrating relationships, our demanding and often crushingly routinized jobs—but the square rigidity of our minds. It's easy to see in others, but hard to see in ourselves, how much the seemingly insoluble problems we fret about are really mental constructs; and most construction is based on the right angles of the square. The real life outside our heads is organic, unpredictable, messy, as wiggly and non-Euclidean as Elvis's hips. Confusion results when we try to impose the square, unhip Euclidean geometry of concepts and expectations on that glorious mess. By relaxing instead and grooving in each shining, never-to-be-repeated moment just as it is, by releasing rigidity, we release ourselves. We stop banging our head against the bars and find freedom right here, wherever we are.

That realization finds its full expression in the final verse, when Shifty Henry suggests to his pal Bugsy that, with no one looking, this would be a good time to escape. Bugsy replies, in the song's climactic exclamation, "Nix, nix, / I wanna stick around awhile and get my kicks." This is the kind of zesty punch line that Leiber specializes in—no, no, the party's so good that the inmates prefer to stay put. In dharma terms, it may suggest the danger of being seduced by samsara, of getting caught up in its raucous pleasures and missing the chance to make a break for nirvana. But it could also hint at something deeper: the Bodhisattva Vow, the determination to abide in samsara and help liberate others, until "all sentient beings without exception"—people, dogs, rats, maggots, inconceivable beings in inconceivable dimensions—are free. Of course that sounds like an impossible, irrational aspiration. But perhaps the point is precisely that, by holding to it, we transcend the limitations of our rational minds.

We've seen that what hems us in is not our existential situation, not the material world, but our limited perspective on it. The most powerful way of expanding our perspective is to give up our usual preoccupation with our own benefit, which, after all, usually amounts to little more than shifting the furniture around in our little cell or occasionally putting a new pin-up on the wall. But to so radically alter our perspective that walls are not walls requires abandoning self-preoccupation. The bodhisattva strategy is to defer the biggest benefit of all—escape—till all others have gained it. The way to stop chafing against the bars of whatever you think is confining you is to make up your mind once and for all that, even if your bars were to fall away tomorrow, you would stick around to help everyone else get out. By devoting ourselves to the ultimate happiness of all beings in the universe, we escape the selfish smallness that is the real prison, and we multiply our possible joy by the number of beings. Then we *really* get our kicks.

THE BODHISATTVA COMMITMENT, which in Judaism is called *tikkun olam*, "healing the world," and in Christianity is *caritas*, the selfless love that ministers to the needs of others, is reflected in the insistent repetition of the word "everybody" in the song's chorus. "Everybody, let's rock." It's a call to universal liberation. On one level that's hopelessly unrealistic because there are only so many people to whom we can minister, whose situations we can improve. But at a deeper level, liberation *can* be universal because it doesn't require changing anyone's situation. We don't need to pull down the prison bars, just see through them. This is what Buddhist texts call "transformation in place"—finding ultimate freedom right where you are. Our burdens may make us feel like Sisyphus rolling his rock endlessly and futilely up the mountain, but if we stop fixating on getting to the top and groove on being wherever we are at each point along the slope, the burden of rolling the rock becomes the joy of rock 'n' roll.

This means that, even as we dot every *i* and cross every *t* of our responsibilities, we can experience life more as play than project, more as Mardi Gras parade than forced march. Happiness and fulfillment and peace of mind are not an eventual destination to be reached; as Thich Nhat Hanh reminds us, "Peace is every step." In fact, steps that positively relish not going anywhere, that we take for the sheer unproductive fun of taking them, are called dance, and the attitude of dancing, applied to anything we do, makes it a means of liberation.

> To dance is to be out of yourself. Larger, more
> beautiful, more powerful. This is power, it is glory
> on earth and it is yours for the taking.
> —AGNES DE MILLE

For a time at least, Elvis embodied that power and glory. We're lucky to have so many radiant moments preserved where he danced and sang and shone it forth for the world. Even Ed Sullivan's proud TV cameras finally bowed to the King and showed him below the waist. His sexy gyrations proved to be something much more than sex. He was making love—*love*—to all of us, and teaching us to make love to the cosmos. Everybody, let's rock.

NOTHING HAPPENS

WALTER [John Goodman]: Smokey, this is not 'Nam, this is bowling. There are rules.
— *THE BIG LEBOWSKI*

If you don't have a sense of humor, it's just not funny anymore.
—WAVY GRAVY

ONCE ON A VISIT TO MY MOTHER IN LOS ANGELES, I WAS helping her unload the dishwasher when a bowl slipped from my hand and shattered on the floor. "Don't worry," she said. "I hate those bowls. I wish they all would break." Without a word, I walked over to the cabinet, took out the offending set, and smashed another one. My mom let out a whoop of shock, then another and another as, one by one, I dashed the bowls to the floor. Soon she was laughing through tears of hilarity and relief. I insisted that she break the last one herself.

I wish I could say that I go through life that way, boldly clearing the clutter, liberating friends and strangers alike from their self-imposed burden of stale attachments. But I'm usually not that daring. That's why I need the Marx Brothers.

Groucho, with his beetle brows, greasepaint mustache, and stream of placid insults; Chico, with his pointy hat and comically larcenous patter; and silent, golden-curled, googly-eyed

Harpo, with his angelic demeanor and his surreal antics—the Marxes are, at their best, the supreme purveyors of anarchic comedy. Perhaps that last phrase is redundant. All comedy contains some element of anarchy. In a night-space that's off-limits to the rational mind's daylight, it brings forth the crazy shapes of our rule-breaking, logic-defying, physics-transcending dreams. Chaplin makes a gourmet feast of his boot, Belushi leads the animalistic Delts to conquer the university, and Bugs pulls sledgehammers, bombs with sputtering fuses, and sexy female bunny suits out of the edge of the frame whenever needed.

> Wild Nights—Wild Nights! . . .
> Done with the Compass—
> Done with the Chart!
> —EMILY DICKINSON

Nothing is more subversive than laughter. It makes the weighty weightless. The things that seemed so oppressively real—our problems and responsibilities, our endless social rituals, our grandiose leaders—are seen as suddenly, hilariously zero: sound and fury, signifying *bubkes*.

The Heart Sutra tell us that this night vision is not merely a dream but the highest reality, the droll fact that form is none other than emptiness. Essays on the nature of comedy are notorious for their overserious theories of what's funny, the throat-clearing professor at his lectern just begging for a pie in the face. So here's *my* serious, dharma-inflected theory: Funny is anything that unexpectedly reveals the emptiness of the forms we took to be life-and-death real. It's the sudden deflation of some puffed-up balloon of conventional reality, which looked so substantial but (we now see) was full of insubstantial air; it's the balloon's crazy flight about the room as the air rushes out the nozzle, emitting (if we're lucky) a nice farting sound.

This is what the Brothers do. They are what the Tibetans call *nyönpa*, crazy saints. By overthrowing our habit of taking things too seriously, of seeing what's fluid as rigid and what's relative as absolute, Groucho, Chico, and Harpo stage the true Marxist revolution. Each film takes on some social institution, the more dignified the better (government, opera, commerce, college before *Animal House* knocked the stuffing out of it), mimicking its outward forms while reducing its inner essence to zip.

But why does that tossing of forms and conventions into the acid bath of absurdity make us *laugh*? Shouldn't it fill us with fear and loathing instead of delight? It would if the existentialists were right, if underlying all forms there was nothing but a gaping, terrifying void. But that void turns out to be our old friend (our best friend, our only reliable friend) shunyata, emptiness, which the existentialists glimpsed imperfectly because for the most part they glimpsed it intellectually, not experientially. Direct meditative experience reveals that shunyata is *luminous* emptiness, self-radiant nonself, not barren but so fertile that it gives rise to the endless stream of forms that are its insubstantial but fully functional manifestations, just as the mind of Shakespeare gave rise to a stream of nonexistent yet immeasurably rich characters. The existentialists correctly intuited the first clause of the Heart Sutra's core teaching, that form is emptiness, but disastrously missed the second clause, that emptiness is form. The ultimate truth is neither emptiness, as they fearfully concluded, nor form, as your average workaday materialist assumes, but rather the nonduality of the two, which is as mindbustingly implausible as Chico's paradoxical patter, Harpo's impossible pranks, and Groucho's greasepaint mustache.

In fact, that mustache says it all. Normally the sign of the serious man, the grown-up engaged in serious business, here the mustache is a sham so flimsy that it should be obvious, yet it's never commented upon. In tragedy we get the gradual buildup of the ordinary schlemiel into the form of the great man, fol-

lowed by his realization of the emptiness of that form and subsequent downfall once more into schlemielhood; it takes five
acts for Macbeth first to become king of Scotland and then to
get himself killed. In comedy the alternation is so fast it's virtually instantaneous, as in *Animal Crackers*, where an admiring
crowd sings to Groucho, "Hooray for Captain Spaulding, the
African explorer," and he answers, "Did someone call me
schnorrer?" (Yiddish for "bum, moocher"). Comedy offers the
complete integration of our sense that we are somebody, and
maybe even somebody special (form, self, Captain Spaulding,
King Macbeth) and our sense that we are nobody (emptiness,
nonself, schnorrer, Macbeth the usurper). Such integration, by
allowing us to function in the world of forms while relaxing
into its essential emptiness, is the basis of sanity, balance, and,
in fact, enlightenment.

As the Sixteenth Karmapa, one of the most revered lamas
of the twentieth century, lay dying in a hospital bed in Zion,
Illinois, he whispered to his attendant disciples, "Nothing happens." Perhaps he was reassuring them that nothing horrendous happens at the time of death, but I suspect that his
meaning was (or was also) more literal than that, that he was
describing firsthand a vision of all phenomenal existence, the
births and deaths of beings and universes—with all the wars
and circuses and intergalactic collisions and species die-offs
and picnics in between—as empty form: a big bunch of nothing,
happening like crazy.

THE STANDARD THEOLOGICAL DEBATE among Marx Brothers
disciples is whether their greatest film is *Duck Soup*, their last
outing with Paramount, or *A Night at the Opera*, their first
with MGM.* *Duck Soup*, like their Paramount films generally, is

---

* I actually belong to the *Duck Soup* sect. I discuss that film in my book
The Zen Commandments.

"purer." The Brothers are given their own mythical country of Freedonia in which to freely run amok, a dream-realm beyond logic and causality, wacky enough to have Groucho as its leader. But *Duck Soup* tanked at the box office, and the Brothers moved to MGM. There the legendary studio mastermind Irving Thalberg decided that their chaos needed more conventional structure to play against, more neatly stacked bowls to break. And incidentally, a conventional, sappy love story and conventional, sappy musical numbers might bring in the notoriously comedy-resistant female audience.

So, to the nirvanic lunacy of the Marxes' hijinks was added a load of sublunary samsara: the story of the modest, handsome young tenor Ricardo (Allan Jones), who longs for success in the opera world and the hand of the demure soprano Rosa (Kitty Carlisle). Blocking both Ricardo's courtship and his success is Lassparri, the mean-spirited, egotistical "world's greatest tenor," who wants both Rosa and all available fame for himself. (Unlike Groucho's, his mustache is real—and, to show he's preening and sinister, pencil-thin.) This is very much the stuff of classical comedy, going back through Shakespeare to the Romans: the journey of two young would-be lovers (preferably with Italian names) as they encounter seemingly insurmountable obstacles and finally overcome them, winding things up with a song, a dance, and a big wedding feast. Depending on which side of the Marx debate you take, the conventionality of this old-fashioned love story demonstrates either the weakness or the genius of the Metro pictures, in that we *don't care* about the samsaric storyline and are relieved every time the Brothers show up to punch holes in it. Samsara is in fact that which we shouldn't take too seriously; nirvana is how we spell relief.

There's also a rich counterpoint between the romantic plot and the Brothers' all-purpose cosmic subversiveness. These two elements propose two solutions to the same problem, posed by the film's featured song, "Alone," sung as a pining duet by Ri-

cardo and Rosa. What do we do about our aloneness, the problem of being one self, all by itself? The conventional answer is
to find a mate and become two. That's the answer that leads to
reproduction and generations, and keeps the world of samsara
spinning. The other solution is to discover that, because self is
empty, you were never one alone to begin with; all along you've
been zero (or infinity—same thing). Most of the Brothers' gags
in this film provoke that discovery, reducing the self to a self-
canceling absurdity and reveling in the all-sufficient nirvana
that's left in its place.

The road that brought the Marx Brothers to become envoys
of nirvana started in turn-of-the-century Jewish-immigrant New
York, where Minnie Marx pushed her talented, rambunctious
boys into vaudeville as their best chance to stay out of jail. Beginning as a musical act called the Four Nightingales, they
originally included Gummo (Milton), who dropped out before
their film careers started and was replaced by Zeppo (Herbert),
who left after *Duck Soup*. They toured the country, evolving into a comedy act in which each brother played an ethnic
stereotype: Chico (Leonard) as an organ-grinder-era Italian,
Harpo (Adolph) as a drunken "harp" or Irishman, Groucho
(Julius) as a scolding, frock-coated German professor, and
Zeppo as the "normal" American straight man. Eventually they
all dropped the ethnic identities except Chico, but they retained
the costumes and wild exaggeration that freed them to become
wondrous, uncontrollable monsters, ever-ready to unleash the
forces of chaos on our formerly settled sense of self. One of the
meanings of the word *atta*, self, is "governor" or "controller";
the doctrine of anatta, no-self, implies that our notion that we
can control the world of outer circumstances or of inner feeling
is sadly—or, as it turns out, joyfully—mistaken.

As monsters of misrule, the Marx Brothers resonate deeply
with something elemental in us. In fact, they correspond closely
to the five elements of traditional cosmology. These are more

than a pre-scientific substitute for the more complex elements of the periodic chart; in Buddhist psychology they're a metaphor for the spectrum of emotions, each of which has an unenlightened aspect when self-grasping is present, and an enlightened aspect when we allow the selfless luminosity of basic existence to shine through. The central teaching is that our emotions, including the so-called "negative" ones, are not obstacles to enlightenment. As we let go of self, they become the *path* to enlightenment. Even without the pretext of misunderstood spiritual teachings, people repress emotions because they perceive them (correctly) as chaotic and uncontrollable, and (incorrectly) as painful. It's actually the repression itself that's painful. It's also, ultimately, pointless: somehow the banished emotions keep showing up, as reliably as earth, water, fire, air, and space. Thus throughout *A Night at the Opera* everyone keeps trying to thwart, banish, fire, or arrest the Brothers, but they keep finding some side door and sneaking back in. Resistance is futile.

The sublime Harpo personifies the earth element. In its unenlightened form, earth signifies greed, the attempt to cope with our intuition of emptiness by accumulating more and more things. In its enlightened form, when we give up the losing battle of trying to prop up empty self with empty possessions, the earth element manifests as omnidirectional appreciation and its consequent equanimity. Rather than try to stop liking the sleek cars and sharp clothes, we can appreciate them without limit by not minding whether it's us or someone else who drives or wears them. With no self, there's no one to possess and accumulate, setting us free to window-shop our way equanimously through the universe. Earthy Harpo is a trickster-thief whose routines frequently parody the absurdity of accumulation: in one film, he's apprehended by a cop and a stolen spoon drops out of his sleeve, then a knife, a few forks, and eventually a whole cabinet's worth of mismatched silverware cascading to the ground, climaxed by a teapot. But Harpo's as happy when his loot is confiscated as when he grabs it—his sweet smile and bulging eyes indicate a delighted appreciation in which having and not having are both great fun. There's a nice example late in the film when he invades a lavish room-service breakfast that Groucho, Chico, and Ricardo are attempting to eat. He helps himself to their syrup, powdered sugar, and jam, but has no interest in eating them—it's much more fun to use them to paint a clown face on himself.

> i laughed when they laughed at me
> 'cause i was dancing happily
> and understood their jealousy
> and forgiveness is freedom is ecstasy
> —DANIEL MOSS,
> "i met my creator in a thrift shop"

The water element in its lower form is anger, which has the surging, destructive nature of a flood. In its higher form it's the crystal clarity of a calm pool. As with all the elements, some of the enlightened form is to be found within the unenlightened; when we're roused for battle our perception becomes very sharp. Groucho personifies the water element, with his constant stream of grouching verbal abuse and the clarity of wit that pervades it. Groucho had a razor-sharp intellect, as demonstrated in his highly literate letters and essays and on his '50s TV quiz show *You Bet Your Life*. Once when a middle-aged contestant claimed she was "approaching forty," Groucho asked, "From which direction?" When a medium invited him to ask a question of the spirits, he asked, "What's the capital of North Dakota?" (In his youth he aspired to be a doctor, and he always suspected he had wasted his life in show business.)

The two sides of the fire element are lust and compassion,

both of which focus on intimacy with others, whether in the service of our own pleasure or of the others' happiness. Here fire is represented by Chico, the lusty, compassionate pseudo-Italian. His name is pronounced "*chick*-oh," not "*cheek*-oh," because of his incessant (and usually successful) onscreen and offscreen chasing of women. Offscreen he was also a compulsive gambler, whose debts kept the Brothers making films well past their prime, and his own daughter has described him as the most seductive person in the world. In this film, when Chico plays his musical number on board a ship headed for America, laughing Italian peasant children crowd around his piano. As he looks up from the keyboard into their faces, it is with the most seductively, irresistibly charming eyes one can imagine, yet he is seducing them not so as to slake his lust with an individual being but to compassionately serve numerous beings by sharing joy with them all—and indeed they're almost beside themselves with delight.

The all-surrounding air element represents the panoramic, security-camera-like, fisheye-lens awareness that in its unenlightened form is paranoia, the feeling that threats to oneself could come from any direction. In the Marxes' earlier films, this is clearly poor Zeppo's situation. The thankless straight man, he is constantly under attack by the ricocheting patter and pranks of the other three, his attempts to hold onto some logical thread as futile as a "normal" basketball player's attempts to hang onto the ball while being triple-teamed by the Harlem Globetrotters. In its higher form, when there is no longer a self to protect, air represents something called "self-accomplished activity," the state in which just walking onto the basketball court of life is so fulfilling that everything's fine whether we get the ball or not. Zeppo seems not to have attained that state—which would explain why he was frustrated enough to leave the act. Certainly Gummo didn't stick around long enough to manifest the ubiquitous intelligence that is the higher form of the space element, instead acting out the retreat and withdrawal (often associated with depression) that are its lower form. Still, in his absence, we could say, he gives an impeccable portrayal of empty space.

A NIGHT AT THE OPERA contains a few scenes in which the explosion of uncontrollable, liberative chaos is especially delicious. The first is a frontal assault on the arrogant tenor Lassparri, standing in for the control-freak self. He enters his Milan dressing room to find Harpo, as his dresser Tomasso, wearing Lassparri's *Pagliacci* clown outfit. Livid at Harpo for encroaching on his own (assumed) identity, his put-on-like-a-costume sense of self, Lassparri orders him to strip. Ever the non-grasping thief, Harpo cheerfully complies, only to reveal the sailor costume (for *Madame Butterfly*?) that he's wearing under the clown suit. With growing anger, Lassparri orders him out of that one, under which Harpo wears a peasant girl's dress, and finally his own clothes under that. This comic demonstration of the artificial, superficial, and ultimately disposable nature of self-identity infuriates Lassparri—it rocks his world. He responds by (violently, shockingly, unfunnily) driving Harpo out of the room with a bullwhip.

Backstage a few minutes later, Harpo gets his revenge, symbolically killing the strutting false self by knocking Lassparri out cold (with a mallet brought in, Bugs Bunny style, from just outside the frame). Groucho and Chico show up, each putting one foot on the supine body as if it were a bar-rail, and order beer from an imaginary bartender. Their physical pose comes right out of Hindu and Buddhist religious art: it's exactly the posture of triumph in which gods and enlightenment heroes are depicted, with one foot subduing a demon or dwarf who represents the ego just as Lassparri does. As Fiorello and Driftwood, a couple of competing flimflam men trying to cut themselves in for a piece of the action, Chico and Groucho negotiate a contract for a tenor, but, furthering the deconstruction of self-identity, they mix up their supposedly individual mental processes as well as their tenors; Chico is representing Ricardo, and Groucho thinks he's hiring Lassparri.

> DRIFTWOOD [Groucho]: Say, I just remembered, I came back here looking for somebody. You don't know who it is, do you?
>
> FIORELLO [Chico]: It's a funny thing, it just slipped my mind. . . .
>
> DRIFTWOOD: What's his name?
>
> FIORELLO: What do you care? I can't pronounce it.

As they examine their duplicate contracts, their negotiations become a full-on parody of our usual process of agreeing to be separate selves, which are reduced here to the malleable legal fictions of "parties":

> DRIFTWOOD: Now pay particular attention to this first clause because it's most important. It says, "The party of the first part shall be known in this contract as the party of the first part." How do you like that? That's pretty neat, eh?
>
> FIORELLO: No, it's no good.
>
> DRIFTWOOD: What's the matter with it?
>
> FIORELLO: I dunno. Let's hear it again.
>
> DRIFTWOOD: It says, "The party of the first part shall be known in this contract as the party of the first part."
>
> FIORELLO: That sounds a little better this time.
>
> DRIFTWOOD: Well, it grows on ya. Would you like to hear it once more?
>
> FIORELLO: Uh, just the first part.

DRIFTWOOD: Whaddaya mean? The party of the first part?

FIORELLO: No, the first part of the party of the first part.

DRIFTWOOD: All right. It says the, uh, "The first part of the party of the first part shall be known in this contract as the first part of the party of the first part shall be known in this contract—" Look, why should we quarrel about a thing like this? We'll take it right out, eh?

FIORELLO: Yeah, ha, it's-a too long, anyhow. [Each tears off the top of his contract.]

The agreement to be separate selves is so insupportably silly that it's quickly breaking down. The party of the first part, in day-to-day life, is always I ("the most important"), and the party of the second part is always you. But now they're dissolving into one big, happy party.

FIORELLO: I no like-a the second party, either.

DRIFTWOOD: Well, you shoulda come to the first party. We didn't get home till around four in the morning. I was blind for three days!

FIORELLO: Hey, look, why can't-a the first part of the second party be the second part of the first party? Then-a you *got* something.

DRIFTWOOD: Well, look, rather than go through all that again, whaddaya say?

FIORELLO: Fine. [They tear off a second piece of the contract.]

The two go on with their legalistic wrangling and happy compromising, tearing off more and more pieces till each is left with a tiny scrap, like the slender, tiny ghost of self left to the enlightened—just enough so they can function in the world, but much too slender to be taken seriously. When it's finally time to sign, even the signing process is deconstructed, shown to be as empty as the selves being signed for.

> FIORELLO: I forgot to tell you. I can't write.
> DRIFTWOOD: Well, that's all right, there's no ink in the pen anyhow.

And then comes the capper:

> FIORELLO: Hey, wait, wait. What does this say here? This thing here.
> DRIFTWOOD: Oh, that? Oh, that's the usual clause. That's in every contract. That just says uh, it says uh, "If any of the parties participating in this contract is shown not to be in their right mind, the entire agreement is automatically nullified."
> FIORELLO: Well, I dunno.
> DRIFTWOOD: It's all right, that's in every contract. That's what they call a "sanity clause."
> FIORELLO: Ha, ha, ha, ha, ha. You can't fool me. There ain't no Sanity Clause!

There ain't no Sanity Clause indeed. Only children believe in Sanity Clause. But with the mature, grown-up wisdom of no-self, we know that since there's no solid ground for being whatever we thought we were, there's none for judging others for being whatever we think they are. There's no perspective of absolute reality or sanity to stand on. The sanest words I've ever heard on this topic came from a lama who told me, "Everybody's crazy, especially me."

The final choice scene (often considered the best routine in any of the Marxes' films) is set on board a ship in which all the principal characters are headed from Milan to New York. Groucho has just checked into his broom-closet-sized stateroom, nearly half of which is taken up by his trunk—which turns out to hold three hungry stowaways, Chico, Harpo, and Ricardo. Stepping out his door, Groucho hails a steward and begins ordering a meal, supposedly for himself.

> DRIFTWOOD: What have we got for dinner?
>
> STEWARD: Anything you like, sir. You might have some tomato juice, orange juice, grape juice, pineapple juice—
>
> DRIFTWOOD: Hey, turn off the juice before I get electrocuted. All right, let me have one of each. And, uh, two fried eggs, two poached eggs, two scrambled eggs, and two medium-boiled eggs.
>
> FIORELLO [through the door]: And two hard-boiled eggs.
>
> DRIFTWOOD: And two hard-boiled eggs. [Tomasso honks his horn.] Make that three hard-boiled eggs. And, uh, some roast beef: rare, medium, well-done, and overdone.
>
> FIORELLO: And two hard-boiled eggs.
>
> DRIFTWOOD: And two hard-boiled eggs. [Tomasso honks.] Make that three hard-boiled eggs. And, uh, eight pieces of French pastry.
>
> FIORELLO: And two hard-boiled eggs.
>
> DRIFTWOOD: And two hard-boiled eggs. [Tomasso honks.] Make that three hard-boiled eggs.

And on the order goes, in its lovely, crazy rhythm, driven along by the insistent choruses of honking and eggs, heaping up absurdly high piles of imagined food, as if to prove that the eaters are infinitely capacious. We have room for an unlimited number of hard-boiled eggs because the boundaries of self are illusory, because the awareness which we are is vast and open like the sky, because the kingdom of infinity is within us.

But as Jesus teaches in the Gospel of Thomas, "The Kingdom is inside you and it is outside of you." So the cramped stateroom, emblematic of the cramped circumstances of our lives, also turns out to be boundlessly capacious. As the Brothers and Ricardo wait for their food to arrive, the four of them already virtually filling the room, one by one an impossible number of additional people join them. First two chambermaids knock on the door, offering to make up the room, and Groucho welcomes them in. Then, in turn, come an engineer to turn off the heat, a manicurist to trim Groucho's nails, the engineer's hulking assistant, a young woman in a stylish hat searching for her Aunt Minnie, a surly washerwoman with a mop, and finally several stewards bearing trays of food (heavy on the hard-boiled eggs). Description does not do justice to this scene. A tone of dreamlike surreality is set by Harpo, who is sleeping the whole time— "Shh, don't wake him up," says Chico, "he's got insomnia, he's trying to sleep it off"—his body flopping and sliding flaccidly over the chambermaids, the stewards, and finally the trays of food. What's wonderful here is how gamely everyone goes about their business, mopping floors and giving manicures, sliding up and over one another when necessary, registering no more than a vague notion that the place might be getting a tad crowded.

It all reminds me of the busier intersections in Katmandu: big, open circles where, without benefit of painted lines or traffic signals, at any given moment a couple of hundred cars, buses, motor scooters, rickshaws, and overloaded jitneys maneuver their way through at maximum speed, with none ever hitting each other. The stateroom scene shows us (at last!) how many angels can dance on the head of a pin: any number you like, since both the angels and the pin are ever-empty and therefore sizeless. And this is more than a metaphysical puzzle—it

speaks directly to our moment-to-moment suffering or nonsuf-
fering. That stateroom is our lives, our world (our ship of fools).
One way or another, it will always be cramped and crowded
with inconvenient circumstances: noisy neighbors, lurking
terrorists, problematic relationships, encroaching disease and
death. Shit happens—that's the First Noble Truth. Of course we
take all practical steps to handle the shit. (We have to keep re-
peating that.) But the ultimate solution is to realize the ultimate
superfluid nature of both self and circumstances—to learn to
use, as Lama Surya Das says, our Teflon mind instead of our
Velcro mind. Then we see that nothing happens—that's the
Third Noble Truth.

The Heart Sutra describes this state as "no hindrance in the
mind" and adds, "No hindrance, thus no fear." Once you know
for sure that your awareness and anything else can frictionlessly slip-slide around or through one another, what can be
done to you? You're free of fear not only of the present situation
but of any conceivable or inconceivable situation, *and* its Aunt
Minnie. There's nothing to fear and no one to fear it. Then, as
Mr. Dylan says, you "walk upside-down inside handcuffs."

The ever-escalating magnitude at which all things seem to
happen in our world can be seen as an opportunity to sound
the capacity of our limitlessly capacious awareness. When Walter Cronkite used to read the news back in the '50s and '60s and
the word "billion" came up, usually in some story on the federal
budget, he invariably gave the first syllable a little extra oomph:
"Ten *bil*lion dollars." This was probably a technique taught in
broadcasters' school to distinguish between billions and millions, but it always came across with a tone of eye-rolling wonder: Can you believe it—we're talking *bil*lions! Nowadays, of
course, *tril*lions barely make us flinch.

THE SIMPLEST, MOST DIRECT application of the wisdom of
comedy in our daily lives is just this: *Smile, darn ya, smile.* Bet-

ter than a hundred books of philosophy, a single smile—or a volley of belly-laughs—can renew your perception of the weightlessness and porosity of all that seemed so heavy and solid. "Enlighten up!" says Lama Surya Das.

Thich Nhat Hanh recommends setting the tone for your day by starting each morning with a smile. I used to have a problem with that advice. I thought there was something sappy and contrived about any smile that was deliberate. In fact, I've got a couple of decades' worth of family photos in which I'm scowling at the camera. But one day a professional photographer trying to get a decent shot of me gave me just the pith instruction I needed: "Smile with your eyes." Once you feel your way into how to do it that way, I discovered, the smile is not glued-on but warm and genuine, maybe because the eyes are directly connected to the brain, and it generates authentic warmth internally as well as externally.

This changed not only my photos but my mornings. Here's what I actually do—if any of this speaks to you, help yourself:

- Start the day by sitting up in bed, just as the "reality" of all you must deal with is starting to resolidify itself after the formlessness of sleep.

- Inhale deeply and intone a long, drawn-out AHHHHHHHH, the mantra of openness, of empty, limitless awareness-space. (If someone else is still asleep in the room, you can subvocalize.) Do this three times.

- Get up and go through your morning routine—the showering, the tooth-brushing, the dressing—but regarding it all as dreamlike and insubstantial.

- Meanwhile, grin like an idiot.

If you need inspiration for that grinning, just look at Harpo in almost any scene of any film he's in, a perfect idiot, idiotic perfection, possibly the wisest and certainly the happiest person you'll ever see, the embodiment of what Sir Thomas Browne called "the unextinguishable laugh in heaven." Smile with your eyes, smile from your heart, smile with each cell of your body. Singing in the shower (preferably something good and raucous) is also recommended. As you go through your day, smiling at others is also recommended. And laughing at yourself at every opportunity is very highly recommended.

> Yes, these are serious times. And serious times call
> for serious laughter.
> —SWAMI BEYONDANANDA

We've all heard those news stories about workplace shootings, usually perpetrated by "a disgruntled former employee." What *we're* becoming, with all this smiling and meditating and awareness practice, is gruntled. (Also combobulated, mayed, and jected.) On the way to permanent gruntledness, I think it's also helpful to cultivate an appreciation of unlikely juxtapositions. In life as in Marx Brothers films, whenever we see the orderly juxtaposed with the chaotic, the obvious with the mysterious, the earthshaking with the trivial, the solemn with the cuckoo, we have a choice. We can reject it as a mistake, too much cognitive dissonance to handle without feeling like we're wearing scratchy wool underwear. Or we can open to enjoy the dissonance of the two things and let it force us to see the third thing, the bigger reality in which opposites are reconciled— where yin and yang, Jesus and Judas, Kennedy and Khrushchev, Pat Garrett and Billy the Kid all knock off from work and take turns buying the next round.

One of the most venerable pilgrimage places I visited in

Tibet was Samye Monastery, the very first monastery to be built in Tibet, founded by Padmasambhava over twelve hundred years ago in a spot that's still remote from roads and towns. (In some of the isolated spots that my group visited, we were so alien that the locals would tug on our arm-hairs—they had never seen that before.) After a difficult trip, first by Jeep over dusty dirt roads, then roasting in open boats as we crossed the Tsangpo River against the current, then bumping over rocks and mud holes in the back of an old pickup truck, we reached Samye in late afternoon. I dropped my bags in my crude little guest room, went down to the courtyard to wash up at the water pump, and found Maggy. Evening was beginning to settle, and we walked around to the front, where we found a couple of monks running a tiny open-fronted monastery store offering the usual incense, rosaries, small *thangka* paintings, and boxes of crackers. A few dozen yards away was the temple, and in the gathering dusk we could hear the solemn sound of chanting monks and the deep drone of long *rag-dung* horns.

That is, we could *just* hear it. Mounted on the doorpost of the store was a scratchy loudspeaker, through which blared American pop music, presumably for our benefit. Playing at that moment was a peppy little song that went

> Boom boom boom boom
> I want you in my room. . . .

As it happened, Maggy had recently filled in for a season as a cheerleading coach and knew a routine for this song. And so, as the rag-dung sounded and the temple monks chanted and the song blared, the store monks looked on in slack-jawed astonishment at this tall, beautiful, blond crazy woman from another planet, folding and refolding her arms across her chest, swiveling her hips, singing "Boom boom boom boom," and laughing.

CASABLANCA
(1942)

YOU MUST REMEMBER THIS

*Nada es nada, a no ser que nosotros mismos convirtamos
ese nada an algo.*
Nothing is nothing unless we ourselves convert that
nothing into something.

> —EMILIA PARDO BAZÁN,
> *"El Revólver"*

One Love! One Heart!
Let's get together and feel all right.

> —BOB MARLEY,
> *"One Love"*

HOW MANY PEOPLE THROUGHOUT THE WORLD, RIGHT
now as we pulse through this moment, are having heart attacks? How many are making love? How many are having terrible violence inflicted on them or are inflicting it on others?
How many are feeling their mouths go dry as they prepare to
dive off a sea cliff or sink their savings into a business venture?
How many have just won the lottery or written the best poem of
their life or learned that they have a terminal illness? How
many are working at a job so boring they want to scream? How
many are taking a perfectly contented stroll around the
block? It's too much to know, and if we could know it it would
be much too much to deal with.

Yet through all this runs a common thread: everyone, in

every moment, is seeking to be happy and free from suffering. So all-embracing is that desire, and even all-consuming, that often our own quest is all we can see. Then it comes as a big surprise when we learn, as Humphrey Bogart says in *Casablanca*, that we're just little people whose happiness doesn't amount to a hill of beans in this crazy world. That's a lonely discovery.

But if there were a way to feel that thread, to find our commonality with the other lonely seekers, and even to join our own quest with theirs, that might somehow lift us out of our isolation. It might change things in some fundamental way.

THE *MONA LISA*, the Brooklyn Bridge, Beethoven's Ninth, *Huckleberry Finn*, the Sermon on the Mount, the '57 Chevy Bel-Air, *Hamlet*, The Spaniels' "Goodnight Sweetheart," Rodin's *Thinker*—some works are so iconic that it's hard to imagine the world without them, as if something in the nature of being human demands their existence. *Citizen Kane* is the textbook answer to the question, What is the greatest American film of all time?, but the more conventional studio film *Casablanca,* though it lacks *Kane's* artistic innovations and political audacity, is more the *necessary* film, the one we need to return to again and again, to get our life straight and keep it straight. You must remember this.

But remember what? During production, *Casablanca's* cast and crew saw it not as anything extraordinary, but one more Warner Bros. film, cranked out like sausages at the rate of one a week. This time there were certainly some excellent ingredients going through the grinder: Bogart was starring, Ingrid Bergman was at her most radiant, and the supporting players (Claude Rains, Sydney Greenstreet, Peter Lorre) were at their smoothest and wittiest. The Epstein brothers' script, frantically written and rewritten even as the film was shooting, was inspired. And Michael Curtiz, who had directed Errol Flynn as Robin Hood, Bette Davis as Elizabeth I, and Cagney in *Yankee Doodle Dandy*, was a master Hollywood craftsman.

But the catalyst for all these ingredients seems to have been a special energy the film drew from the great change that was in the air. America had just entered the war, but the film takes place over three days in the week *before* Pearl Harbor, while we were still maintaining our isolation. (This important time element is established with subtlety. The first time we see Rick he is signing a credit slip dated December 2, 1941.) Viewers could watch Bogart as Rick Blaine, *Casablanca*'s archetypal American, resist committing himself to the cause just as they themselves might have resisted not long before, yet know which way he must ultimately go.

And Bogey was in a parallel transition of his own. After years of being typecast as heavies and already at mid-career, he was now playing his first sympathetic lead (and only after Warners couldn't get George Raft). The freshness of his encounter with the possibilities of acting out of altruism informs the whole film with yet another kind of special energy. Wisely, he retains much of his gangster hardness; the power of the role and much of the power of the film derive from his not being a bland good guy from whom virtue is naturally expected. *Casablanca*'s great theme is the discovery, within one's own damaged, suffering, imperfect self, of perfect *bodhichitta*—utter commitment to the liberation of suffering fellow beings. Precisely because Rick, like us, is not a Sunday school paragon, his discovery makes us believe we can make that same discovery within our own imperfect, damaged selves.

Politically, the Casablanca of 1942 is ruled by the French, whose own country is split between free France and the Nazi-collaborationist Vichy government. As the principal city of French-ruled Morocco, Casablanca reflects this conflict, ostensibly independent yet beholden to the Gestapo, just as, before liberation, we are beholden to our own inner Nazi, the impulse of unkindness and rigidity that ever seeks world domination, one person at a time. And with thousands of refugees pouring out of war-ravaged Europe, Casablanca is also an uneasy stopping-off point, awash in black-market visas and all kinds of vice and corruption as people desperately seek passage to America, the tranquil far shore beyond the reach of the Nazis. As such, Casablanca suggests what has been called "the restlessness of the seeker," the unease of those who have learned of the existence of a nirvanic realm beyond samsara but who have not yet secured their passage.

RENAULT [Claude Rains]: Nobody is supposed to sleep well in Casablanca.

Casablanca's faraway, offscreen America, then, is nirvana, the land of peace and freedom, and Rick's saloon, significantly called the Café Américain, is like a dharma center, a jumping-off point to freedom from the world of bondage. Even the name Casablanca, which literally means "White House," suggests that samsara has a covert affinity with nirvana. As we've been saying in different ways for the last couple of hundred pages (because, finally, what else is there to say?), by penetrating to the true nature of samsara we see that it's none other than nirvana—what we've been seeking so passionately has been right before our eyes all along. Interestingly, the Russians have a saying when someone states something that should have been obvious: "You just discovered America."

THE PLOT (IN CASE you've just dropped in from Pluto and have never seen this film) turns on a couple of stolen "letters of transit" that are "unconditional," that "cannot be rescinded, not even questioned"—a silly device on the face of it, as if there could really be a magic piece of paper that rendered both the Gestapo and the French authorities powerless to detain whoever happened to get his hands on it and fill in his name. As a spiritual metaphor, though, it makes perfect sense. *Moksha,*

liberation, does in fact ensure our transit out of samsara, unquestionably and unconditionally, no matter who we are or
what particular corner of the samsaric morass we're sunk in.
No one is beyond the pale—that's the wonderful promise of all
the Christs and Buddhas. Ironically but logically, the infinite is
more accessible than the finite. Some people, because of the circumstances they were born into or subsequently stumbled into,
will never have the finite blessings of money, or health, or edu-
cation, or love, but the infinite by definition can never be out of
reach. A lot of things in this world are, let's face it, very seriously messed up. The Israelis and Palestinians—maybe those
guys will *never* work it out, and just go on and on, slugging
away at each other in perpetuity. Yet all their drama and trauma
takes place within the arena of the infinite (where else could
it be?), and every single participant has the potential in every
single moment to look up, see that endless space, and make the
transit, liberated from the grip of his appalling finite situation.

Appropriately, the petty criminal Ugarte (Lorre), who has
stolen the transit letters, leaves them for safekeeping with his
American friend. Rick's nationality is central to the film—
surrounded by people who speak in accents, he is, with one important exception, the film's only American. Viewers are rarely
bothered by the fact that Claude Rains, who plays a Frenchman,
and Sydney Greenstreet, who's supposed to be Italian, are both
undisguised Brits—Rains pulls it off by wearing his cap at just
the right jaunty angle—while Peter Lorre, another supposed
Italian, speaks with his native Hungarian accent. Conrad Veidt,
as the Gestapo's Major Strasser, was a real German (and Universal's first choice to play Dracula) but a staunch anti-Nazi
whose first wife was Jewish.

Rick's Americanness comes across in the contrast between
his characteristic Bogart brashness and the Europeans' fussi-
ness. The oily civility of his rival saloonkeeper Ferrari (Greenstreet), the weaselly furtiveness of Ugarte (who is soon arrested

and killed), the cheerfully shameless corruption of the local prefect of police, Captain Renault (Rains), and the bullying bluster of Major Strasser are all foils to Rick's blunt, unassuming honesty. He is an emissary from the land of freedom, with an aura of godlike aloofness established by our initial view of him. First we see only his hand in close-up (signing that credit slip with the most American of expressions, "OK"); then, as he raises a cigarette to his lips and squints against the smoke, we pull back to see him in his white dinner jacket, seated commandingly at his private table at the Café Américain, returning to his solitary game of chess.

Rick, we soon learn, is secretly a god in pain, but even in his evasions there's incipient dharma wisdom, as in the here-and-nowness he uses to deflect the demands of his latest casual girlfriend:

> YVONNE: Where were you last night?
> RICK: That's so long ago, I don't remember.
> YVONNE: Will I see you tonight?
> RICK: I never make plans that far ahead.

The slogans that are repeated around the café like articles of religious faith—"Rick is completely neutral about everything," "Rick never drinks with the customers"—all speak to America's pre–Pearl Harbor neutrality, but also to the transcendental quality of the nirvana with which America is identified.

The film's central question then becomes, How can infinitely neutral nirvana, which is by nature not of this world, be mobilized to solve the world's problems? How can America/Rick be induced to join the good fight? Clearly, everyone wants to claim him as their own, as we see by the way they coin their own variations on his name: Carl, the German waiter, calls him Herr Rick, Ilsa (Ingrid Bergman) calls him Richard, and Renault (who confesses that if he were a woman he would be in love with him) calls him Ricky. Even the sneak thief Ugarte, in his backhanded way, tries to draw on Rick's integrity: "Somehow, just because you despise me, you are the only one I trust." But as the film begins, Rick is having none of it, keeping his American freedom to himself, a lone Hinayanist: "I stick my neck out for nobody." "I'm not fighting for anything anymore except myself. I'm the only cause I'm interested in."

But that's a lonely stance. It's clear that Rick needs engagement with the world as much as the world needs him. He is missing the joy, the juiciness of life, which consequently feels flat and dry, like a desert that stretches hopelessly in all directions forever.

> RENAULT: What in heaven's name brought you to Casablanca?
> RICK: My health. I came to Casablanca for the waters.
> RENAULT: The waters? What waters? We're in the desert.
> RICK: I was misinformed.

Things start to change, though, when Ilsa shows up. ("Of all the gin joints in all the towns in all the world, she walks into mine." Yes!) Rick's onetime lover from pre-occupation Paris, the cause of the broken heart he has been marinating in booze and bile ever since, she represents a time before his present isolation, when he knew love and commitment—a hint that Hinayana detachment is not in our true nature but is a kind of perversion of life, an expression of our damage rather than a wholesome impulse toward its healing. When Ilsa comes in on the arm of the heroic resistance fighter Victor Laszlo (Paul Henreid), Rick breaks his own ironclad rule of isolation and joins them for drinks, a gesture that marks the beginning of his conversion.

A little earlier he has a revealing exchange—disguised, again, as merely clever, evasive banter—with Major Strasser and Captain Renault:

> STRASSER: What is your nationality?
> RICK: I'm a drunkard.
> RENAULT: That makes Rick a citizen of the world.

These lines indicate the start of a deeper exploration that will lead to the rediscovery of a crucial universalist Mahayana principle: the very pain that seems to isolate us actually unites us with our fellow beings. Even Rick's complaint about Ilsa's return inadvertently affirms that the little gin joint in which we cower, licking our wounds, is an inseparable part of "all the world."

The most powerful technique I know for piercing through this illusory isolation is a variety of the popular Tibetan practice of *tonglen* ("sending and receiving"). It's a specialty of Lama John Makransky, a wonderful American lama and professor who combines an extraordinary academic mind with a big dharma heart, and with whom I've been privileged to study.

- Sit in meditation for a little while.

- Then bring to mind some difficult or problematic feeling that you have been dealing with, such as anger, fear, loneliness, or grief. Allow yourself to really *feel* the feeling— not getting too embroiled in the story of the situation that produced it, but experiencing the feeling itself, simply and directly, as if it were a flavor or a texture.

- Now reflect on the fact that countless others before you have had the same feeling of (let's say) grief, or are having it right now, or will have it in the future. Amazing! Billions of beings, with stories and situations all so different, yet the feeling is exactly the same.

- Next, allow yourself to sense the presence of those countless others. This is not a matter of imagination—they are actually out there, all around you—and feel the unity, the connection, between your grief and theirs. It's as if you're feeling it for them. In fact, take theirs upon you, opening yourself to receive all the grief in the universe, drawing it away from the other beings and bringing it to your heart center.

- See or feel your heart center as if it's encrusted with a hard shell (this is ego) and now use the powerful energy of all that grief to *crack* it open. Out through the cracks shines an intense white light, the light of realization, healing, love, pure being. Allow it to radiate throughout your body and then continue in all directions, filling the universe, bathing all beings—including yourself—and healing them of all their grief and all their damage.

- Repeat the whole process a few times if desired, then let it dissolve and simply rest in open awareness.

This phenomenon of healing and clearing through perception of our inseparability with all others is inexpressibly profound. Using the technique above as a starting point, you may also intuit other ways to cultivate that perception.* The most important sentence in the New Testament, Luke 17:21, is usually translated "The kingdom of God is within you," but it can

---

* More on this and related practices can be found in Lama John's book, *Natural Great Compassion* (Wisdom Publications, 2005).

also mean "The kingdom of God is *among* you." I like both versions, the one that locates the space of boundless freedom in the awareness within each of us, and the one that locates it in the connectedness among all of us. Together they point to the possibility of a universal mutuality of healing. Or, as my daughter Tara, then age two, put it:

> Every children get the dollies from every people,
> and they hug them like this,
> and they don't cry.

NOW THE PROCESS of Rick's conversion picks up steam. More plot summary for visiting Plutonians: Laszlo must get to America to continue his fight against the Nazis. He is a marked man, especially after the terrific scene in which he drowns out the Gestapo officers' noxious anthem by leading the café's band and patrons in a stirring rendition of "La Marseillaise." Through several scenes of rising tension, Laszlo and Ilsa seek the transit letters and Ilsa and Rick trade bitter recriminations over their broken romance. Finally, Ilsa explains to Rick why she abandoned him in Paris. Secretly married to Laszlo, whom she admired for his idealism, she thought he had been killed in a concentration camp when she met Rick; then Laszlo escaped and she found him alive on the day she and Rick were to leave Paris together. Now, as deeply in love as ever and unwilling to leave Rick again, Ilsa tells him he'll have to decide the future for both of them, whether they'll choose personal happiness together or she'll stay by Laszlo's side to help him carry on the fight for social good.

This paralyzing conflict recalls the choice faced by Arjuna the warrior, hero of the Bhagavad Gita. Moments before the commencement of an apocalyptic war against the Hitlerian tyrant Duryodhana, Arjuna has his charioteer drive him to the middle of the battlefield to survey the enemy. There he is shocked to see that Duryodhana has somehow recruited many of Arjuna's beloved friends and relatives into his army. Declaring "I will not fight," Arjuna throws down his bow. Like Rick, he is torn between personal affection and a larger sense of duty. Fortunately, his charioteer happens to be Krishna, the incarnation of the infinite, who gives a long discourse on the infinite and the finite and how the two are reconciled in realization. The core of his teaching is *Yogastah kuru karmani:* established in enlightenment, perform action. Having found refuge in the vast, serene ocean of being, vigorously participate in the turbulent waves of doing.

Rick's Krishna is Sam (Dooley Wilson), the black piano player who is the star of the club's floor show. (Interestingly enough, Krishna literally means "dark one.") Sam is subject to the casual racism of the day—Ilsa refers to him as a "boy" and Ferrari tries to buy him—and he has a seemingly minor role, but he's the film's only American besides Rick and thus important in the quest for nirvanic freedom. He is clearly the wisdom-giver in Rick's life, nursing him through his drinking jags and advising him from the start to let Ilsa go. He spends most of his screen time seated at his upright piano, like a Buddha on his teaching throne, and it is in Sam's piano that Rick hides the stolen transit letters, as if they must cook in that oven, incubate in that wisdom womb, to attain their full, liberative potency.

"As Time Goes By," the song that first Ilsa and then Rick makes him play, "their" song from their Paris days, is on its face a standard romantic ballad, but it's also Sam's enlightenment hymn, the equivalent of Krishna's discourse, beginning with the teacher's admonition "You must remember this."* Sam educates us about the nature of *sukha* and *dukkha,* the pleasure and pain

---

* Both Ilsa and Rick tell him merely to "Play it." "Play it again, Sam" is the most famous line never said in this film. It's actually from the Marx Brothers parody *A Night in Casablanca.*

of life—the kisses of romance and the sighs of separation—and how to handle them wisely. He tells us that a kiss is *just* a kiss, a sigh is *just* a sigh: everything is exactly what it is, no less but no more. Each wave of happiness or suffering has its own value, its experiential reality, but then it passes as all waves do. Our grief and anger (like Rick's drunken self-pity and recriminations against Ilsa) arise when we become attached to particular waves, perversely nurturing our traumas and clumsily clinging to our fleeting joys—missing the crucial fact that time does indeed go by.

But as it goes by, the fundamental things apply: the fundamental ocean of existence that underlies all our drama completes and fulfills every wave on the surface. The flawless, timeless, absolute nature of life applies to every moment of apparently flawed, time-bound, relative phenomena. Knowing this, you can do what you gotta do (*yogastah kuru karmani*). You can fight for love and glory, and, win or lose—no matter what the future brings—everything is OK. So do it. Don't retreat from life. The world will always welcome lovers: it will always need and therefore embrace those who passionately embrace it in its wholeness, including the kisses and the sighs and that which transcends both. On that you can rely.

RICK'S COURSE, THEN, becomes clear. He must follow the dark one's advice and give up Ilsa. As with Arjuna, the transcendental vision makes doing the right thing viable. By transcending the self, we transcend self-interest. Of course Arjuna has the benefit of the greatest meditation teacher in the universe, but Rick has something just as good in its way: love. Ilsa tells him this during their Paris sojourn. "Only one answer can take care of all our questions"—and she kisses him. Just as powerful a teaching is his toast to her: "Here's looking at *you*, kid." Love, in the Jewish philosopher Martin Buber's terms, means escaping from I-centeredness to Thou-centeredness. By relaxing my preoccupation with me and my needs and paying attention to you and yours, I am freed from the narrow attachments that inevitably bring pain. If I really *look* at you, kid, I see you as you truly are, as a fellow being—not just part of the scenery of my own little drama of happiness and pain, but one whose pain and happiness are as important and real as my own. Then I rediscover my true nature, our true nature, which is unsullied kidlike innocence, nirvanic pure awareness. (As Jesus teaches, to enter nirvana, the kingdom of heaven, we must become like little children—kids.)

Which brings us (at last, in this last chapter) to one of the most crucial points I can try to convey:

Service is bliss.

It took me a long time to learn this, being a man. (Women generally get in on the secret early.) Certainly I knew it in a theoretical way and had even taught and written about karma yoga, the way of action in service to others as a path of realization. But I never really experienced it until my wife became ill with cancer. My attention and energy increasingly had to be focused on caring for Maggy at all times; work, play, writing, my so-called meditation, everything else had to give way. And that was great. There was so much I no longer had to think about. I found myself melting into each moment of service, letting go of past and future, hope and fear, including the hope that my efforts might do any good. (Krishna tells Arjuna to focus on his actions only—their results are out of his control.) Maggy was a great dharma practitioner, and through her months of illness she taught me by the way *she* abode without hope or fear, refusing to indulge in speculation about the future or longing for the past, instead resting aware of each moment as just another way of being, finding its naked OK-ness. To serve her, I had to emulate her.

Service is bliss. Service is serene freedom from the lifelong ping-pong game of sukha and dukkha. It is the acid bath in which desire and self dissolve.

This is the true joy in life, the being a force of
nature instead of a feverish selfish little clod of
ailments and grievances complaining that the
world will not devote itself to making you happy.
　　　—GEORGE BERNARD SHAW,
　　　　Man and Superman

Casablanca, being a crackerjack Hollywood creation, works
out Rick's epiphany through several delightful twists and surprises, culminating in the night scene at the airport, where, in
the thick, romantic fog, he tells Ilsa, who thinks she's staying on
with him, that she must go with Laszlo—in what must be the
most famous profile two-shot, with the two best-looking hats,
in the history of cinema. Everyone, all together now:

> **RICK:** Inside of us, we both know you belong with
> Victor. You're part of his work, the thing that keeps
> him going. If that plane leaves the ground and you're
> not with him, you'll regret it. Maybe not today.
> Maybe not tomorrow, but soon and for the rest of
> your life. . . . Ilsa, I'm no good at being noble, but
> it doesn't take much to see that the problems of
> three little people don't amount to a hill of beans in
> this crazy world. Someday you'll understand that.
> [Ilsa cries.] Now, now. Here's looking at *you*, kid.

This is the way of the bodhisattva. Every time you choose to
put Ilsa on the plane, every time you let go of what you wanted,
you see more clearly how small is the self's hill of beans and
you release yourself and everyone else further into the freedom
of selflessness. My Ilsa was Maggy, and I had little choice. (I was
like John Kennedy, who, when asked how he became a war
hero, replied, "It was involuntary. They sank my boat.") During
the writing of this book, Maggy flew away. The only options her

death left me were to let go or create suffering, and I let go. Of course there is sorrow; there are songs I still can't hear without crying, and I can't pass a flower stand without wishing I could bring a bunch home to her. But in our time together we learned, through love and letting go, that when you look into one another's eyes you're looking through a window at the light that's everywhere. Then, when the window shatters, it's shattering but it's also all right.

> My heart
> is broken
> open.

IN THE COURSE of getting the couple safely off, Rick also winds up shooting Major Strasser, thus committing himself to the struggle and ending both his and, symbolically, America's isolation. It is by committing to service that we transcend self-interest and integrate nirvana into samsara, mobilizing it to solve samsara's problems. Once we embark on that path of commitment, we might note that it takes many forms—we can forgo self-interest for our family, our team, our country—and we might start to wonder if it has an *ultimate* form. One of the film's most mysterious details hints at the answer. For reasons that are left pointedly vague, Rick can't go to back to America, at least until the war is over. He is committed to exile from the land of freedom until the pandemic of chaos and suffering comes to an end. Again we are reminded of the Bodhisattva Vow, recited daily in various versions by those on the Mahayana path:

> As long as space remains
> As long as sentient beings remain
> May I too remain
> And dispel the miseries of the world.

The bodhisattva, in other words, vows to be the last one out of the burning building of samsara—to defer his own final exit into nirvana, sticking around no matter how many years or lifetimes it takes, until every single being has been led to liberation. Sound attractively noble? To maintain my perspective, I like to shop at an Asian food market near my home, looking at all the piles of cuttlefish and squid that I will need to guide to enlightenment, and especially the big bins of dried baby shrimps, pale pink with their pairs of tiny black eyes, hundreds of them in each tin scoopful that customers pour into their plastic bags, tens of thousands of them in each bin, each one a sentient being, each as precious as I am, to each one of which I vow, "After you."

Everyone you encounter—the janitor sweeping up the restroom, the girls in the Internet porn, the guy who cuts you off on the turnpike, the murderous dictator on the evening news—are the ones you've vowed to save, the ones whose welfare you've put before your own. Can you measure up to that? Of course not. But at the least it means you can't write any of them off, as just incidental or as beyond the pale. You can't close your heart to anyone.

Save everyone. Very noble. But often when I recite the formula, I hear a small, cynical voice—not unlike Bogart's—asking, "Oh, yeah? What's your plan?" It's all very well to make grandiose cosmic pledges to clear all the sand off the beach, but then there's the grunt work, the business of taking tweezers in hand and starting the job, grain by grain. That must be done in the real world, and it takes a realistic, worldly attitude to do it. Laszlo is the famous freedom fighter, but in a way he's too noble to be real, too pure, and he runs off to the pure freedom of America (which has always seemed odd to me—is he going to fight Nazis in Connecticut?). Rick, meanwhile, stays in the war-torn world, the bodhisattva passionately engaged in a fight for love and glory. We see the difference in the way they kiss

Ilsa. When Rick does, it's full on the mouth and it sizzles. Victor kisses her a couple of times, but always primly on the cheek, preceded by a thoroughly sexless "I love you very much." He's like the idealistic spiritual aspirant who's so pure he lacks the funky pragmatism to see the muck we're living in and what it's going to take to slog our way out of here.

Throughout the film this funk is embodied in Renault. He takes bribes, he uses visas to extort sex from desperate women, he's lazy and corrupt in the administration of his duties ("Round up the usual suspects"), but he's so frank in his corruption and so twinkle-in-the-eye charming that we (and Rick) always enjoy his company. He's built to survive, and survive with French élan, in the real world; when he's threatened, his soupçon of sleaze is his best defense:

> RICK: And remember, this gun is pointed right at your heart.
> RENAULT: That is my least vulnerable spot.

Spiritual idealists often talk about affirming the "higher self," but Renault is a reminder that we need the lower self onboard too. We need an alliance between the higher and the lower, our head in the clouds and feet on the ground, bodhisattva aspiration to set our course and street smarts to keep it real. This alliance is cemented when Rick and Renault, now both committed to the resistance, their backs to us (facing the same direction as us, leading us), walk off into the fog as the camera swoops upward and Rick speaks the film's final line:

> Louie, I think this is the beginning of a beautiful friendship.

Much has been written about this last scene: how Bogart was recalled to loop in the tagline weeks after shooting wrapped, and how Curtiz ingeniously dealt with his cramped set by using an undersized cardboard cutout for the plane and midgets for the ground crew. What's little noted is that the scene is meteorologically impossible. There is no fog in the desert. But we like impossible things—they're also known as miracles. I like to think that what we're seeing is the absurd fulfillment of Rick's earlier absurd crack about coming to Casablanca for the waters. Now that he has embarked on the path of altruism and entered into the most beautiful of all friendships, the friendship of fellow feeling with all fellow beings, he's no longer in an emotional and spiritual desert. The air is suddenly, miraculously full on all sides with life-giving water. He has found what he came to Casablanca for, and now, his health restored, he can move on.

OK, THEN, LET'S ALL be bodhisattvas, or at least try to be good people. How? Every spiritual tradition offers useful guidelines. I take particular inspiration from Buddhism's how-to for budding bodhisattvas, known as the Six Paramitas, the transcendental virtues. In a sense, the phrase "transcendental virtue" is a contradiction, since transcendence is the nature of nirvana and virtues must be practiced in the field of samsara. But the Six Paramitas are precisely of such quality that practicing them transforms samsara into (or, rather, shows samsara to be) nirvana. They are modes of selfless behavior that help reveal the endless, open space where we thought we had a self. This is their classical order, along with typical affirmations for their development:

- *Generosity: Dana paramita.* May I be generous and helpful.

- *Morality: Shila paramita.* May I be pure and virtuous.

- *Patience: Kshanti paramita.* May I be patient and forbear the wrongs of others.

- *Diligence: Virya paramita.* May I be strenuous, energetic, and persevering.

- *Meditation: Dhyana paramita.* May I practice meditation and attain oneness to serve all beings.

- *Wisdom: Prajna paramita.* May I gain wisdom and give the benefit of my wisdom to others.

Putting them like that, however, sounds just a bit Sunday school–ish, a bit Victor Laszlo–ish. It might be useful to try to rephrase them as they would sound in Bogey's street-hard voice. Being a salty character, and being a Westerner, he would probably frame them, like most of the Ten Commandments, in negative form, as thou-shalt-not's. There's some wisdom to that: the negative form emphasizes that practicing the Paramitas is not a matter of constructing some artifice, of imposing something unnatural on ourselves, but rather a letting go of the unnatural things we've *been* doing. If we empty ourselves of the confusing, complicating, aggravating patterns we've fallen into, the luminous emptiness of existence shines through of its own.

- *Generosity: Don't be a cheapskate.* As you lay the tip on the table, let go of that *next* dollar, the one you're not sure about giving. Feel that space of liberation? Now find that space in as many places as you can—keep opening it up by giving to others.

- *Morality: Don't be an asshole.* You should be an expert on this topic by now. How many times have you said this or thought it about others? And if you're honest, don't you recognize it in yourself? We don't need elaborate ethical systems to tell us how assholes behave—we know it when we see it, and it's painfully obvious how much unnecessary suffering it ultimately brings to everyone, including the perpetrator. Breathe in, breathe out, and let that behavior go.

• *Patience: Don't be pushy.* Your doddering dad tells you the same anecdote for the twenty-seventh time. Or your fidgeting, distracted toddler makes drying off from the bath and putting on her jammies take half an hour. Or the clock takes forever to reach 3:00 P.M. for the end of your crummy school day or 5:00 P.M. for the end of your crummy workday. Or you're still sick, or still having to deal with that trying relationship. Whatever the situation, you can create suffering for yourself by pushing impatiently (and uselessly) against it, or you can let go and find freedom by relaxing into it and respecting the karma that seems to require it for now. This virtue must be carefully balanced by the next . . .

• *Diligence: Don't be flaky.* Pay your bills, take care of business, be a grown-up (someone who knows that the stuff we evade doesn't go away but festers). "See the job, do the job, stay out of the misery," Maharishi once said. The trick is to notice how evasion is rooted in aversion. For example, I never minded taking out the trash, but I always found replacing the plastic liner in the trash can to be, for some reason, mildly annoying. *Notice* the aversion, then let go and replace the trash bag anyway, relaxing into that action and recognizing it as just another way of being, no worse or better than doing anything else. Diligence also implies diligent application of the teachings in all moments, whether you're tranquil or agitated, sober or drunk, not just as a luxury when you're in a philosophical mood.

- *Meditation: Don't be picky.* This is a complete instruction for both formal and informal meditation. Whether sitting on your cushion or going through your daily life, let go of picking and choosing what needs to be present or absent for you to be satisfied. Let go of nitpicking and faultfinding, and rest in the perfection of whatever appears. We used to have a very old refrigerator whose motor ran constantly, making lots of annoying sounds. Finally, while our daughter was away at college, we traded it in for a nice, new, quiet one. When she came home on break, she was aghast—what were annoying sounds for me were, for her, the cozy, comforting sounds of home. Who was picking and choosing? Both of us. It's all good—be a praiser, not an appraiser. And that will lead you to . . .

- *Wisdom: Don't be stupid.* Let go of the habitual stupor that keeps you from seeing that this is *it*—that life is perfect and complete in every moment, just as it is.

These virtues are developed over time, so while practicing them sincerely don't beat yourself up for not having perfected them (yet). An interviewer was once praising the Dalai Lama for his great forbearance in the face of the Chinese takeover of his country. "You don't get angry at the Chinese, who've tortured and killed your teachers and friends and forced you into exile for over forty years," she said. "I get angry over being stuck in traffic." The Dalai Lama replied, "Sometimes when the traffic doesn't move, I get angry too."

THE END OF *CASABLANCA*, with Rick and Renault walking off together into the fog and their beautiful friendship, seems like a good place for us to walk off too. Perhaps this book has inspired you to watch other movies in glorious DharmaVision.

For starters, you can find plenty of juicy material in *King Kong, Lawrence of Arabia, Groundhog Day, Fatal Attraction, Frankenstein, Gone With the Wind, Heathers, Repo Man, The Great Escape, North by Northwest* (hint: what's Roger Thornhill's middle name?), *Rear Window, Strangers on a Train,* everything else by Hitchcock, *The Wizard of Oz, Zardoz, Gattaca, Touch of Evil, The Blob, The Sting, The Third Man, The Player, McCabe & Mrs. Miller, Raising Arizona, Fargo, Cast Away, Annie Hall, Rebel Without a Cause, Zorba the Greek, Raging Bull, RoboCop, Chinatown, Cool Hand Luke, Adaptation, Blue Velvet, Papillon.* Conveniently, our cinematic quasi-religion is a universal one, with temples almost everywhere, including Tibet—just ask for the *log-nyen-khang* (electric shadow house).

More important, I hope you'll be inspired to practice. Certainly some kind of dharma awareness seems to be seeping into our culture, sometimes in unlikely places. Recently I opened my newspaper to an ad that actually told me the efficient gas mileage of the new Lexus would help my karma while its high-performance engine would give me nirvana. The next day, right here in central New Jersey, I drove (not in a Lexus) past the grand opening of the Zen Nail Spa. But even if the words are rendered meaningless, I think the practices will always attract us because they're basic to being human, and maybe even more basic than that. Dr. Jane Goodall observed that wild chimpanzees, when they come to a waterfall, go into an extraordinary display lasting as long as twenty minutes, swinging from vines and vocalizing with great excitement. Then they sit quietly before the waterfall with tranquil eyes, just gazing.

So I hope you're inspired to be at least as motivated as a chimp, and to take some time, after all the excitement, to just sit and gaze. I hope you'll take up dharma practice in some form, or continue your present practice with diligence (lighthearted diligence), and not just go on to read the next book.

Even if he is fond of quoting appropriate texts,
the thoughtless man who does not put them into
practice himself is like a cowherd counting other
people's cows, not a partner in the Holy Life.
        —DHAMMAPADA

Don't be overwhelmed by the number of teachers and teachings. Just start by doing a little bit of something, even five minutes of meditation, but do it every day. And don't worry about
how screwed up beyond help you may think your life is. An
electric cord may be frayed, it may be twisted, it may lie in tang-
les in the dust under the rug, but as long as it stays plugged into
the wall it gets the juice.

Once you put one foot in front of another, the dharma path
has a way of leading you where you need to go. Sometimes you
may keep looking right past the next step just because it's so
stupidly obvious. When I was eight or nine, I had raging insomnia. For hours into the night, I would stare up at the ceiling. Finally one night it occurred to me, "Hmmm, maybe I should try
closing my eyes."

And sometimes the logic of things is more obscure. In my
town there's a fleet of cabs with YELLOW TAXI painted on the
side. They're all green. Beats me, but nevertheless the taxis roll
on, taking folks unfailingly to their destinations.

Don't overlook the obvious. Relax about the obscure. Be
grateful for this human life and the opportunities for limitless love and freedom it unfolds. And meet me in the movie
temple—sixth row, right aisle. Here's looking at *you*, kid.

INDEX

THE WIZARD
[as he floats away in the balloon]:
I can't come back!
I don't know how it works!
Goodbye, folks!

—*THE WIZARD OF OZ*